THE
NEW
RIGHT

ALSO BY MICHAEL MALICE

Dear Reader:
The Unauthorized Autobiography of Kim Jong Il

THE
NEW
RIGHT

A Journey to the
Fringe of American Politics

MICHAEL MALICE

ALL
POINTS
BOOKS

www.allpointsbooks.com

Designed by Meryl Sussman Levavi

Library of Congress Cataloging-in-Publication Data is available upon request.

ISBN 978-1-250-15466-8 (hardcover)
ISBN 978-1-250-15467-5 (ebook)

Our books may be purchased in bulk for promotional, educational, or business use. Please contact your local bookseller or the Macmillan Corporate and Premium Sales Department at 1-800-221-7945, extension 5442, or by email at MacmillanSpecialMarkets@macmillan.com.

First Edition: May 2019

10 9 8 7 6 5 4 3 2 1

For Harvey

TABLE OF CONTENTS

THE
NEW
RIGHT

1

★

THIS IS YOUR WELCOME

> And, indeed, what is the State anyway but organized
> banditry? What is taxation but theft on a gigantic,
> unchecked, scale? What is war but mass murder on a
> scale impossible by private police forces? What is con-
> scription but mass enslavement? Can anyone envision
> a private police force getting away with a tiny fraction
> of what States get away with, and do habitually, year
> after year, century after century?
>
> —MURRAY ROTHBARD

I made it my goal to bring sanity and clarity to north Korea.

I traveled to the DPRK in 2012 partly for the purposes of doing research for my book *Dear Reader: The Unauthorized Autobiography of Kim Jong Il*. At the time much of the press was focused on how "suicidal" and "crazy" the north Korean regime was. Through my work I sought to demonstrate how absurd this is. If they were suicidal they were very bad at it, having outlasted the rest of the communist dictatorships other than Cuba.

As for crazy? Sure they had their idiosyncrasies, such as their insistence that Korea is one nation, indivisible, with the south being a *region* under occupation by the "U.S. imperialists" (hence their usage of lowercase "north" Korea and "south" Korea, a convention I follow). To call something crazy is to confess that one doesn't understand it. By now, few are calling the DPRK crazy. There is an understanding that this most evil of countries works logically and coherently. Their depravity is moral, not psychological.

Being an anarchist, it is no surprise that I set my sights upon the worst government in the world. But being an anarchist also gained me entrée into the New Right as it was developing, and I watched the same sort of dismissiveness to their ideas that I've seen regarding north Korea (which is, incidentally, the most racist and homogenous nation on earth).

From concentration camps to leader-worship and an obsession with racial purity, north Korea shares much in common with Nazi Germany. But to equate Kim Jong Un with Hitler would not be very fruitful. So too is it inaccurate to dismiss an entire subculture as neo-Nazis—especially when they are having far more profound influence with our society than the Nazis ever did. Any attempt to reduce them to a single demographic—the troll in the basement or the white supremacist next door—is inaccurate.

Thomas Sowell once wrote, "Nobody is equal to anybody. Even the same man is not equal to himself on different days." Jim's Blog took this one step further and laid out the central thesis of the movement as:

> The fundamental realization [. . .] is that all men are *not* created equal, not individual men, nor the various groups and categories of men, nor are women equal to men, that these beliefs and others like them are religious beliefs, that society is just as religious as ever it was, with an official state religion of progressivism, but this is a new religion, an evil religion, and, if you are a Christian, a demonic religion.

If taken at face value, "unequal" can have the benign meaning of "celebrating our differences." More often, however, it has been used in far more nefarious senses, ranging all the way to full-blown racism. Therefore, though terms like "New Right" and "Alt-Right" are used in various ways in various contexts, for the purposes of this book the New Right is defined as:

> A loosely connected group of individuals united by their opposition to progressivism, which they perceive to be a thinly veiled fundamentalist religion dedicated to egalitarian principles and intent on totalitarian world domination via globalist hegemony.

This is a broad definition that encompasses several subgroups. The most well-known faction is the Alt-Right, which includes members of the New Right who perceive race (*not* "racism") to be one of the most important sociopolitical issues if not *the* most important one. The Alt-Right isn't wholly composed of neo-Nazis, white nationalists, and white supremacists, but those groups do have significant representation within it.

In the 1940s, more white supremacists and white nationalists gave their lives fighting the Nazis than did urban male feminists. To say the Alt-Right and the Nazis are synonymous—especially when the press does so—can have profoundly dangerous consequences. At the very least, an innocent media mistake or misrepresentation can be taken as proof that the press is lying—and from there it is fairly easy to convince the listener to write off the media entirely.

The question of what to do with the government once progressive hegemony is destroyed forever is where the New Right is perhaps at its weirdest. Racism and white nationalism can safely be described as reprehensible by today's standards, but the ideas are hardly unusual or unfamiliar. What's unusual is finding people who advocate such principles openly. Though the Alt-Right is the faction that gets the most press, for reasons both obvious and obscure, it's the other types that I personally find more intriguing. I once had dinner with another anarchist who had also been watching this movement come into being. "So what are their actual answers?" I asked him.

"They want to restore the stewards," he told me.

This didn't seem particularly new or controversial. It sounded like typical Rudy Giuliani law-and-order Republican-ism. "So who would be these stewards?"

"Oh no no no no," he laughed. "Not the stewards. The *Stuarts*. They want to restore the *Stuart* dynasty to reign over Amer-ica. See, they think that we anarchists are crazy, utopian, and unrealistic. So the sane, *realistic* option is to bring back *monar-chy* to the United States."

The New Right is not a geographically proximate movement. It's more frequently represented by that one kid in his town networked with his counterpart in another state or another country. As such, in a milieu that's relatively new and sort of a Wild West when it comes to ideology, all sorts of factions emerge as alternatives to the status quo—including monar-chism, though not a *new* king. No, only a descendent of the old one will do. Once one dismisses the mainstream or even mar-ginal worldviews within a culture, *something* has to take their place. The New Right is of the fringe (and I say that as an anar-chist), and the fringe is where both innovation and insanity lay. Sometimes, innovation seems like insanity because one hasn't encountered such concepts before and can't quite port them to one's own frame of reference. And sometimes they're just genuinely batshit.

As the union leader Nicholas Klein said in 1914, "First they ignore you. Then they ridicule you. And then they attack you and want to burn you. And then they build monuments to you."[1]

Cranks are a byproduct of free thought and a consequence of liberation from orthodoxies. In other words, it takes work to determine whether an ideology is insane or innovative or a mix. Even if the New Right's solutions were all incorrect, that wouldn't mean their criticisms were inaccurate as well.

Many of my friends expressed concern as I began swimming in New Right circles. I was amiable with people who were amiable with Nazis, and on more than one occasion I met someone who thought that the JQ—"the Jewish Question"—was the most important thing when it comes to politics.

I am very fortunate to live in New York City for many reasons. One of these is the privilege of having to deal with anti-Semitism far less than I would in many other parts of the world. I do empathize with leftists when they talk about how pernicious racism—*actual* racism—can be. I recall vividly how my father told me that one of his college professors back in the Soviet Union patted him on the back and said, "You're one of the good ones!"

"You're flying close to the sun," my buddy Kmele warned me one night at dinner. It wasn't a judgment but a statement of fact, and frankly one that I agreed with. Kmele was an anarchist as much as I was (is it "crazy" that he's Jamaican but doesn't identify as black?), and very contemptuous of how accusations of "racism" play into American culture.

"Well," I told him, "that's kind of my thing." The cover of my biography, *Ego & Hubris*, depicts me flying over the sea, blissfully unaware that my wings have ripped away. Whether I'm meant to be Icarus or Lucifer fallen from Heaven, the danger remains the same.

"Why do you want to talk to these people?" he wanted to know.

It was a question I had asked myself many times.

I have a friend who is a very successful entertainer. He grew up in south central Los Angeles and by all accounts should have been just another young black male statistic. He couldn't finish high school because he kept getting into fights with people, at one point even getting into it with the cops. This led to him getting expelled from school after school until he had no place left to go.

Now, however, he's a family man who has made a real name for himself. He is also one of the most admirable people I know, and he has taught me a great deal about both show business and life in general. We frequently discuss politics, and since his upbringing was so different from mine, I always try to listen. He never fails to have something insightful to say, even when I disagree with him, because his perspective is so much unlike my own in many ways.

"No one ever feels sorry for black men in this country," he said one day.

The statement seemed like an absurdity. After all, how many people marched when Trayvon Martin was killed? But later I understood what he was getting at. There's a television series called *Beyond Scared Straight*, and (I think) these are the black men he was specifically speaking about. The series deals with at-risk kids who are going down a dangerous path. They're sent to spend a day in jail, living with the inmates, in hopes of knocking some sense into them.

Overwhelmingly these teens are black males. They are aggressive and usually violent, often boastfully so. They brag about being in gangs, about using violence to settle disputes, about the weapons they have, the thefts they've committed. They all sound somewhat less than erudite, to put it mildly. In Alt-Right parlance, each of these teens is always proclaimed by the press as a "good boy who didn't do nothing wrong" (hence the slur "dindu") and who is somehow simultaneously "starting to turn his life around." Given how many of them end up shot or in jail, the vicious joke is that being an aspiring rapper is the most dangerous job in America.

It's hard to feel sorry for these young men because they are violent predators by their own admission. The way they laugh about the crimes they've committed against other people is downright sociopathic. The remorselessness they proclaim does not speak to having a sense of hope for their future. They claim to be dangerous, their actions have been dangerous in the past, and there is every reason to believe that they are going to be dangerous in the future. Their own families send them to the Scared Straight program as a last resort, often being afraid of sharing homes with them.

The overwhelming majority of these young men seem irredeemable. Time and again, the updates at the end of the show demonstrate that they haven't changed their ways and have continued to engage in their violent, criminal behavior. It is hard if not impossible to feel bad for someone who steals from, threatens, or actually lays a hand on their own mother or grandmother. I am not a Christian, and the idea that every person can be saved, that every person is *worth* saving, is a view that I was never taught and personally do not hold.

Yet one of the things I found compelling about the series is how these young men's demeanors changed when speaking to the inmates. These were criminals who had similar upbringings, came from the same streets, and exhibited the same behaviors. Every so often, the inmates managed to get through to the kids because they spoke the same vernacular and lived the same experiences.

This is how I feel when I interact with members of the Alt-Right. Some of them are irredeemable, horrible people. Yet, in my view, to be defined by one's ideology is already "problematic." To be unable to associate with those you disagree with (within limits), to think there is an absolute correlation between one's politics and one's character, is something I find reprehensible. "The personal is the political" is a totalitarian progressive decree that I reject entirely.

To reduce every individual one encounters to their race, gender, or ethnicity is something that is unacceptable in one's friends. I find it vile that for many of these people anything I do or say is simply a function of being a Jew. Whether I act one way or in the complete opposite, either would somehow be taken as a function of being Jewish. Just as with the left, if you can ascribe motivations to others, then it is easy to "prove" what those motivations are. I knew going into this project that the anti-Semites—the undiluted ones—would regard anything I did as illegitimate. There was simply nothing I could do that they would be satisfied with, since their worldview—much like progressives'—is strongly grounded on impugning their foes' intentions.

Some in the Alt-Right like to accuse Jewish people of "shapeshifting," meaning identifying as Jewish when it's convenient but then identifying as white when that suits us. This isn't a function of Judaism so much as it is a function of language. For a long time it was commonly believed that eating high-fat foods would make a person fat; hence all the low-fat foods clogging supermarket aisles. It seemed to make sense because the words are identical.

Judaism has a genetic component and a cultural one—as does whiteness. It is the terms that are imprecise, not the speaker. One can be Jewish and white (or not-white) in the same way that being tall doesn't preclude someone from being, say, left-handed. Let's add to the fact that it is not at all clear whether Middle Easterners are considered white. Many contemporary racists say they aren't due to hue; many historic racialists said yes due to features. Similarly, "white" can mean of European descent, or it can specifically refer to WASPs.

For some people—not just in the Alt-Right—Jews are simply an abstraction. It's Jon Stewart and Debbie Wasserman Schultz and Chuck Schumer on their televisions not merely disagreeing with them but condemning them as stupid or evil or both. The left is very big on optics but feels—with reason—that to acknowledge and adjust for the wrong kind of prejudices is granting them power. The problem is that in a democracy prejudices have power regardless. They influence how people vote and how they contribute their money. The right wing deals with tradeoffs, while the left simply pretends costs don't exist or don't/shouldn't really matter.

I remain convinced that among the Alt-Right there exist young people, especially young men, who are not lost to the world. I am certain that *some* can be turned away from the path they are currently on, that for myriad reasons they haven't been able to or haven't felt able to choose better, and that they aren't beyond hope. Like with the *Scared Straight* kids, many or even most are a lost cause. But what's the point of being an author and a pundit if I can't persuade people? Even if 98 percent of people who hear me out dismiss what I have to say, 2 percent is still a huge number.

One of the biggest ways that gays and lesbians achieved acceptance in the United States was through a sort of ambassador program. As more and more men and women came out of the closet, it became harder and harder to stereotype and dismiss an entire population. An ambiguous "them," defined only by sexual practices that many felt were unappealing and therefore bad and therefore wrong, are easy to ostracize—they only exist as an abstraction, after all. It's far harder to hate one's uncle or cousin, even if they act in stereotypical ways. The more common impulse—especially among young people—is to seek common ground and understanding of one's loved ones rather than condemning and alienating someone who doesn't seem to be causing any harm whatsoever. If I have to be the lesbian sister that gets a Nazi or two to question their anti-Semitism, then so be it. Perhaps I am being naïve, but I would much rather be naïve than cynical. The cynic is the man without hope, who projects his hopelessness to the world at large. (Or perhaps I will be the Jew who validates their anti-Semitism after all.)

What statistics teach us is that within any group there will be a distribution. A group of tall people will have someone be the shortest. Politically, every group will have a relative right wing and left wing as well. There were Bolsheviks and Mensheviks among the revolutionary communists, for example, which translate to "Mores" and "Lesses."

In late 2015 I was preparing for a public debate with an intellectual from the tradition of anarchist Murray Rothbard. Curious as to just how bad Rothbard got at his nadir, I came upon a thread on the neo-Nazi message board Stormfront. It had the pithy title of "Murray Rothbard (Jew) defending David Duke." In fact Rothbard wasn't defending Duke so much as making the case that the criticisms of Duke were unfounded, that like the protagonist of Camus's *The Stranger* he was actually being condemned for reasons other than his purported sins. It's the same sort of thinking as when I told an employee of the Innocence Project—a nonprofit dedicated to using DNA to exonerate falsely convicted killers—that their new slogan should be "Not every rapist is a murderer."

On the thread, one Nazi (the left-wing, inclusive iteration in the group) opined, "Finally, a Jew I'd be willing to invite into my house." Against him was the right-wing exclusionary user, who insisted, "Are any of us really stupid enough to be snuckered by a jew pretending to be on 'our side'? I would hope not and most real White activist [sic] here are a little more sauvy [sic] and intelligent to be took in [sic] by these conartist [sic]." Finally there came the moderate position, which attempts to take the best from both sides but ends up being ineffectual in the long run: "There are some good decent jews out there that are not evil or corrupted, and aren't zionists. But they are few and far between. It's much safer trusting no jews at all than trying to pick which few you should trust."

When dismissing an entire group, even the Alt-Right, one effectively denies its individual members' humanity. Even within an ideology, whether Nazism or progressivism, one will find a continuum of thought and adherence to the worldview— and one's adherence might change constantly. Conservatives, blind to history, tout the nuclear family as the height of stability. Yet the nuclear family is rarely "stable." There are deaths and births. Children go through puberty and leave the home. Dad loses his job or Mom gets sick. The relationships are dynamic. So to condemn people for their ideas in a blanket way—as opposed to condemning ideas or actions themselves—is to miss certain opportunities.

One of the great accomplishments of Martin Luther King (and apologies for invoking him, since it has become so banal) is that he managed to bring prejudiced people to his side. Attitudes in the South toward blacks and their place in society were changed by viewing well-dressed men and women attacked by dogs and blasted by fire hoses. The starry-eyed might claim that prejudice was thereby eliminated, and in many cases that was surely true. But a more modest view is that many people, *still maintaining antipathy toward black Americans*, found the visuals to be repellent. They didn't like King and his supporters, but they disliked what they saw even more. Such thinking, that humans frequently have to select between two bad choices, is part and parcel of the right-wing view of humanity and seems a far more realistic explanation of human behavior than the idea that prejudice was or can be somehow totally or even largely expunged from a culture grounded in it.

In January 2017, shortly after Trump's inauguration, I was disturbed to see Richard Spencer (who coined the term "Alt-Right") getting sucker-punched in the face. He obviously didn't suffer major damage, wasn't knocked out, and I doubt even had a bruise. Yes, Spencer is pretty much actually a national socialist. But I still wrote an article attacking the violence. My main point was that we live in a culture where everyone working for President Trump is brazenly referred to as a White Supremacist or a Nazi, even Jewish advisors like Jared Kushner. If punching "Nazis" becomes permissible in any sense, that means actual Jewish people—not to mention, say, Sarah Huckabee Sanders—can be slugged in the face at random. That's a very difficult position to defend on ethical grounds or (if one is a complete Machiavellian) on strategic grounds. There are very few people in America who are comfortable seeing their fellow citizens being assaulted. Yet if we don't understand people's needs and wants, if people—especially young men—feel unheard, violence is the only other way for them to express themselves.

As such, I present this intellectual time capsule of the New Right as it burst into the popular consciousness. As the Virgil in this Inferno, I will be attempting to present logical, rational explanations for the New Right's foundational beliefs. They're not crazy. They're not suicidal. They're as American as apple pie.

2

★

THE LURKER AT THE THRESHOLD

Mike Wallace: You are out to destroy almost every edifice in the contemporary American way of life: our Judeo-Christian religion; our modified, government-regulated capitalism; our rule by the majority will. Other reviews have said that you scorn churches and the concept of God. Are these accurate criticisms?

Ayn Rand: Yes.

It all started with the Trollboard.

On November 11, 2011, I went to the FEE mansion in Irving ton, New York, to hear Yaron Brook, executive director of the Ayn Rand Institute, speak about Rand's philosophy. Founded by Leonard Read in 1946, FEE—the Foundation for Economic Education was the first free-market think tank in the post FDR era, an early proponent of free-market views, and the nexus for those principled right-wingers who would be derided as extremists or kooks or both.

In 1946 Milton Friedman and George Stigler—who both later won the Nobel Prize in Economics—coauthored a pamphlet for FEE titled "Roofs or Ceilings?" They argued that rent control (as any other price control) artificially leads to a shortage of supply and exacerbates housing problems rather than helping them.

The novelist-philosopher Rand, an early FEE advisor, did not take kindly to the publication, claiming it "without exception, the most pernicious thing ever issued by an avowedly conservative organization." She insisted on grounding capitalism in moral terms, not merely utilitarian ones, and wondered "why did Leonard Read hire two reds" (i.e., communists, meaning Friedman and Stigler)? She went on in her resignation letter to say (emphasis and capitalization in original):

> *Their basic premise is that everything belongs to everybody—and that the arguing among various factions is only about methods of dividing it up. NOW I SUBMIT THAT IN A CIVILIZED SOCIETY ONE DOES NOT INCLUDE THE SOCIALIZATION OF PRIVATE HOMES AMONG THE SOCIAL "POSSIBILITIES"— AND ONE DOES NOT DISCUSS IT IN THAT TONE OF CALM, ACADEMIC DETACHMENT, AS IF IT WERE A COURSE AS PROPER TO CONSIDER AS ANY OTHER.*[1]

It's because of things like this that I hesitate to describe myself as being influenced by Rand. In my personal experience, for a certain percentage of the population greater than 10 percent but less than 50 percent, being a Randian is perceived as identical to being a Scientologist. My position is that Rand doesn't have all the right answers, but she does have all the right questions—and that puts her far and away ahead of many other people.

One of the big differences between Rand and myself was that she was a minarchist, a believer in minimal, limited government. I am an anarchist, someone who does not believe in the legitimacy of government at all. There's a joke in these sorts of circles: "What's the difference between a minarchist and an anarchist? Six months." What usually takes people over the line is the work of nineteenth-century abolitionist Lysander Spooner, whose 1869 essay "The Constitution of No Authority" argues that

> [t]he Constitution has no inherent authority or obligation. It has no authority or obligation at all, unless as a contract between man and man. And it does not so much as even purport to be a contract between persons now existing. It purports, at most, to be only a contract between persons living eighty years ago. And it can be supposed to have been a contract then only between persons who had already come to years of discretion, so as to be competent to make reasonable and obligatory contracts. Furthermore, we know, historically, that only a small portion even of the people then existing were consulted on the subject, or asked, or permitted to express either their consent or dissent in any formal manner. Those persons, if any, who did give their consent formally, are all dead now.[2]

Therefore, Spooner concludes, the Constitution "has either authorized such a government as we have had, or has been powerless to prevent it. In either case, it is unfit to exist."[3] Spooner's thought has been condensed into one simple meme, his photo overlaid with the caption "Social contract? I didn't sign shit."

Anarchism in this sense does *not* mean no police, for example. It holds that security would be handled more safely, cheaply, and effectively by private companies, in the same way that UPS had trackable packages for years while the government post office monopoly routinely lost mail and millions in taxpayer dollars.

Rand died in 1982, Read in 1983, Stigler in 1991, and Friedman in 2006. The Soviet Union was dead and gone, and central planning completely discredited intellectually. It was a different world by 2011, and through it all that lighthouse of freedom that was the FEE mansion stayed atop that little hill in Irvington. Having Brook speak there sixty-five years after Rand and Read fell out could be seen as nothing else but a long-overdue rapprochement.

The crowd at the cold and drafty mansion skewed older and white. As Brook spoke about the moral case for capitalism ("Does anyone really think Bernie Madoff was ever truly happy?"), many of them nodded out for a spell. After the question-and-answer period, everyone mingled around. I asked Brook if he had read *Ayn Rand and the World She Made*, Anne Heller's authoritative 2009 account of Rand's life. "I am more interested in Rand's philosophy than I am in her biography," he insisted, a bit at variance with Rand's repeated claim that her life was evidence that her system of Objectivism "corresponds to reality."

One of the people in the crowd was a young man by the name of Jesse. He was tall, portly, and wearing a trilby, the official hat of internet geeks worldwide. Between his shoe-polish-black hair and (as I later learned) a wardrobe consisting almost entirely of Superman t-shirts, he looked like a factory-reject Clark Kent.

We quickly got to talking and realized that we shared the same irreverent sense of humor, admiration for Rand, and complete contempt for establishment politics and government in general. He was very bright and quick-witted, the latter often lacking among the all-too-humorless Rand crowd. It turned out that Jesse lived two train stops away from me in Brooklyn, so we took the Metro-North back to Grand Central with a couple of others, had a late dinner at a diner, and then headed back to Brooklyn.

Shortly thereafter, he added me on Facebook. And shortly after that, he added me to the Trollboard. The Trollboard was a Facebook group set to "secret," meaning it was not searchable and one had to be added by someone who was already an existing member. The board was young but quite diverse, with members from all over the country and a few from overseas. It was a place to post articles and mock things in our culture that the trolls found humorous or contemptible or both. It was also a safe space of sorts, with the biggest rule being that you can't "take Trollboard off of Trollboard."

Having formed in the aftermath of the 2008 Ron Paul campaign, the Trollboard had a membership composed almost entirely of anarchists. But unlike myself, they were anarchists in the tradition of the late Murray Rothbard. It was a name I was somewhat familiar with, but I had never encountered many Rothbardians before. During his lifetime, Rothbard was nicknamed "Mr. Libertarian" for good reason. Much of the modern libertarian movement was influenced or founded by him directly—something which many modern libertarians are somewhat uneasy with, due to Rothbard's own idiosyncrasies.

I had read *An Enemy of the State*, the Rothbard biography by Justin Raimondo, several years prior and had been unimpressed. I too became more interested in his philosophy and his influence than I was in his biography. I learned that—especially online—there was a population of people heavily influenced by his philosophy of "anarcho-capitalism." They called themselves "ancaps" for short, and their colors were black and yellow—black being the traditional flag of anarchy (in other words, a flag with nothing there) and gold being the symbol of free enterprise and trade.

As time went on with the Trollboard, I became close friends with many of the members. Once a week we even got together for Hoppe (pronounced "Hop-uh") Hour, named after Rothbard's protégé Hans-Hermann Hoppe (author of *Democracy: The God That Failed*). Conversations about the most esoteric of cultural and political issues lasted way into the night.

At some point, however, certain members began making references I had never heard and posting links to blogs I was unfamiliar with, such as Jim's Blog and Xenosystems. VDARE .com focused on immigration, while AmRen.com was about "race realism" (i.e., "scientific racism"). They would bring up "HBD," meaning "human biodiversity," the idea that different human populations have important inherent biological differences. They spoke of NRx—short for neoreaction—and the Dark Enlightenment, right-wing strains of thought that were more skeptical of contemporary culture than even the ancaps. The term Alt-Right was not yet a thing, certainly not like it would become within a few short years.

The biggest and most innovative name by far in this internet scene was Mencius Moldbug, the pseudonym of programmer Curtis Yarvin. Moldbug's blog was called "Unqualified Reservations," and it was as remarkable for its radical ideology as for Yarvin's use of seemingly interminable prose. It was Moldbug who formulated the concept of the Cathedral, pointing out that "the left is the party of the educational organs, at whose head is the press and universities. This is our 20th-century version of the established church. Here at UR, we sometimes call it the *Cathedral*."

He goes on to explain that

> in post-1945 America, the source of all new ideas is the university. Ideas check out of the university, but they hardly ever check in. Thence, they flow outward to the other arms of the educational system as a whole: the mainstream media and the public schools. Eventually

they become our old friend, "public opinion." This process is slow, happening on a generational scale, and thus the 45-year lag.

The Cathedral, with its informal union of church and state, is positioned perfectly. It has all the advantages of being a formal arm of government, and none of the disadvantages. Because it formulates public policy, it is best considered our ultimate governing organ, but it certainly bears no responsibility for the success or failure of said policy. Moreover, it gets to program the little worm that is inserted in everyone's head, beginning at the age of five and going all the way through grad school.

If anyone is in an obvious position to manufacture consent, it is (as [legendary commentator] Walter Lippmann openly proposed) first the journalists themselves, and next the universities which they regard as authoritative.

For example, we can ask: which set of individuals exerts more influence over American journalists? American professors, or American CEOs? American diplomats, or American generals? In both cases, the answer is clearly the former.

Which means that

you have *no rational reason* to trust anything coming out of the Cathedral—that is, the universities and press. You have no more reason to trust these institutions than you have to trust, say, the Vatican. In fact, they are motivated to mislead you in ways that the Vatican is not, because the Vatican does not have deep, murky,

and self-serving connections in the Washington bu-
reaucracy. They claim to be truth machines. Why
wouldn't they?

As a result, Moldbug claims, cultural movement is always
leftward. "The leftward direction is, *itself,* the principle of organization. [. . .] So, for instance, if you take the average segregationist voter of 1963 and let him vote in the 2008 election, he
will be way out on the wacky right wing."

Moldbug is not enthusiastic about our future: "There is simply no power in the world, not even obviousness, that can dis-
place our present economics faculty, or dislodge them from
their lock on policy. They have tenure, after all. They're scientists, which means that if you oppose them you're an ASS. And
they will remain in power until someone drives a tank or two
into Harvard Yard—which, come to think of it, doesn't sound
like such a bad idea at all." Here Moldbug is channeling Rand,
who explicitly said that "the universities are the real villains in
the picture" and that "those who didn't go to college are more
intelligent and better informed and less easily fooled than the
people who did go to college."

By now, this concept of the Cathedral has seeped into common parlance, with both sides of the aisle frequently discussing media-constructed "narrative." The late Andrew Breitbart
saw this as essential, writing, "The left does not win its battles
in debate. It doesn't have to. In the twenty-first century, media
is everything. The left wins because it controls the narrative. The
narrative is controlled by the media. The left is the media. Narrative is everything. I call it the Democrat-media complex." But
the jeers against Jeb and the other Republican contenders during the campaign showed that this framework was about much
more than merely hating the Democratic Party (which is itself
not synonymous with "the left").

One book that feeds into New Right thought is *The Nurture Assumption* by Judith Rich Harris. Unlike the left-wing premise that we are all malleable by society, Harris points out that much of the development of the individual is genetic, innate, and internal. She also demonstrates that children define themselves not by *unity* but by *opposition*. "They don't identify with their parents because parents are not people like themselves—parents are grownups. Children think of themselves as kids." However, "if there are enough of them, [they think of each other] as girls and boys."

> When only one group is present, groupness weakens and self-categorization shifts in the direction of me and away from us. That's when you get within-group differentiation—that's when members of a group jockey for status, and choose or are chosen for different roles.

This applies just as easily to adults. When it comes to progressivism, the New Right is united. But without that common enemy, there was very little in common to be had.

I knew enough about how ideas permeate the culture to see that this movement was going to go *somewhere*. The ideas were not new per se, but they were novel in how they were being discussed and promulgated. At its most basic it was both a healthy and a toxic approach to confronting leftist talking points of the moment. For all of progressivism's blather about confronting racism and racists, it is very rare for a progressive—very rare for *anyone*—to find a coherent "racist" (in some sense of the term) who can challenge them on their views and have a rational, intelligent conversation about them. Some racists do still have all their teeth, after all. Soon enough, I found myself invited to go down the rabbit hole.

Twin Peaks: Fire Walk with Me was the 1992 prequel to Lynch's iconic (and recently resurrected) television series. At one point in the movie FBI agent Dale Cooper (Kyle MacLachlan) walks into the office hallway and stares up at the security camera. He walks into the adjoining room with the security monitors and sees the empty hallway on the screen. He returns to the hall, stares up at the camera again, and then goes back to the monitors. The officer manning the station looks over his shoulder at Cooper, wondering what he could possibly be looking for.

As Cooper tries for a third time, the long-lost agent Phillip Jeffries (David Bowie) steps off the elevator behind him. Now, when Cooper returns to the monitor room, he sees himself standing in the hallway on the screen. Understandably panicked at the seemingly impossible visual, Cooper rushes down the hall calling for his supervisor. Putting Cooper off for the moment, the rest of the team wonders where Jeffries has been for all the intervening years.

"Listen," Jeffries tells them ominously. "*I've been to one of their meetings.*"

The scene then cuts to a roomful of characters who are meant to be spirits of evil. The actors had been filmed moving in reverse, even speaking in reverse, and then that reverse-footage was played backward. The end result is a nightmarish analogue to the way people actually speak and move: every motion, every syllable is not quite correct.

I might be one of the few people who knows how Agent Jeffries felt, because I too had "been to one of their meetings." Although the *Twin Peaks* entities lived "above a convenience store" (the nature of which is never made completely clear), the meeting I had attended was inside a Chelsea townhouse. It was held in October 2014, when the movement's identifier on Twitter was #NRx.

"Salutations my motley crew of reactionaries, monarchists, thought-criminals, rapscallions, scip-scaps and scalawags," the invite began. Already I was a little confused. I didn't know what a scip-scap was, and I wasn't sure that scalawags existed outside of a nautical context. My biggest idol is Alexander Hamilton, which I guess makes me monarchist-adjacent, but I most certainly was a thought-criminal and a rapscallion, perhaps even in that order.

There were about eighteen of us, all of us males but not all of us white males. This included several of my friends, one of whom I can't tell to this day if they're of Indian, Pakistani, or Arab descent. None of us lived in a basement, unless a New York garden apartment can be considered a basement. There was only one overweight person, further defying the stereotype that the subculture was full of perpetual-adolescent fatties living with mom and dad while spilling rage online. Everyone was highly educated and very bright, and immediately and obviously so.

The men began eyeing one other to see what was safe to say. As thought-criminals, we were used to biting our tongues. As scip-scaps—well, I don't know. "I'm part Native American," one guy said in response to another's gently probing questions.

"Sorry," the other man laughed. "I guess everyone is trying to figure out everybody else's genotype and phenotype."

"You mean like Mark Shea?"

It was the most insider of references possible. As uncomprehending and credulous media types began sniffing around the scene, many NRx members decided to play into their preconceptions and make fools of them in the process. A blogger named Mark Shea accordingly posted on the Catholic site Patheos:

I was initiated into the first stages of the Dark Enlightenment, which involved me stripping down naked so

> people could "inspect my phenotype." I was then given
> a series of very personal questions, often relating to
> sexual matters. I was then told to put on a black cape.
> (I really regret doing this but at the time I was younger,
> more impressionable and eager to please.)

"Phenotype" refers to how an organism presents visually, whereas genotype refers to an organism's genetics. Many genetic illnesses come about when both parents are genotypic carriers but phenotypically display as the norm. The idea, however, that one's phenotype is open to inspection via stripping down is basically a dick joke—and yet it was taken at face value.

As we gathered around for steaks around a long wooden table, I thought back to a previous dinner party I'd attended, one held in Brooklyn a couple of months prior. Depending on one's perspective, it was either a fortuitous coincidence or a sign of America's demise that every single individual there was either a first- or second-generation immigrant from a different country. Being somewhat of a dick, I knew better than to let such an opportunity go to waste.

"Let's go around the table," I suggested, "and tell one another who our people hate."

"We don't hate anyone," one girl insisted.

This was not how human beings operate. "Well, who borders your home country?"

"Oh, we don't *hate* them. We just think they're dumb."

As a lifelong New Yorker, I enjoyed that diversity. Actual diversity, not a euphemism for "having one black person there." But as an intellectual, I also enjoyed the diversity of the neoreactionary dinner. I knew that everyone would have their own unique and well-thought-out (to the point of tunnel vision) philosophy. Still, I felt a bit like an imposter, a tourist, and a dilettante—and not for the first time.

The Jewish Question is a never-ending topic in Alt-Right circles, especially given the vocal group that insists that "the JQ" is the only question that matters. As such, anyone in this loose subculture will frequently be tweeted at about the issue. Some are so convinced that their worldview is inseparable from anti-Semitism that they assume that I must share their perspective. More than once I've had to reply, "Is this where I tell you that I went to yeshiva?"

As we went around the table making introductions, my concern was that I didn't want the hassle of trying to speak for all Jewry. Nor did I want to talk to someone, have an interesting conversation, and then have to discover that he was an anti-Semite. Finally, I didn't want to validate the common anti-Semitic trope that Jews are sneaky and deceptive.

One of the techniques I use in my general life is to utter a marginally provocative statement upon first meeting someone. Their reaction will be visceral and more importantly it will be sincere. A funny person will laugh or build upon my comment, perhaps with some sort of comeback. An eyeroll is fine too, registering disapproval but also recognizing an offhand comment isn't a big deal. The ones who make some face are the dangers. These are the ones who are unable or uninterested in refraining from demonstrating their distaste.

One by one, everyone stood up and introduced themselves: who they were, what industry they were in, where they were from. Finally it came to me. "I'm Michael Malice," I announced, "and I'm here representing ZOG." ZOG is an acronym for "Zionist Occupied Government." Many in the New Right are *philo*-Semites, viewing Jews as the acme of intelligence and admiring the Jewish people's ability to survive millennia of assault. They recognize that American Jews are frequently progressive, but they also recognize that Jewish contributions to culture and politics cover all political persuasions. Most importantly, they perceive being Jewish as akin to being like any other sort of ethnic American, largely a non-issue—especially on an individual level.

Then there are the rest.

When I made my triply absurd comment, I quickly scanned the room for everyone's reactions. Most burst out laughing. The rest either made an expression of displeasure or had no reaction whatsoever. Immediately I could guess who I was dealing with, who would perceive me as a person and who would think of me in the context of the identity politics that they supposedly abhorred. I knew that my presence there would make the latter types uncomfortable: What is *he* doing here? I knew that, and I was delighted by it.

In the conversations that followed, both at dinner and in the study afterward, I encountered ideas that I'd never heard before, and they were being backed up. Godwin's Law states that "as an online discussion grows longer, the probability of a comparison involving Hitler approaches 1." Invoking Godwin is an assertion that someone has gone off the deep end in terms of hyperbole. Only Hitler was Hitler; not even Mussolini was Hitler.

With neoreaction there is a similar law, almost a corollary. It doesn't have a name, but the law can be stated that "as a neoreactionary discussion grows longer, the probability that the conversation becomes 'We never should have entered World War II!' approaches 1." Pat Buchanan even wrote an entire book on the subject. His 2008 *New York Times* bestseller *Churchill, Hitler, and "The Unnecessary War"* argued that both world wars could have been avoided not just by the United States but by *England*. (For some reason, the quotation marks around "The Unnecessary War" are on the title page and official book listing but not on the cover.) When dealing with the New Right, one starts to notice things and wonder if they are coincidental or mistakes—or clues to some hidden, deeper truth.

The argument against World War II is not hard to grasp, though it seems insane for many to hear even as a hypothesis. The starting point is simple: We did not prevent the Holocaust. Therefore, if we hadn't entered World War II, all those millions of people would have perished regardless. As unpleasant as it is to hear, it's a wash. Neither in actual history nor in a parallel universe is Auschwitz prevented.

The orthodox view is that FDR and later Truman sided with Stalin because the enemy of my enemy is my friend. The neoreactionary view is that, given the choice between totalitarianism and democracy or even democratic progressivism, the choice is pretty clear. But a better alternative is not therefore somehow clean and pure. Neoreactionaries do not view World War II as a victory of good over evil. The popular presentation as such is a testament to past and current leftist education. Despite right-wing rhetoric to the contrary, few on the left generally regard Stalin as a good guy. Yet Hitler is such a bad person that, perhaps, next to him anyone else comes off as *relatively* good.

For neoreactionaries, World War II was a battle of three rival ideologies made manifest in three respective rival gangs: the fascists, the communists, and the progressives. Stalin's reign was longer, bloodier, and just as evil as Hitler's was. Despite his rhetoric of "equality," Stalin had no issue with the forced migration of entire ethnicities throughout the Soviet Union. The Holodomor—his intentional starvation of millions of Ukrainians—is increasingly being recognized as an act of genocide. Finally (and crucially in terms of comparison), Stalin was planning an assault on the Soviet Union's Jewish population right before his death in 1953—years after the Holocaust was public knowledge. As one person put it, "Which murderous ideology should I be worried about: the one that won or the one that lost?"

In the logic of the evangelical left, to claim someone is as bad as or even worse than Hitler is literally incomprehensible. It's almost like asking if Judas was in fact a hero because his betrayal is what allowed Christ to fulfill His earthly mission and redeem all of humanity. To bring someone to parity with Hitler is perceived as mitigating Hitler's unique evil or even downright defending him. It's a very touchy subject; Hitlerism didn't happen all that long ago and all that far away. It remains the slipperiest of slopes, and understandably so.

The neoreactionary view is that the United States should have bided its time and let Hitler and Stalin battle each other to the death or at least to a stalemate. Then it would have been far easier for America to come in and finish them both off. Alternatively, we could have finished off Hitler at a later date, in which case the outcome would still have been an Allied victory albeit with a far weaker Stalin. A weaker Stalin might have meant a free north Korea, different outcomes in Maoist China (or even a non-Maoist China, saving 45 million Chinese in the process), and freedom for the Soviet satellite countries like Czechoslovakia and Hungary.

None of this is plausible if one thinks of World War II as a Crusade, a religious war between the progressive children of the light against the fascist children of darkness (with some Stalinist moral ambiguity that we don't need to talk about at the moment because it ruins the story). This is also to ignore the fact that it was Stalin's forces that reached Hitler's bunker first, not ours.

But once one starts questioning fighting Hitler, one might start questioning fighting some of Hitler's ideas. One of the most heretical buzzwords in contemporary culture is the specter of eugenics. The science or "pseudoscience" of eugenics holds that some genes are better than others and that we should encourage the better ones to reproduce and discourage the worse ones. Expanded, this means that certain people—often those of a given race, but not always—shouldn't reproduce for the sake of humanity. Taken to its logical conclusion (i.e., divorced from moral reasoning), this leads to things like forced sterilization and even genocide. The Nazis were the most famous and thoroughgoing practitioners of eugenics in human history, and as such in common parlance Nazis = eugenics = worst thing ever.

Yet eugenics is practiced every single day all over the world. It is practiced in its horrific sense, as with selective-gender abortion and the killing of female infants in societies that view male children as more desirable. But it's also practiced in populations with low genetic diversity (this is not a slur or a euphemism), such as Hasidic Jews. The Hasidic Jewish community, due to inbreeding, has a higher than average rate of genetic diseases such as Tay-Sachs. Yet there's a workaround. As *Tablet* magazine reports, "After conducting genetic screening, [an organization called] Dor Yeshorim assigns identification numbers that correspond to its clients' genetic data. Before or soon after meeting, potential partners exchange ID numbers and dial an automated hotline to check genetic compatibility—a phone call that almost always determines if a relationship will move forward or end."

As of 2012 approximately 67 percent of infants with Down syndrome have been aborted. Does that mean that inside the breast of every expectant mother beats the heart of a Nazi eugenicist? This subject has become so riddled with taboo and outrage that it has led to some truly odd outcomes. In 2014 Fredrick Brennan authored an opinion piece titled "Why I Support Eugenics." Brennan was the founder of the message board 8chan ("Twice as good as 4chan!"), and suffers from Osteogenesis imperfecta. As a result of this genetic disease, he has severely stunted growth and is confined to a wheelchair—hence his handle of "Hotwheels."

The common name for Brennan's condition is "brittle bone disease." It is heartbreaking to read his contention that Osteogenesis imperfecta "is one of the most painful conditions in the world" knowing that he's speaking from firsthand experience. Many know the extreme pain of breaking a bone once or twice in one's life. Few have to endure that pain over and over, or the stress of living in constant fear about when it will happen again.

Brennan suggests offering carriers of extreme genetic diseases like his a cash sum in order to undergo sterilization, arguing that this would save millions in future medical costs alone. Such genetic testing is easily done, and in his view this would be a very humane way to make sure no child has to live a life where they will never know the fun of running around outside due to Osteogenesis imperfecta. "Eugenics is a humanitarian idea," he concludes, "not a national socialist one."

So where did Brennan run this piece? A page as far from removed from humanitarianism as possible: the neo-Nazi site Daily Stormer. "I could find no other publication which would publish this article," Brennan reveals, "and I am far from a neo-Nazi." For the evangelical left, those who suffer largely exist as mechanisms for others' salvation, but not as beings with consciences of their own—or more precisely, they are allowed to have their own conscience if and only if it fits into their salvation model. Else, they can be considered as corrupted.

The black man loses his "blackness," which is a state of grace and nothing to do with skin color. Clarence Thomas isn't "really" black but Bill Clinton is, in the same way that the Eucharist literally becomes the body of Christ. Similarly, the disabled object of empathy and veneration becomes a hateful heretic, and eugenics remains a taboo that must be enforced rather than an idea to be discussed. Brennan's piece is calm and reasoned. He is speaking from personal experience and has an informed point of view. The shame that Brennan had to be driven into the hateful arms of the Daily Stormer kicking and screaming (or screaming at least) is lost on progressives.

As the evening wound down, the conversation turned to what each of us would do if we were given a billion dollars. "I would discover the virus for homosexuality," one man said, "and fund a vaccine."

The idea that homosexuality is caused by a pathogen sounds crackpot at first. It's a strange welding of the old "homosexuality is a disease" argument with the more contemporary "people are born gay." The fact of the matter is that we don't know what causes homosexuality; we don't even know what causes *hetero*sexuality. It's unclear how the human mind becomes attracted to what it is attracted to. This also ignores the eternal question of whether homosexuality refers to the attraction or to the act itself. Are you really gay if you get on your knees but your heart isn't in it?

Gay people very frequently claim that they were born gay, but this is a claim no one can make with precision. "I was born gay" is a looser way of saying "I've been gay since I can remember." In terms of memory, being born gay and having one's sexuality crystallize at, say, six months would be recalled in identical terms. On this point, gay people have as little insight as heterosexuals do about why they're attracted to what they're attracted to.

Due to twin studies, we do know that homosexuality has a genetic component of some kind. Identical twins are genetically the same person, naturally occurring clones of one other. Surveys of identical twins have found that in many cases both twins are gay or straight, but in some cases one is gay and one isn't. This holds true both among twins raised separately and together. Meaning, twins with the same genes and same environment often have different outcomes with regard to sexuality. So there is *some* genetic effect but not enough for a guarantee.

The issue with homosexuality and genetics is that it's extremely evolutionarily disadvantageous. Those who prefer to have intercourse with their own gender are far, far less likely to pass their genes along for obvious reasons. It's funny to point this out to the evangelical left, because even a word as literal as "disadvantageous" sets some of them off, because "dis-" sounds bad and saying anything bad about gay people is homophobia and "it took Reagan five hundred years to even say the word AIDS" and "OMG go back to Bible school with that crap." That basically seems to be the reasoning, although it's rarely expressed even that linearly and coherently.

Given all of the above—it's not genetics and it's not environment and it's really a problem in terms of reproduction—where does that leave us in terms of causation? Well that brings us to the pathogen theory, espoused by such mainstream scientists as Gregory Cochran. It sounds more controversial than it needs to be, and obviously combining the words "virus" and "homosexuality" is touchy and laden with bad connotations and historical references. Yet it's as good a theory as any, and would have absolutely no effect on claims about the morality of being gay.

There are many infections that are known to cause their hosts to act in certain ways for reasons that are not clear. The zombie fungus *Ophiocordyceps unilateralis* causes ants to leave their colony, attach themselves to a leaf, and stop moving in order to function as a living host for the fungus to exploit. *Toxoplasma gondii* causes "crazy cat lady disease," which can trigger schizophrenia, bipolar disorder, OCD, and aggression. A pathogen that causes humans to be attracted to their own gender frankly seems far less upsetting than either of those two.

Yet if this pathogen were discovered, we might very well see the end—or near end—of homosexuality within a generation. One of the most insightful things Rosie O'Donnell ever said was during her time coming out of the "glass closet" in 2002 (meaning, when a person is technically still closeted but everyone in their personal life knows that they are gay). During her publicity tour, she was asked by Diane Sawyer if she wanted her children to be gay or straight. "[I]f I were to pick," O'Donnell mused, "would I rather have my children have to go through the struggles of being gay in America, or being heterosexual? I would say heterosexual. [. . .] I think life is easier if you're straight."

One of the first "out" gay people, Quentin Crisp (1908–99), agreed. As recounted in *The Independent*, "In 1997, he told *The Times* that he would advise parents to abort a foetus if it could be shown to be genetically predetermined to be gay: 'If it (homosexuality) can be avoided, I think it should be.'" And while there are many parents who genuinely don't care if their child is gay or straight, there are plenty who, if given the chance in private, would opt for the same preference as O'Donnell or Crisp.

I listened to all this with a great deal of interest. It was the sort of intellectual conversation that would cause many New Yorkers to go apoplectic—yet most of them would be unable to articulate why. As for myself, I had a guess as to why having the issue discussed in such terms would lead to awkwardness. "Can we please have a conversation," I suggested, "that *doesn't* end in advocating genocide?"

"I just think it would make the progs go nuts."

"Don't you understand that it's not about the gays?" I said. "If gay people never existed, they would find some other group to champion in order to dominate society. There are an infinite amount of tools in their toolbox, and each is disposable. Besides, if you got rid of gay people, who do you think is going to be creating culture? The Catholic Church?"

Apparently that was precisely who they thought would be creating culture. Sure, the Catholic Church was the be-all and end-all of culture for quite a long time. Yet it's hard to imagine a world where it can produce something to compete with *It's Always Sunny in Philadelphia* or even Lena Dunham's *Girls*. The argument is that the Catholic Church and other bastions of traditionalism are only regarded as passé due to the progressive control of entertainment. I found this absurd, even on New Right terms. What I didn't realize at the time was to what extent the New Right was creating its own culture at that very moment—and had been since its inception.

3

*

THE STRIKE

> If you look at the great philosophies and ideas that have
> moved the world; if you look at the great religions—
> and the Judeo-Christian religion has been the origin of
> human rights and the significance of the individual—
> do you think you would have ever had those great
> guidelines had people gone out and said, "Brothers,
> I believe in consensus!" Of course you wouldn't. You
> would've had nothing great, nothing of value.
>
> —Margaret Thatcher

Every movement has a creation myth. Conservatives have the
Founding Fathers. Liberals have the civil rights movement. But
for the New Right, Genesis starts a little more than twenty-five
years ago. The dirty little secret is that the New Right actually
isn't all that new. Rather, this subculture has its roots in what
was known as the Old Right, emerging at the moment when the
"paleolibertarians" (meaning Rothbard and his people) teamed
up with the "paleoconservatives" (i.e., Buchanan et al.).

"There is a religious war going on in our country for the soul
of America," Pat Buchanan told the 1992 Republican National
Convention. "It is a cultural war, as critical to the kind of nation we will one day be as was the Cold War itself."

While we do know that First Lady Barbara Bush was wearing pearls at the time, it's unclear as to whether she literally clutched them at that moment. She wouldn't have been the only one. The reaction from the Cathedral—the press, the political establishment, and everyone else who shaped acceptable opinion—was quick and unanimous: "What do you mean by 'culture'?" wondered three-time New York governor Mario Cuomo. "That's a word they used in Nazi Germany."

As Buchanan recounted at the time,

> Mario is not the only one to have recoiled in fear and loathing. Media who have burbled all over Mario's locutions in class warfare found my Houston speech "divisive," "hateful," and the old standby, "racist." Carl Rowan told his co-panelists on *Inside Washington* it was the closest he had ever heard to a Nazi address. Bob Beckel thought my remarks might have been ghosted by Satan himself. The savagery of the reaction—ongoing—underscores my point: As polarized as we have ever been, we Americans are locked in a cultural war for the soul of our country.[1]

It wasn't as much what Buchanan had said as how he said it. Others had taken similar positions before: protectionism; putting the American workers first; cultural conservatism. None of these were particularly objectionable, even in combination. But to dub political disagreements as a war, to imply that those on the other side were an enemy to be defeated, was a bridge too far. It's 1992! *How could we be having this conversation?*

The Cold War had ended, and it had given way to a New World Order. America was supposed to be a "kinder, gentler" nation. Everyone knew that it was time to melt down the knives and put the pitchforks away. "Everyone," that is, except for those completely outside the mainstream of political discourse.

In other words, everyone except for people like Rothbard, who had been in the audience in Houston and watched Buchanan with more than a bit of glee. Buchanan's fellow traveler Sam Francis once wrote an essay titled "Capitalism the Enemy." For Rothbard, it was precisely capitalism that was the one and only savior of mankind. Whereas Buchanan was a strict constitutionalist and a strong patriot, Rothbard was opposed to government itself—and not just the American government, but *all* government. According to Rothbard's anarcho-capitalism, all state functions could be served cheaper, better, and more effectively by the free market. This included the police and even national defense.

Whereas Buchanan's views were informed by a sense of earnestness, humility, and respect, Rothbard's every breath was laden with irreverence for authority. Buchanan was an Irish Catholic who regarded 1959's liberalizing Vatican II Council as a surrender of the forces of good (meaning orthodoxy) to those of decadent modernism. Rothbard, on the other hand, looked and sounded so much like a stereotypically Jewish New Yorker that if he had played himself in a movie it would have read as an anti-Semitic caricature.

Rothbard wasn't a misanthrope so much as he regarded very few people as worthy of his respect and admiration. As a Columbia University student, Rothbard had the luck to have George Stigler as one of his professors. Impressed with the very same pamphlet that so offended Rand, Rothbard began visiting the FEE mansion. On staff at the time was the man who would be the most important influence on Rothbard's life: Ludwig von Mises. It was on July 8, 1948, that Rothbard met him at the fabled estate.

Mises (pronounced Mee-zis) was by far the most important

figure of the Austrian School of economics. The Austrians es-
chewed economic calculation for a more philosophical approach
to issues of finance and trade. They viewed modern theories as
highly mathematical, heavily conceptual, and largely divorced
from reality. For them, virtually every contemporary economist
is akin to a geocentrist using increasingly complicated models
to predict how celestial bodies circled the Earth. Difficult math
doesn't make a calculation true, and neither does it make its
practitioner smart. This disdain for statistics can be seen in the
New Right's contempt for using numeric data as a mechanism
of persuasion. It's about the story, not the numbers.

Mises was born in 1881 in my hometown of Lvov, in what is
now Ukraine. He emigrated from Eastern Europe to New York
in 1940 and became perhaps the most thoroughgoing American defender of laissez-faire capitalism. Years later Milton Friedman would recount a story about the first meeting of the Mont
Pelerin Society, held in 1947. The group was meant to bring
together what Europeans would call liberal intellectuals and
what Americans would describe as libertarians. As Friedman
recalled, "We were discussing the distribution of income, and
whether you should have progressive income taxes. Some of the
people there were expressing the view that there could be a
justification for it." Furiously and famously, Mises declared,
"You're all a bunch of socialists!" and stormed out.[2] Much like
Rand with rent control, Mises felt that once income distribution is on the table, the jig is basically up. It simply becomes a
matter of haggling over how much socialism there is.

Mises's masterpiece was 1949's *Human Action*, a very long,
very densely written book. Mises uses "praxeology" as the basis
for human activity and seeks to answer why humans behave
the way they do in an economic sense. His work gathered the
ire of bisexual ex-Communist and *National Review* writer
Whittaker Chambers, who did not take kindly to Mises's

view that anticapitalism was rooted in envy. As his biographer put it,

> To Chambers this "shocking" thesis epitomized "know-nothing conservatism" at its "know-nothingest." In his own years as a Communist, Chambers stiffly said, he had not envied capitalists in the least.[3]

Rothbard became an attendee at Mises's New York University economics salon. He later briefly fell into Rand's orbit and was strongly influenced by her worldview as well. She would fare even worse at Chambers's pen than Mises had. When Chambers reviewed *Atlas Shrugged*, he proclaimed, "Out of a lifetime of reading, I can recall no other book in which a tone of overriding arrogance was so implacably sustained. [. . .] From almost any page of *Atlas Shrugged*, a voice can be heard, from painful necessity, commanding: 'To a gas chamber—go!'" Then as now, certain types have no problem comparing right-wingers to Nazis, even Jewish ones, as Rand (née Alice Rosenbaum) was.

Rothbard's own 1962 masterpiece, *Man, Economy and State*, was basically *Human Action* made clearer and more readable. He codified Rand's political principle that no man can initiate force against another man (which led to her advocating such things as "voluntary taxation") into the non-aggression principle or "NAP." (It is therefore a pun when anarchists refer to the Rothbardian author and pundit Andrew Napolitano as "Judge Nap.")

For Rothbard, "*no government interference with exchanges can ever increase social utility*," and "[w]e are led inexorably, then, to the conclusion that the processes of the free market always lead to a gain in social utility." Therefore, "capitalism is the fullest expression of anarchism, and anarchism is the fullest expression of capitalism. Not only are they compatible, but you can't really have one without the other."[4]

For Rothbardians—as opposed to their archenemies the neocons—the worst of all government activity is war: "It is in war that the State really comes into its own: swelling in power, in number, in pride, in absolute dominion over the economy and the society." There is no difference between a Lois Lerner and a beat cop. They are both enforcers of the state, albeit in different clothing.

Rothbard eventually made his mark in academia as well. His 1963 book *America's Great Depression* is still taught in many universities by professors who have no idea what an ancap is. As his official online biography puts it,

> Far from being a proof of the failures of unregulated capitalism, the 1929 Depression illustrates rather the dangers of government interference with the economy. The economic collapse came as a necessary correction to the artificial boom induced by the Federal Reserve System's monetary expansion during the 1920s. The attempts by the government to "cure" the downturn served only to make matters worse.[5]
>
> In making this argument, Rothbard became a pioneer in "Hoover revisionism." Contrary to the myths promoted by Hoover himself and his acolytes, Hoover was not an opponent of big government. Quite the contrary, the economic policies of the "Engineer in Politics" prefigured the New Deal. Rothbard's view of Hoover is now widely accepted.

For the evangelical left, equality and fairness are universally shared goals. Rothbard's response was a book titled *Egalitarianism as a Revolt Against Nature*. The idea that freedom and democracy are not only compatible but downright synonymous is taken for granted in contemporary American culture, but here Rothbard disagrees as well. The popular conception of democracy is one in which every voter envisions their ideal society and then votes us in that direction. In the anarchist perspective, this is akin to everyone imagining themselves as a totalitarian dictator and then selecting the politician who will best implement their plan into reality. Rothbard thought of the vote in a different way. By regarding all state action as illegitimate, he viewed the two political parties as *literal* rival gangs whose power needed to be curtailed as much as possible and hopefully destroyed altogether. He regarded the air of prestige around Congress as akin to a Mafia don's three-piece suit, a pretense of civility masking the murderous thug within. Accordingly, the New Right still regards vulgarity toward and disrespect for the elites as important mechanisms for revealing their true inner evil. Let them drop their masks and expose themselves as the moral abominations that they really are.

Though he doesn't use the word, Rothbard saw "trolling" as a way to bring down the establishment:

> Since these elites are also the hitherto unchallenged opinion-molding class in society, their rule cannot be dislodged until the oppressed public, instinctively but inchoately opposed to these elites, are shown the true nature of the increasingly hated forces who are ruling over them. To use the phrases of the New Left of the late 1960s, the ruling elite must be "demystified," "delegitimated," and "desanctified."[6]

In other words, irreverence will free us all.

It is this radical perspective on the legitimacy of voting and the state that led Rothbard to make such seemingly unpredictable political alliances. As a Columbia graduate student he had once founded a Students for Thurmond group. "I showed up at the first meeting," he recalled, "which consisted of a group of Southern students and one New York Jew, myself. There were a brace of other New York Jews there, but they were all observers from the Henry Wallace Progressive Party, puzzled and anxious to find out to what extent fascism and the Ku Klux Klan had permeated the fair Columbia campus." This was of course in 1948, not 2016. Rothbard insisted that during this period he "never once encountered any anti-Semitic hostility," yet he admitted that "there were unfortunately very few Jews."[7]

Later in his life, Rothbard wrote that he had "naively" supported the segregationist Strom Thurmond's Dixiecrat presidential candidacy in 1948, hoping at the time that "the States' Rights Party would continue to become a major party and destroy what was then a one-party Democratic monopoly in the South." By combining this bloc with Midwestern antiestablishment Republicans, a new majority party could be born. Rothbard was already anticipating Richard Nixon's notorious—but victorious—1968 "Southern strategy," twenty years ahead of time.

And it was Nixon who formed the first link between Rothbard and Buchanan, though both men found themselves on opposite political sides. After barely losing the presidency in 1960, former vice president Nixon went on to a humiliating defeat in 1962's California gubernatorial election. The press could barely hide their delight, and the contempt was more than mutual. People remember the angry "you don't have Nixon to kick around anymore" during his concessional press conference, but they forget that he prefaced it with a plea for the media to do their job without an underlying agenda. "I would hope that in the future," he said, "as a result of this campaign, that perhaps they would try at least simply to see that what both candidates say is reported, that if they have questions to ask of one candidate they ask the same questions of the other candidate."

By 1966 the former vice president (and current loser and

laughingstock) was pondering another run for the White House. A twenty-seven-year-old Pat Buchanan was the first advisor Nixon hired for his 1968 campaign, joining the team after working at the *St. Louis Globe-Democrat* as an editorialist. At first, Buchanan held a more nuanced view of the media than his new boss did. This view did not last. "The press," Nixon told him bluntly, "is the enemy."

Just like Nixon, Rand had her own cadre of enemies, breaking relationships with one follower from her inner circle after another. "Miss Rand" was nothing if not opinionated. She insisted that all her views were derived from and demonstrable by reason, and that her *Atlas Shrugged* was so tightly argued that to accept one part was to accept it all. Given her sexual peccadilloes and the claim that *Atlas* integrated economics, morality, and sex, the logical corollary was that the purely rational man demanded laissez-faire from Washington and BDSM from his women. As she described one of her characters, "the diamond band on the wrist of her naked arm gave her the most feminine of all aspects: the look of being chained."

Finding no room for intellectual discussion in Rand's sphere (and years later satirizing her in his embarrassingly juvenile and unpublished play *Mozart Was a Red*), Rothbard searched for other alliances. So while Buchanan was joining with Nixon, Rothbard was singing the praises of Tricky Dick's archenemies: the New Left. Sometimes it was hard to tell if the anarchist Rothbard was simply looking for people to take him seriously, and at other times it was hard to tell how they *could*.

For Rothbard, the way to freedom was to destroy the only thing that ever stood in its way: government. He praised the Black Power movement at first, seeing it as a useful opponent to the state (though spending little time writing about race per se, being an ultra-individualist). In 1967 Rothbard wrote that Che Guevara was "an heroic figure for our time" and "the living embodiment of the principle of Revolution." In other words, my enemy's enemy is my friend—a principle that the New Right struggles with to this day.

These sentiments were not exactly shared by Nixon the candidate or Nixon the new president in 1969. As recounted by libertarian author Radley Balko in *Rise of the Warrior Cop*, Nixon and his team had recognized that there existed a Venn diagram in the minds of his base, the so-called Silent Majority (a term Buchanan coined). They hated crime, and they hated the civil rights movement, and they hated the counterculture. What did all these things have in common? *Drugs*. Correlation might not *logically* mean causation, but politics and voting were anything but logical. As simple as that, the Drug War—the centerpiece of the ever-growing modern police state—was born, with Buchanan working in the White House as it was all being formulated.

Regardless of a politician's inclinations and even their stated intentions, they almost always kneel at the altar of internationalist trade. No one could call Nixon soft on communism. The Senate candidate who had smeared his foe as a pinko in 1950 was the vice president who had poked Soviet premier Nikita Khrushchev in the chest in the 1959 kitchen debate. This gave Nixon the cover necessary to be the president who raised a glass in 1972 to Chairman Mao, the worst mass murderer in history, in a toast written by Buchanan himself. "Only Nixon could go to China," the saying became. Similarly, as president, Nixon pushed forward much of the left's domestic legislative agenda. It was not despite his reputation as a right-winger but rather *because* of it that he was able to get away with it.

Nixon oversaw the implementation of such projects as forced school busing, Title IX, and the creation of the Occupational Safety and Health Administration (OSHA). Rather than relying on Congress, he used executive orders to create the Environmental Protection Agency (EPA) and to implement affirmative action—progressive ends implemented by progressive means. Buchanan saw firsthand that the idea that the Republicans were a strong bulwark against progressivism was usually just that: an idea. The data suggested that the opposite was true. In fact, Republican politicians were far more effective at putting over progressivism than the Democrats because there was no one to their right to criticize them for doing so.

Recognizing this, a small group of activists founded the Libertarian Party in 1972 as an alternative to the "two-party duopoly." This new "party of principle" compromised on its most basic principle: namely, whether it would advocate for an absolute minimal government or the total anarchism that Rothbard and his followers desired. Despite some early hesitation (perhaps akin to "I don't want to belong to any club that will accept me as a member"), Rothbard soon came on board to join the LP.

It was that same year that Rothbard released his most popular (though hardly mainstream) book, *For a New Liberty: The Libertarian Manifesto*, making such fair and balanced claims as, "[T]aking the twentieth century as a whole, the single most warlike, most interventionist, most imperialist government has been the United States." From there, he went on to cofound the Charles Koch Foundation in 1974, later renamed the Cato Institute per his suggestion. Yet despite his intellectual journey, Rothbard the *personality* never changed. After having broken relations with the Ayn Rand circle and then grown disenchanted with the New Left, Rothbard naturally proceeded to have a falling out with Koch and Cato president Ed Crane. As Rothbard wrote in 1981, "[T]he dominant spirit at the Cato Institute was one of paranoia, intense hatred, back-stabbing, and endless crises." He compared Crane to Nixon and laid the blame for this atmosphere solely at Crane's feet. "Either all the rest of us are Bad Guys," he insisted, "or Crane is the Bad Guy.

The movement must choose." You're either with me or you're against me.

In 1982 Rothbard cofounded the Mises Institute to help spread ancap ideas and ideals. When a *New York Times* reporter came to Mises headquarters in 2014 requesting a tour, chairman Lew Rockwell ejected him from the premises in no uncertain terms: "You're part of the regime." Rockwell correctly predicted the article would be a hit piece, and indeed *the very first sentence* defined the "libertarian faithful" as "antitax activists and war protesters, John Birch Society members and a smattering of 'truthers' who suspect the government's hand in the 2001 terrorist attacks." In other words, a collection of kooks as opposed to a group of men and women united by their opposition to Washington. After several paragraphs of trying to equate Senator Rand Paul with his father, Congressman Ron Paul, and those who attend Mises, the authors are forced to admit that "Mr. Paul says he abhors racism, has never visited the institute and should not have to answer for the more extreme views of all of those in the libertarian orbit."

Rothbard worked closely with Congressman Ron Paul's 1988 Libertarian presidential campaign, to no real avail. Having burned bridges with Rand, the Koch brothers, and Cato—and having long since been banished from *National Review*—Rothbard left the Libertarian Party after the Paul campaign as well.

Things weren't all that much better for Pat Buchanan. After Watergate, the taint of Dick Nixon followed most of his cronies. Buchanan managed to parlay his political experience into a career as a columnist and pundit, playing the right-winger on talk shows like *The McLaughlin Group* and CNN's *Crossfire*. But by 1988 his particular brand of "conservatism" had grown distinctly out of favor.

William F. Buckley had spent the previous decades decreeing

what conservatism meant—and purging entire classes of dissenters who argued to the contrary. "Ayn Rand is dead," he wrote with typical class in 1982. "So, incidentally, is the philosophy she sought to launch dead; it was in fact stillborn."[8] Buchanan's anti-immigration views increasingly came under suspicion from Buckley. Virtually every leftist program was later adopted and championed by *National Review* after a couple of decades: the Civil Rights Act; Social Security; semi-open borders, to name a few. Conservatism is progressivism driving the speed limit.

As Rothbard biographer Justin Raimondo put it,

> When *National Review* was founded in late 1955, Buckley and his circle initially refrained from criticizing or even differentiating themselves from the rest of the right-wing movement in this country. [. . .] Whereas the Old Right had been a diverse and loose coalition [. . .], Buckley and the *National Review* crowd soon put an end to this peaceable kingdom. In a series of polemics, they sought to purge American conservatism of every dissident group and subgroup.[9]

For the New Right, so-called "conservatives" have been willful or witless dupes of the left for *decades*. In contemporary terms, examples include Mitt Romney delivering to Massachusetts what would become the basis for Obamacare, President Bush appointing David Souter to the Supreme Court, and John McCain sponsoring campaign finance "reform."

This argument about principle versus expediency is not a new one in politics and hardly limited to the right wing. As one author put it, the history of northern conservatism

> has been that it demurs to each aggression of the progressive party, and aims to save its credit by a

respectable amount of growling, but always acquiesces at last in the innovation. What was the resisted novelty of yesterday is today one of the accepted principles of conservatism; it is now conservative only in affecting to resist the next innovation, which will tomorrow be forced upon its timidity and will be succeeded by some third revolution; to be denounced and then adopted in its turn. American conservatism is merely the shadow that follows Radicalism as it moves forward towards perdition. It remains behind it, but never retards it, and always advances near its leader.[10]

The author was pro-Southern intellectual Robert Lewis Dabney, and his words were written in 1897 just as progressivism was gaining a hold on the American psyche.

In this sense, the contemporary New Right can be defined as precisely those who were driven from mainstream conservatism. VDARE's Peter Brimelow, John Derbyshire, the Rothbardians, the Randians—all were driven into the wilderness. This is why many on the New Right see Bill Buckley as the archenemy. As author Vox Day put it, "When the Alt-Right comes to power, one of its first acts should be to dig up the corpse of William F. Buckley and burn it."[11]

In 1960 Buckley's *National Review* was proclaiming that "Leadership in the South [. . .] quite properly, rests in white hands" because "[in] the Deep South the Negroes are, by comparison with the whites, retarded[.]" In 2013 (and far earlier), the editors recanted by claiming that *NR* in the past "worried about the effects of the civil-rights movement on federalism and limited government. Those principles weren't wrong, exactly; they were tragically misapplied, given the moral and historical context."[12] Yet the claim that comparatively "retarded" Americans should not have their views heard in political discourse is still precisely how both progressives and *National Review* conservatives regard populists to this day.

The problem is that conservatives use the same mask of class and sophistication that the evangelical left does to barely disguise their rage-fueled need to control. It is their use of erudite language to express the crassest sentiments, such as *National Review*'s 1996 essay about *the politics of fucking dead bodies*: "Necrophilia is the erotic attraction to corpses," the article cheerfully begins. "There is no exclusivity here. The corpse may be old or young, male or female, human or animal, stranger or relative, one's own recently departed mother or a sheep taken at random from the abattoir." The claim that this—and in fact any—kink wouldn't have internal preferences is both false and bizarre, but that's hardly the least of it.

Fifteen years before *Fifty Shades of Grey* broke publishing records, *National Review* saw fit to equate its peccadilloes with having sex with the dead: "The idea of a campaign to promote necrophilia is not as fantastic, if I may use that word, as it might seem. Currently there is a case before the European Court concerning the 'rights' of sado-masochists to hurt each other in various perverted ways."

The main thrust of the piece is to sarcastically compare necrophilia with the gay rights movement, laying out a plan to normalize sex with the dead:

> A classical liberal economist could easily be found to talk impressively about costs imposed on others, externalities, private and public goods, and Pareto optimality. He would reach a conclusion similar to the philosopher's: it hurts no one. A psychoanalyst would go further and point out that necrophiliacs were more likely to hurt others if their desires were repressed than if they were indulged. Indeed those desires might be

transferred to live objects. Necrophiliacs should be not only allowed to practice but encouraged to talk about their practices. Assorted necrophiliac activists would then sift through history to find all sorts of generals, kings, bishops, and scientists who were necrophiliacs or would have been had they not lived in societies irrationally prejudiced against necrophilia. They would produce a survey which showed that 27 per cent of the American population had had or had fantasized a necrophiliac episode, and that these included taxpayers and men who had fought for their country. The final card to win the game would be a statement by a leading sculptor or novelist that the denial of necrophilia was a denial of artistic and creative freedom.[13]

The piece concludes with the assertion that "Many of the homosexuals who have died from AIDS were killed, in part, by society's rush to endorse homosexual behavior as normal." In fact it was the stigma of what was at first called "gay cancer" and "Gay-Related Immune Deficiency" that led to deaths, since so many men were scared of being outed by the outward symptoms of AIDS instead of feeling comfortable seeking treatment and being visible as ill. It was when children like Ryan White began being diagnosed that AIDS came to be seen as a disease that could not be localized to a marginalized community.

The point isn't how offensive such an article might be in retrospect. The point is how blithely conservatives will adopt progressive ideas and not bat an eye about it, considering the new stance a mere evolution. To no surprise, the same *National Review* ran an article in 2015 titled "Why We Should Recognize Same-Sex Marriage." What, then, are they conserving, other than the progressive accomplishments of the prior generation?

Yet Buckley did still have a point, if only when it came to elections. It was all well and good for Barry Goldwater (in words ghostwritten by anarchist Karl Hess) to proclaim in his 1964 convention speech that "extremism in the defense of liberty is no vice" and "moderation in the pursuit of justice is no virtue." Yet that campaign also led to the biggest anti-GOP landslide in history. The reasonable conclusion was that extremism in the defense of liberty is no electoral winner.

Matters finally reached a boiling point between Buckley and Buchanan after the latter wrote a 1990 *New York Post* article questioning some aspects of Holocaust history. Nixon went on the air to defend Buchanan, insisting that he's "not an anti-Semite"—which was fairly indisputable proof that he *was*. Holocaust denial is far more often couched as Holocaust skepticism ("just asking questions!"), and Buckley was having none of it. He devoted an entire issue of *National Review* to an essay lambasting Buchanan titled "In Search of Anti-Semitism," which he expanded into a short book the following year.

So it was that by 1991 both Rothbard and Buchanan were pariahs in their own way—and had nothing to lose. It seemed inevitable that George H. W. Bush would be the Republican nominee again. In the wake of the Gulf War he had posted approval ratings of around 90 percent, an unprecedented number. It also seemed rather certain that Bush would be reelected, as no one on the Democratic side had anything close to his political stature.

For Rothbard and Buchanan, all this seemed an enormous—and possibly permanent—step backward after the Reagan years. Reagan had famously denounced the Soviet Union as an "evil empire," but George H. W. Bush was quite the opposite. As historian Victor Sebestyen recounts, President Bush at times "tried desperately to keep Communist governments in power when he felt that Eastern Europe might be careening out of control." "No one wishes to see the disintegration of the Soviet Union," Bush explicitly wrote to Gorbachev in 1991.[14]

The collapse of the USSR had been the world's greatest leap forward for freedom in over half a century. But rather than pressing the issue and fighting for even greater liberty, Bush had decided to change tacks. Within months of half the globe being changed forever, Bush was prepared to assert American strength to ensure that such changes would never again be repeated. The former director of the CIA advocated for a New World Order—by which he meant a stable international regime. And since the current international regime was heavily progressive, for Buchanan and Rothbard this meant *and could only mean* world domination by a globalist elite.

The outcasts decided to make a move from the fringe, targeting disenchanted working-class whites who had been cast aside by both political parties. This antipathy is paralleled even today. In 2016, *National Review*'s Kevin Williamson explicitly wrote, "The truth about these dysfunctional, downscale communities is that they deserve to die. Economically, they are negative assets. Morally, they are indefensible."[15] This meant inevitably courting people who were angry and often felt victimized by affirmative action as well as by the failure of the political establishment to control illegal immigration. Then and now, American society was strongly dominated by a progressivism that declared "racist" views to be invalid. While this was true in a moral sense, in a democracy it wasn't quite the case. Mathematically, the vote of a racist is precisely as valid as that of a liberal; the Holocaust denier and the concentration camp survivor count for exactly the same at the ballot box.

It might be unreasonable to say that Rothbard and Buchanan consciously sought out such followers. Yet it is certainly reasonable to point out that seeking out voters alienated from the

mainstream would inevitably lead to drawing in such types. It would be impossible to separate out the wheat from the chaff—what would be the point, anyway? Respect from the left? Buchanan had seen that despite Nixon's liberal agenda—even socialist Bernie Sanders wouldn't dare advocate the wage and price controls that Nixon had implemented!—the president had still been called a fascist. As a right-winger, a person would similarly be condemned as a "racist" regardless of their actions.

It also made sense politically. Buchanan had been a front-row witness to how the evangelical left exploits race to further its hold on power. He'd watched Martin Luther King's beatification over the decades. "That there would be a national holiday for King was unimaginable in that spring of '68," Buchanan would write in 2014, "as would be the claim by twenty-first-century conservatives that Dr. King was somehow one of us."[16]

Rothbard now also found himself courting the same types of people who had venerated Strom Thurmond in 1948. His old buddy Ron Paul seemed to agree with this approach. *Ron Paul's Political Report* featured several eyebrow-raising turns of phrase, such as the claim that "[o]rder was only restored in L.A. [after the 1992 riots] when it came time for the blacks to pick up their welfare checks three days after rioting began." Rothbard also saw fit to, if not exactly *champion* ex-Klansman David Duke, at least denounce his critics. That a former KKK official's sincerity would be in doubt seemed shocking to Rothbard: "It took a campaign of slander that resorted to questioning the sincerity of Duke's conversion to Christianity."[17] One wonders how Rothbard would have grappled with the "repentant" Mr. Duke's 2003 book, *Jewish Supremacism: My Awakening to the Jewish Question*, which included the claim that Jews literally shapeshifted to fit in among Christians.

The enemy of my enemy is my friend, both Rothbard and Buchanan decided. So it was that Rothbard came on board the

1992 Buchanan presidential campaign. Buchanan remained a pro-labor, religious protectionist. ("Pat Buchanan is not a conservative," Rush Limbaugh would later insist. "He's a populist.") Rothbard was still an anarchist, opposed to the government always and in all ways. Both were far more united in what they were against—namely, progressivism in all its forms—than in what they were for. But both also shared a complete contempt for the political establishment, left and right. Both presaged the New Right in its entirety.

Contempt flowed in both directions. Despite receiving a significant percentage of the primary vote, the Buchanan campaign was mocked and reviled by right-thinking people who knew better. The acme was a *Saturday Night Live* sketch parodying the *McLaughlin Group* program on which Buchanan had been a frequent panelist.

"Is there any one person in the universe who could not get a 30 percent protest vote against an incumbent?" asked host John McLaughlin, played by Dana Carvey in all his smirking glory.

"David Duke?" "Al Sharpton?" "I don't know, maybe a cartoon character?" the panelists guessed.

"Wrong!"

"Okay, how about Adolf Hitler?" said Buchanan, as portrayed by Phil Hartman.

"Correct answer," McLaughlin replied. "Hitler would only have gotten 25 percent. Good work, Pat!" It was *SNL* at its best, as hilarious as it was scathing. "Prediction: A new state will be created that Pat can actually win a primary in. It will be made entirely of Swiss cheese and float in the Atlantic. It will be peopled by little fairies and be called Fantasyland and exist entirely in Pat's head." Carvey spoke as McLaughlin for the media establishment at large. Their verdict on the Buchanan run was explicit: "He had no impact whatsoever."

Buchanan was grudgingly invited to speak at the 1992 Republican convention, and his speech remains its most memorable moment by far. Kinder? Gentler? Motherfuckers, this was *war*, and Buchanan addressed it as such by name. Just as with Trump in the 2016 campaign, the establishment hope was that Buchanan would have his say and then go back to his corner, never to be heard from again.

That wasn't quite what happened.

Billionaire H. Ross Perot coopted many of Buchanan's protectionist views and, in the opinion of many Republicans, delivered the presidency to Bill Clinton. The middling success of Buchanan's campaign did irreparable damage to his union with Rothbard, as Buchanan's views hardened away from their areas of agreement. Rothbard died in 1995, and Buckley was quick to piss on his grave: "We extend condolences to his family, but not to the movement he inspired. [. . .]" He closed the obituary by comparing him to the pedophile Branch Davidian cult leader: "Yes, Murray Rothbard believed in freedom, and yes, David Koresh believed in God." (Hey, better than comparing him to a stillbirth.) Buckley insisted we were "leaving him, in the end, not as the father of a swelling movement that 'rous[ed] the masses from their slumber,' as he once stated his ambition, but with about as many disciples as David Koresh had in his little redoubt in Waco." In fact, as of 2018 Rothbard's Facebook page has 22,000 likes—as compared to 3,600 for Buckley.

As for Buchanan, Rothbard's protégé Hans-Hermann Hoppe declared their alliance null and void. Taking aim at Buchananism, he said, "For obvious reasons this doctrine is not so named, but there is a term for this type of conservatism: It is called social nationalism or national socialism."[18] In other words, he was claiming that Pat Buchanan was a Nazi—the kind of attack that has become all too common in contemporary America (though sometimes accurately).

Though Rothbard might have been dead, his spirit of antag-onism, aggression, and personal vindictiveness filled the halls of the Gingrich Congress in 1995. Appropriations chairman Bob Livingston took to the House floor on December 23 and promised, "We will never, never, never give in. [. . .] We will stay here until doomsday! *Merry Christmas*." The Republicans shut down the federal government and forced Bill Clinton to balance the budget, something that would have been regarded as a fringe daydream even a year prior. Taking matters one step further, they then impeached the man as well. To this day, the corporate press claims (and perhaps even believes) that the Republicans were more upset to learn that, as one example, President Clinton had jerked off into a White House sink than that he had committed the felony of perjury.

There were feeble attempts to build bridges again between Buchanan and Team Rothbard. In his 1996 presidential cam-paign, Buchanan took a gratuitous dig against "reading too many books by these dead Austrian economists"—a comment for which he would later get on his knees (literally) to beg for-giveness from the executor of Rothbard's estate.[19] It didn't work. My enemy's enemy was once again my enemy.

For a while, it seemed that both Rothbardian anarchism and Buchananist nationalism were dead and gone. In 2000, George W. Bush, grandson of a Connecticut senator and son of a president, campaigned for the White House as a demilingual hick that Americans would love to have a beer with. After 9/11 even Ron Paul voted to give the president a blank check, autho-rizing him to "use all necessary and appropriate force against those nations, organizations, or persons he determines planned, authorized, committed, or aided the terrorist attacks."

Yet by Bush's second term, things were a little bit different on the right. The president and his philosophy were increasingly reviled by the public at large, barely squeaking out a win in 2004 over John Kerry despite being involved in two simultaneous wars (and setting the stage for Democratic landslides in 2006 and 2008). In 2007 Ron Paul once again ran for the White House, this time as a Republican. Gone were the racist dog whistles of the newsletter days, replaced by a strongly anti-interventionist foreign policy. Paul stood on the debate stage and told former New York mayor Rudy Giuliani to his face that the United States bore some complicity for the 9/11 attacks—pure Rothbardian thinking.

By 2012 Ron Paul was giving establishment candidate Mitt Romney a run for his money in yet another race. Of course, the press didn't spin it that way at all, since the radical Paul didn't fit neatly into their box of what a Republican should look like. It was hard for the media to portray Mitt Romney as an extremist when an actual extremist—i.e., a man of principle—was standing alongside him, sounding perfectly reasonable (if not exactly polished).

Yet despite the establishment propaganda, every time the Republicans have run a right-winger in the last forty years they have won the White House—and every time they've run a moderate they have lost. George H. W. Bush was especial proof of this, winning as Reagan II in 1988 before hiking taxes and moving to the center in time for a 1992 defeat. Further, in the last thirty-five years, the only times budgetary concessions have been wrested from the left were via utter Republican intransigence (namely, the Gingrich federal government shutdown and the debt-ceiling crisis of 2011). These tactics were straight out of the Rothbard playbook. According to Rothbard, complete gridlock is the best one can hope for in Washington. A paralyzed government was fairly close to his anarchist ideal. In this vein, political insanity is not a bug; it's a feature, and also the goal and a realistic short-term approach to bringing about the end of government.

For many right-wingers, there also came a realization that Andrew Breitbart was correct. "Politics is downstream from culture," and electing the correct people was the *consequence* of the right strategies and not the goal. One of the great techniques used by the evangelical left is its claim that all decent, sane people are basically progressives at heart. It was only within such a context of presumed unanimity that Starbucks could launch a 2015 campaign encouraging their employees to discuss matters of race with their customers.

The New Right is not only opposed to civil discourse; it's opposed to pretty much *any* discourse with those it considers the enemy. It's a working strategy. Peter Thiel secretly funded a legal battle between Hulk Hogan, a man he didn't even know, and the gossip website Gawker, one of the mainstays of sneering media progressivism. The result was the personal bankruptcy of Gawker's owner and editor and the destruction of the site, a major New Right victory.

By 2015 it was Donald Trump who had once again melded the combative Rothbardian style to Buchananite ideology. Trump did not simply defeat Jeb Bush; he humiliated him and his family on a personal level. Ditto Ted "Your father shot JFK" Cruz, and Marco "Google 'gay rumors'" Rubio. Many in the thinking class assume Trump doesn't know what he's doing, believing in what *Dilbert* creator Scott Adams calls the "Lucky Hitler Hypothesis." The facts imply something quite different.

Few Americans understand what the Federal Reserve is or what it does, and it hardly seems like Donald Trump should be among them. Yet Ron Paul had pushed for a Federal Reserve audit every year until he left Congress in 2015, including writing a bestselling 2009 book titled *End the Fed*. It's telling that Trump had promised to audit the Fed via executive order. It's almost as if he was trying to co-opt the Liberty Movement that came about as a result of Ron Paul's last two presidential campaigns.

Trump was not alone in trying to pick up the Rothbardian Paul's coattails. There was Paul's son, Kentucky senator Rand Paul, who ran as a Manchurian candidate for the Republican nomination. Run as a Republican, govern as a Rothbardian was the plan. Yet Trump was onto him and cut him off at the pass. This was the backdrop to the September 16, 2015, Republican primary debate. The very first question was to Carly Fiorina, asking whether she trusted Trump with his finger on the nuclear button. After she demurred, moderator Jake Tapper turned to Trump for his thoughts. Trump opened his response with an apparent non-sequitur: "First of all, Rand Paul shouldn't even be on this stage. He's number 11 and has 1 percent in the polls and how he got up here . . . there is far too many people anyway." As with much of Trump's discourse, this could have been random. But at a certain point, chance can only explain so much. He wanted those Ron Paul voters, and he needed the younger Paul out of the way. "I never attacked him on his looks," the future president went on to say. "And believe me, there is plenty of subject matter right there. That I can tell you."

For years, the New Right has had little political representation and been treated as beneath notice by the mainstream press. This is no longer an option, especially in a social media world. Its members are smart, they are organized, and, most importantly, they do have a very coherent worldview. Illiterately tweeting "YOUR RACIST" over and over at one's enemies is not enough to silence millions of people. Simply because the New Right was unheard didn't mean that its members had nothing to say. Simply because their ideas may be wrong or abhorrent doesn't make those ideas poorly thought out or based on nothing. In fact, the more the New Right's ideology is dismissed by the progressive mainstream culture as stupid and crazy, the more appealing it seems to the marginalized—and as soon as one of their ideas seems reasonable, *just one*, then the whole tactic of blanket dismissal falls apart.

An example of how this works—and how it often backfires on the left—can be seen in discussions of crime. Blacks commit far more violent crime than whites do. (They are also far more likely to be the victims of violent crime.) To criticize African Americans in any sense raises up leftist antennae. It might give them an opportunity to puff out their chests and defend black people. For the evangelical left, every Facebook update can be a personal march on Selma.

By equating racial discussion with racism, the conversation immediately takes on an emotional and toxic tone. Then by dismissing views as "outdated" and "pseudoscientific," the left hopes to give the impression that there is nothing more to say, that these views are absurd and downright evil—and that this is something "everyone" agrees on. So when a New Right thinker comes along and offers a logical, coherent explanation, it can be highly persuasive *even if it is not true. An* answer will often sound better than *no* answer.

THINGS THAT HAVE BEEN CALLED RACIST IN THE PRESS

- Engaging with other cultures
- Not engaging with other cultures
- Noticing other races
- Not noticing other races
- Moving out of minority neighborhoods
- Moving into minority neighborhoods
- Repeating what a racist said
- Ignoring what a racist said
- Expecting people to show up on time
- Milk

- Brownies
- Picnics
- Peanut butter and jelly
- Barbecue
- Soul food
- Certain dinosaurs
- Crime surveillance videos
- The Walt Disney statue
- Marble
- Believing in hard work
- The term "marijuana"
- Automatic soap dispensers
- Grammar
- Math
- "Reason itself"

Though the two broad factions of the New Right have differing goals, they share several things in common. They have a completely identical perspective on our culture and a completely identical view of the enemy: the progressive ideology, as forced on our children in progressive schools and as taught to our students on progressive campuses, who then disseminate the ideas either explicitly in the media or implicitly in entertainment.

Twenty-five years later, Pat Buchanan has been proven correct. There *is* a religious war going on in our country for the soul of America. On one side of the battlefield is the religion known as progressivism. On the other stands the New Right.

4

*

MEME MAGIC IS REAL

Every time I speak of the haters and losers I do so with
great love and affection. They cannot help the fact that
they were born fucked up!

—Donald J. Trump

Rush Limbaugh's reinvention of talk radio brought about a re-
surgence of aggressive conservatism. Similarly, the New Right
has four major conduits through which their ideas are promulgated to the broader culture, each of which are different in their
approach. To explain the first, 4chan.org, to outsiders is effectively to violate the ethos of the board and to render oneself
an outsider too—hence the frequent comments of "Normies,
get out! REEEEEE!" The site is a group of message boards devoted to specific topics. There is a health-and-fitness board
called 4chan.org/fit/, or "/fit/," where young men compare
tips on building good physiques—and share their despair upon
realizing that achieving said physique does not get them
laid. The /fit/ board's archrival is /fa/, dedicated to fashion and
dressing well.

When the press discusses "4chan," they very frequently use

that as (incorrect) shorthand for the /b/ board. The letter doesn't stand for anything but the board (officially labeled as "Random"), which is the site's main repository of memes, jokes, and random taboo subjects. It's also where various movements have been formed. When a bunch of female celebrities' naked photos were leaked in 2014, it was on /b/ where users shared the pics and created mirror sites in order to make sure there were enough copies online that could never be taken down. This event was known as "The Fappening," "fapping" being slang for masturbating after the "fap" sound a male makes when doing so. Again, to explain 4chan to outsiders is effectively to violate the ethos of the board and to render oneself an outsider—but also to render oneself ashamed and feeling dirty.

The Fappening led to clueless news reports, including a CNN interview leading with the question, "Who is this 4chan person or website?," to which their "technology analyst" replied, "He may have been just a system administrator who knew his way around and how to hack things." As a result, the meme asking "Who is this hacker known as 4chan?" flooded the site, alongside pics of a man in a ski mask superimposed over a wall of green digital text in typical scare-news fashion. CNN never did learn its lesson. In the aftermath of an internet hoax that said school shooting survivor David Hogg was actually an actor, the network announced on February 22, 2018, that "CNN reached out to 4chan for comment twice about these false posts about Hogg, but has not yet received a response." This is the equivalent of learning about a prank phone call and asking Sprint for comment.

It is on /pol/ "Politically Incorrect"—where the New Right congregates. The board is representative of all types of political perspectives, from communist to Nazi to anarchist and everything in between. It is from this board that the expression "God-Emperor Trump" (frequently misquoted by Ann Coulter as

"Emperor God Trump") came into being, the title taken from a book in the *Dune* series in which the protagonist merges with one of the planet's gigantic sandworms, achieving near immortality in the process.

What all of 4chan has in common is a love of breaking taboos. As such, users refer to each other with the -fag suffix. New users are therefore "newfags," and those who have been around are "oldfags"—and, of course, gay people are "gayfags." The term "4chan troll" is a shorthand for users on the site, and it is not an inaccurate one. The board is a breeding ground for anti-mainstream thought; consequently, there is virtually no support for, say, Mitt Romney. What is amazing is how diverse and well-trafficked the site is, with users from all over the world. Though users are anonymous and threads vanish after they become inactive, 4chan allows users to customize their posts with a flag. This can be either the flag of an actual country or one that connotes an ideology, such as the black-and-red flag of anarcho-communism, the Nazi swastika flag, or the "Don't tread on me" Gadsden rattlesnake flag.

The fact that Donald Trump was so effective at trolling the entirety of the establishment earned him the strong—though hardly universal—support of the /pol/ community. It became a hub for the latest news of the is-this-shit-for-real Trump campaign, from which users could spread the information throughout their own personal social media orbits. Every day found a new Trump post "stickied" to the top of the first page, which would have to be replaced after receiving too many replies. The tributes went both ways, as memes that originated on /pol/ were occasionally retweeted by Trump and others in the campaign.

In contrast to the anything-goes content of 4chan, there are the tamer pages on Reddit. There are far more subforums ("subreddits") than on 4chan, and users must create an account before posting. One of the largest subreddits on the site is reddit

.com/r/The_Donald, with more than 600,000 subscribers as of June 2018. By contrast, the Rothbardian /r/Anarcho_Capitalism has 57,000 subscribers while /r/Conservative has 135,000—which is amazing given how frequently conservatism is represented in the media compared to Rothbard's near invisibility. (/r/National-Review is private and invite only.)

Unlike /pol/, /r/The_Donald is quite welcoming to new-comers. There's a list of ten rules on the right-hand column, including "Racism and Anti-Semitism will not be tolerated" and "No type of trolling will be allowed." Explicitly, "This fo-rum is for Trump supporters only." In addition to the rules is a list of convenient links, including "What do all those memes mean?" (the opposite of the 4chan ethos), explanatory pages about Trump's border wall and his accomplishments, and the official White House social media pages.

Unlike 4chan, where posts vanish after being inactive, Red-dit posts are permanent (until deleted) and may be sorted in various ways, such as by recency, popularity, or momentum. Posts or comments may be "upvoted" or "downvoted," much like Facebook's "like" feature. If a comment gets sufficiently downvoted, it will be obscured, and enough downvotes make a post vanish without having a direct link to it. Posts can also be tagged with various categorizations, such as "Trump tweet" or "2nd Amendment." Unlike with 4chan, to explain Reddit to outsiders is to render oneself helpful and without any feelings of shame whatsoever.

Typical posts on /r/The_Donald include links to articles de-fending whatever Trump happened to say that day, as well as interesting news clips and polls undermining whatever the me-dia narrative of the moment happens to be. Many ideas and memes originate on /pol/ and reach their way over to /r/The_Donald—far more than the inverse—and the cross-pollination is not a source of conflict between the two. Meaning, a /pol/ post on /r/The_Donald won't be denigrated, and vice versa. This is despite the fact that a broader rivalry exists between the two sites in general.

Sometimes the two sites' users work together, and it is often unclear who is originally behind the hijinx that ensue. After Trump's election, actor and activist Shia LaBeouf started a "He Will Not Divide Us" movement, with the slogan being displayed on a wall or, later, on a flag. After being driven from a couple of locations for various reasons, LaBeouf in February 2017 placed the flag at an undisclosed site with a webcam displaying it. It took less than a day for users to discover where it was. First, they compared airplane flight patterns against the stars to narrow down the location. Then one user drove in the general area honking his car horn until the webcam picked up the sound. The flag was then taken down and replaced with a MAGA hat and Pepe T-shirt.

In March the flag was moved to Liverpool; allegedly a pair of /pol/lacks used the wall-climbing technique parkour to get access to its rooftop location. The subsequent flag locations were similarly uncovered and interfered with. By the time LaBeouf was arrested for public drunkenness in July 2017 he had been driven off the deep end—he told the arresting (black) officer that he was going to hell and that he had arrested LaBeouf for being white, and he complained that the policeman was "eating dumbass fucking sandwiches, you racist."

If Reddit and 4chan are the juveniles, *Taki's Mag* is the adult in the room. It was founded in 2008 by Taki Theodoracopulos, who had previously cofounded *The American Conservative* magazine with Pat Buchanan, and is currently edited by his daughter Mandolyna. *Taki's Mag* bizarrely features an Audrey Hepburn–esque girl with a tiara and cigarette holder as the icon beside the slogan "Cocktails, Countesses & Mental Caviar." Taki claimed he wanted to "shake up the stodgy world of so-called 'conservative' opinion,"[1] which is pretty blatant code for "We're the opposite of *National Review*."

It was in *Taki's Mag* in 2012 that John Derbyshire wrote what *Gawker* understandably called the "Most Racist Article Possible." Derbyshire had previously authored the book *We Are Doomed*, which is a good exposition of the pessimistic side of the New Right. In response to the idea that black parents have to give their children "The Talk" about how to behave in a white-dominated culture, Derbyshire wrote his own fifteen-point version for white children, including things such as

> while black-on-black behavior is more antisocial in the average than is white-on-white behavior, average black-on-*white* behavior is a degree more antisocial yet.
>
> Avoid concentrations of blacks not all known to you personally.
>
> If you are at some public event at which the number of blacks suddenly swells, leave as quickly as possible.
>
> You should consciously seek opportunities to make friends with [intelligent and well-socialized blacks].[2]

Derbyshire was swiftly and understandably purged from *National Review* by editor Rich Lowry, who wrote:

> Derb is effectively using our name to get more oxygen for views with which we'd never associate ourselves otherwise. So there has to be a parting of the ways. Derb has long danced around the line on these issues, but this column is so outlandish it constitutes a kind of letter of resignation.[3]

Other writers at *Taki's Mag* include Jim Goad and, until 2017, Gavin McInnes. Steve Sailer writes there as well, taking on issues of race, ethnicity, and culture from an articulate Alt-Right perspective. In short, it is almost impossible to find a single article on the site that wouldn't cause the median American—or even the median right-winger—some modicum of discomfort.

The biggest New Right site by far, however, is Breitbart, named after its late founder Andrew Breitbart (who I'll here refer to as Andrew to avoid confusion). Andrew cut his teeth on the internet by helping Arianna Huffington develop the Huffington Post. His big revelation was that "Politics is *downstream* from culture." As one Breitbart writer later put it, "The first time I heard the phrase, 'Politics is downstream from culture,' I had no idea what it meant. After figuring it out, and explaining it to a few Conservatives, they dismissed the concept."[4]

Andrew was as focused on the media itself and how it gets over as he was on politics. In 2010, civil rights legend and Democratic congressman John Lewis claimed that he was berated by racial slurs—including the big one—as he entered Congress. Andrew got footage from several different angles that showed nothing of the kind. Further, he found that congressman Jesse Jackson Jr. was himself filming the entrance.

Andrew challenged Lewis, Jackson, or anyone to provide proof of what Lewis was saying. The story then became "Andrew Breitbart calls civil rights legend a liar." To be totally pedantic, it was the footage itself that was making the claim. There was no analysis necessary. When Andrew was confronted by a reporter, it was obvious to him that the insistent challenge was to get Andrew to say the right quote, which he obliged in doing—but he called the journalist out on it. "I said it strains credulity," Andrew replied, "and the second I said 'Yes, he's a liar,' [. . .] you go, 'Cut, we got it!'"

Following Andrew's death at age forty-three in March 2012, Steve Bannon became executive chairman. Under Bannon's reign Breitbart became a haven for what the corporate press indiscriminately describes as "alt-right," "far-right," "populist," or "white supremacist" views. Conservative wunderkind—and purported ghostwriter of Andrew's book—Ben Shapiro and Milo Yiannopoulos both rose through the ranks at Breitbart, with Shapiro becoming increasingly upset by Breitbart's editorial direction and the many not-so-good-natured jabs thrown his way by coworker Milo on Twitter.

One of Breitbart's big breaking moments was in March 2016, when Breitbart reporter Michelle Fields claimed that Trump campaign manager Corey Lewandowski assaulted her. Subsequent video footage showed that he clearly grabbed her by the arm and pulled her away from the candidate. The degree to which this was assault and to which it was akin to Corey acting as a bouncer was a source of enormous dispute. At the very least, laying your hands on another person is battery in the legal sense. Yet prosecutors declined to pursue the case.

Enough was enough. Fields resigned over the perceived lack of support and Shapiro followed suit. Shapiro minced no words, later writing:

> Andrew Breitbart *despised* racism. Truly despised it. He used to brag regularly about helping to integrate his fraternity at Tulane University. He insisted that racial stories be treated with special care to avoid even the whiff of racism. With Bannon embracing Trump, all that changed. Now Breitbart has become the alt-right go-to website, with Yiannopoulos pushing white ethno-nationalism as a legitimate response to political correctness, and the comment section turning into a cesspool for white supremacist mememakers.

Yet the members of the New Right don't simply receive their news in alternative ways from the median American. News is ostensibly fact based. The rift exists even further when you examine humor and imagery, two things that are ambiguous and subjective by their very nature.

⋆ ⋆ ⋆

On September 12, 2016, an anonymous HillaryClinton.com staffer took it upon xirself to explain some of the iconography of the New Right: "Let me get this straight," the page asked. "Trump's presidential campaign is posting memes associated with white supremacy online?

"Yes," the page answered. To make it perfectly clear: "That cartoon frog is more sinister than you might realize." Given that cartoon frogs are decidedly unsinister, this is not a very bold assertion to make. Describing Pepe the cartoon frog as "associated with white supremacy" is akin to describing the Stars and Stripes as "associated with flag burning." It is technically correct, factually true—and utterly clueless.

Andrew Stroehlein, European media director of Human Rights Watch, later reacted in horror to an official Russian government account tweeting out Pepe's image. "This is pretty much the modern equivalent of Russia raising a swastika flag over the Kremlin," he decreed.[5] I would argue that even tweeting out a swastika wouldn't be the "modern equivalent of raising a swastika flag over the Kremlin." Maybe, just maybe, the Russians hate the Nazis as much as we do (if not more), and maybe, just maybe, the Soviets sacrificed far more to defeat Hitler than we ever did despite the patriotic mythology that claims otherwise. While I can see how Mr. Stroehlein would think that the Nazis' siege of Leningrad is basically the equivalent of some collegiate antifascist hunger strike, I suspect that my former countrymen remember it a bit differently.

The Cathedral isn't content with merely controlling what people say and think. A ubiquitous tactic is to *ascribe* meaning to the communication of others. When then–Texas governor Rick Perry referred to the national debt as a "big black cloud that hangs over America" in 2011, commentator Ed Schultz immediately took this as a reference to Barack Obama. Though no one would accuse President Obama of being "big"—let alone a floating mass of water vapor—it was still enough for Schultz to launch a kneejerk attack. As Politico reported at the time, Schultz said, "Perry comes from the radical country club that loves to remind white America that President Obama is other: not like you" and "that big black cloud Perry is talking about is President Barack Obama."[6]

This inability to contextualize communication is emblematic of the provincialism that underscores so much of progressive ideology: it's the same mindset that looks at an Andy Warhol or Jackson Pollock painting and declares, "I can do that!" If said speaker could, in fact, paint a soup can and sell it for millions, one can only wonder why they were choosing to mutter in annoyance instead of getting out an easel.

In 2008, Obama had his sublime Shepard Fairey "Hope" poster and a volunteer internet army to spread his message. Today, the New Right has its own iconography and its own huge internet subculture, one driven heavily by maintaining an obscurant pose toward the hated mainstream. It's not enough to have Hillary Clinton staffers find it confusing. The higher goal is for such types to bring their own mental baggage to the communication—and to render themselves fools in the process.

This is what is known as trolling.

To no surprise, "trolling" is defined incorrectly by the corporate press. It is not synonymous with taunting, and it doesn't simply mean insulting someone in virulent or racist terms. Trolling is meant to be clever. At its best, it is the art of turning an audience into a performer by exploiting their flaws for comedic effect. There is, in contemporary times, a huge overlap between racism and trolling. But this is in large part due to race being such an easy way to get the sensitive to act out.

A good way to understand trolling is to look at the original troll: Andy Kaufman. Kaufman often performed in costume as his alter ego, the foul-mouthed and foul-voiced lounge singer Tony Clifton. At one point during a 1978 show, Clifton mused about how his wife passed away, and then invited his twelve-year-old daughter to join him on stage for a duet. As recounted by Kaufman associate Bob Zmuda:

> It was a wonderful, heart-touching moment, at least until the kid made a mistake by singing over Tony's part.
>
> Suddenly his hand shot up, and the loud smack it made against her cheek couldn't have stunned the audience more had it been a gunshot.
>
> "What are you, a fucking idiot?" screeched Tony. The stunned child began to cry. "Shut the fuck up or I'll give you another one."

As the audience booed what they were seeing, Tony turned and asked the crowd to stop booing lest the child think they didn't like *her*. Yet the singer, it turned out, wasn't Kaufman's child. In fact she wasn't even a child at all, but a young-looking actress who was in on the whole thing. In one sense, then, Kaufman was "associated with child abuse." Kaufman—as well as the audience and every sane person on earth—thought that genuine violence against children was a horrific subject. It was precisely this universal repulsion to such actions that drove the comedic tension.

For nonreligious people, the preference is to view things as acceptable until and unless they must be forbidden, to err on the side of freedom. For the evangelical left, however, the world is defined by what is acceptable, and everything outside this acceptability is wrong and bad. The scales are tipped heavily against anything outside their norms. For them, humor follows the same principles as music or home décor. There are approved parameters, and anything else is simply wrong, as "everyone" (i.e., everyone they associate with and approve of) knows.

Progressives often insist that certain subjects are off limits to humor. Rape or slavery or the Holocaust are all issues that currently make the list. Asking someone if they think rape is funny only has and can only have one legitimate answer. But this misses the point entirely. No one thinks knocking on a door is funny. No one laughs when a chicken crosses the road, or when a priest and a rabbi walk into a bar. Not understanding a math problem would certainly not be taken as evidence that one is good at math. Yet it is almost unheard of for someone who dislikes a joke to recognize that maybe the problem lies with them and their poor sense of humor.

Few (if any) subjects are inherently funny, in the same way that many ingredients aren't inherently a meal in and of themselves. Asking if rape is funny is more akin to asking if flour is food. No one actually eats flour. On the one hand, everyone *has* eaten it. Similarly, the more taboo a subject, the more exotic an ingredient, the more difficult it is to make it palatable—and some subjects will never be palatable for everyone, no matter how skillful the presentation. A joke is like a person: you can't dissect it and expect to put it back together again and have it breathe.

From the Holocaust ("What's the difference between Hitler and Michael Phelps? Michael Phelps knew how to finish a race") to slavery ("Why do black people hate cruises? They're not falling for that trick again") and even to crib death ("What's eighteen inches long, purple, and makes women scream?"), there are jokes to be found. As of this writing, my friend is announcing her pregnancy by telling people she has "a little Jew in the oven." When comedian Bonnie McFarlane roasted broadcaster Jim Norton by saying his show was so unlistenable that "I'd rather hear my daughter drowning," there is little ground to criticize her as either a professional comic or a loving mother. A person who decrees "That's not funny" isn't in a position to define that for *anyone*, let alone *everyone*.

Selling females, including underage girls, into marriage is a very real contemporary cultural practice that horrifically offends Western sensibilities. Yet the internet is replete with jokes about Melania Trump being a mail-order bride, with the hashtag #FreeMelania being openly used by the left. Slavery, on the other hand, has been eradicated from the West. Yet joking about Michelle Obama being sold would cause unimaginable outrage.

Two months before she died in 2014, comedian Joan Rivers was challenged during a CNN interview about making jokes concerning subjects that "seem off limits to a lot of people." Rivers is the woman who suggested to a reporter that they conduct their post-9/11 interview at "Windows on the Ground." "Life is very tough," Rivers snapped at the questioner, "and if you can make something easier and funny, do it! [. . .] Winston Churchill said if you make someone laugh, you give them a vacation. And maybe you take the worst thing in the world, make it funny and give them a vacation from horror." She then walked off the set, herself offended at the interviewer.

Rivers's mindset is very central to the Jewish tradition, especially the Eastern European Jewish tradition that she came from. The expression "laughing to keep from crying" is universally known and understood. I've found this to be the case in other situations where people are escapees from horrible situations. One north Korean refugee I know said that *The Hunger Games* was her favorite book and movie, then jokingly asked

how the author knew so much about life in the DPRK. Another
refugee managed to escape and go to high school in the United
States. When his schoolmates were reminiscing about liking
Pokémon as kids, he quipped, "Yeah, only instead of Pokémon
I watched my father starve."

It's not unreasonable to say that joking about someone's
father dying, let alone starving, is not a ripe source for comedy.
But it is universally understood that everyone grieves in different ways, and though grieving through wisecracks and making
other people uncomfortable is most certainly not common, neither is it (in the internet cliché) "not OK." Thankfully we live in
a country where virtually no one will ever have to experience
what my refugee acquaintance did. The idea that he is to be condemned for how he handles his grief—as opposed to being
given carte blanche to react as he sees fit—is hard to defend.

Laughter can obviously be a bonding experience. In 2017 I
attended an Alcoholics Anonymous meeting where my friend
was commemorating her ten-year anniversary of being sober.
One by one, the addicts who were also celebrating that day got
up and told stories of the travails they had suffered. "Eight years
ago I was in a mental institution," one man recalled. "I was
homeless, I was in the hospital, I was in jail, I was in the shelter.
I did the whole tour!" The room burst into laughter. It would be
safe to say none of those four experiences is a laughing matter.
Yet in this case each one quite literally was—especially given
the man's grateful caveat that the one stop on the tour he managed to avoid was death.

In many cases, someone might see the humor in a joke or
anecdote but for valid personal reasons be unable to find something funny. Yet for the evangelical left, with humor as with
everything else, if it's not for *everyone* then it's not for *anyone*.
The insistence is on universalism and inclusion regardless of
context. This shrill admonition as to what is and isn't fair

grounds for humor is precisely what fuels trolls. Loudly announcing that certain subjects will provoke a reaction, thereby turning audience into performer, lets trolls know exactly which buttons to press. The cost/benefit ratio could not be more favorable.

In 2012, for example, Mountain Dew had a campaign to name their new flavor of soda. The public would vote, and then judges would pick from the top ten names. It barely took any time for trolls to vote in large enough numbers to guarantee that the top ten choices would be as unpalatable as the glowing poisonous beverage itself. The top result? "Hitler did nothing wrong." In the same way that Kaufman was not endorsing child abuse or even laughing at it, this option wasn't about Holocaust revisionism as much as it was about trolling a corporation. The company would be forced to react in *some* embarrassing way. Sure enough, Mountain Dew pulled the contest within forty-eight hours, tweeting out that "Dub the Dew definitely lost to The Internet."

Similarly, in March 2017 an eleven-year-old autistic boy by the name of Hughie Malone appeared on Ireland's *Late Late Show* to discuss his condition and how it affects him. "What is your aim in life?" asked host Ryan Tubridy. "What would you like to be doing in, say, ten years' time? Have you thought about it?"

"Driving planes into buildings," Malone replied.

"Driving what?"

"Driving planes into *skyscrapers*."

"Right. Well, let's say that's not a career option. What else would you like to do?"

"Um . . . move to Iraq and become a terrorist."

It's very easy to say 9/11 jokes aren't funny. It's also easy to say that what little Hughie was doing wasn't very funny either. But to call it offensive as opposed to tasteless seems a bit of a stretch. If anything it calls for more of an eyeroll than a gasp, though there is something to be said for the visual of a smirking autistic kid clowning a late-night television comedian.

On the other hand, there most certainly are many examples of genuinely racist iconography online. Under the pen name of "A. Wyatt Mann," artist Nick Bougas has drawn many explicitly racist, homophobic, and anti-Semitic cartoons where there isn't even a pretense of humor. His most famous anti-Jewish image, that of a hook-nosed man rubbing his hands together and nicknamed "le happy merchant," comes from a drawing that flatly states that a world without Jews and blacks would be like a world without rats and roaches. The internet term "bix nood" to describe black vernacular comes from Bougas's image where a genderless black person babbles into their cell phone: "Mup da doo didda po mo gub bidda be dat tum muhfugen bix nood cof bin dub ho muhfugga."

It is when the dark humor and racism interact that we see the world of internet trolling isn't as black and white as some would like it to be. One of the most prominent gray-area cases is that of Ben Garrison, a longtime cartoonist from Montana. The targets of his illustrations were exactly what one would expect for a libertarian political cartoonist: the police state, global corporations, the Federal Reserve.

Starting in 2010, however, his drawings took on an unexpected life of their own. If there's one thing people who spend all day on their computer are good at, it's technology. Starting with actual Nazis and spreading to trolls, his cartoons began to be edited without his permission or even his knowledge. Anonymous users took Garrison's works and switched out key elements with Bougas's anti-Semitic drawings. Rather than having then–Federal Reserve chairman Ben Bernanke's face captioned as "The Great and Powerful Wizard of Debt," the new version had a Jewish stereotype holding a fistful of dollars. The Photoshop work was flawless. For all intents and purposes, it looked as if the substitutions had been the originals.

After turning all his drawings into cartoons straight out of the Third Reich, trolls then began writing a fictitious Nazi backstory for Garrison and spreading that fake biography as truth. Breitbart.com reported the whole story under the self-explanatory headline of, "How the Internet Made a White Supremacist." As Garrison told them, "Do an internet search of my name and you'll see me in a Nazi uniform, which can be a tad off-putting to potential commercial art clients."

It's fair to say that this is a bit of an understatement, but Garrison's subsequent internet aliases were anything but. The website Encyclopedia Dramatica (basically a troll's version of Wikipedia) lists over one hundred troll nicknames for Garrison, ranging from Ben "Causing Hysteria in Every Black Area" Garrison to Ben "Goin' Mental on the Oriental" Garrison to Ben "Three Reichs and You're Out" Garrison. The most often used, however, is the simple "Zyklon Ben." Ah, *le mot juste*!

Which brings us back to Pepe the cartoon frog. As with most iconography, the backstory and context is quite complex. So when HillaryClinton.com flatly declares that "Pepe's been almost entirely co-opted" by "white supremacists," this is simply false, and an attempt to impose meaning rather than to understand—an extremely common and decreasingly effective weapon of the evangelical left. Why engage in discourse when one can simply speak for one's opponent, dismiss their words as "hate speech," and end the conversation before it has even begun?

Before there were emojis, there were image replies. If, for example, a message board user wanted to respond to a funny post, he could simply post a picture of someone laughing as his reply. Over time the images used to connote specific emotions became largely standardized. Tom Cruise laughing hysterically and Don Draper chuckling as he sips from a tumbler were both popular alternatives to writing "LOL." There's no particular reason why Tom Cruise and Don Draper gained currency, let alone those two specific Tom Cruise and Don Draper images. It's as essentially random as football fans watching a "giant" battling an "eagle" who had competed with a "viking" or a "tiger" a week earlier.

As he explained on Time.com, illustrator Matt Furie created Pepe the frog in 2006 as a character in his comic *Boy's Club*. A panel of Pepe exclaiming "feels good man" became a popular reaction to stories people shared, or even attached alongside posts where the author had a happy outcome. He was the troll's version of the smiley face or the :-) emoticon. And thanks to the principle of comedic inversion, it didn't take long until an image of a downcast Pepe muttering "feels bad man" gathered traction as well. :-(As such, Pepe was part of a huge cast of image archetypes for close to a decade, and never had any political connotations whatsoever.

But meanings change over time. LOL used to mean "laughing out loud" but is now much closer to writing "ha ha," in the same way that "scuba" is a word in itself and not literally regarded as an acronym for Self-Contained Underwater Breathing Apparatus. And because jargon serves as a signifier in internet culture just as much as it does in every other aspect of human existence, the mainstreamed term LOL became "LEL," which begat "KEK" (one letter higher!) for long, complicated reasons. Trolls claim to "do it for the LULZ," but by 2015 they could be said to be "doing it for the KEKs."

Then, at some point in 2015, a random user discovered that there actually was an ancient Egyptian deity named Kek. If this weren't coincidence enough, there was an image of Kek next to a hieroglyph that resembled a man at a computer, as well as a double-strand (as in DNA) and . . . a frog. As such, the satirical

Cult of Kek was born. Kek was a chaos god who reveled in sociopolitical carnage, always with hilarious consequences, and Pepe was now regarded as his avatar.

The claim became that "meme magic is real," that internet posters could literally alter reality through their computers. For example, every post on the 4chan message boards is automatically assigned a sequential nine-digit code (since there have been over one hundred million posts to date). If the last two digits happened to be identical (i.e., 102522433), this one-in-ten result was called "dubs" as in "doubles" (as well as "trips" for, say, -555, "quints" for -33333, etc.). Since the code is only generated after any given message has been posted, 4chan began to be used by posters as a Magic 8-ball: "If this post gets dubs, Hillary will get a coughing fit in the next debate. Praise be to Kek." The tongue-in-cheek idea that memes were causing reality to warp was as rational an explanation as anything out there during the 2016 presidential campaign. Trump's use of humor and trolling was without any historical precedent—and not only was it unprecedented, it was actually making him *win*.

The left has historically had a virtual monopoly on American humor. The use of humor to put over one's political views can be traced back at the very least to the 1920s and the legendary Algonquin Round Table. For over a decade, a core group of now-forgotten media heavyweights would gather daily for lunch at the Algonquin Hotel and engage in the search for the perfect retort.

Like many (if not all) such scenes, it's almost certainly the case that the prism of nostalgia has given their "ten-year lunch" a sublime glow that the reality didn't exactly match. Years later the Algonquin Table's most famous member, Dorothy Parker, said as much herself: "The Round Table was just a lot of people telling jokes and telling each other how good they were. Just a bunch of loudmouths showing off, saving their gags for days, waiting for a chance to spring them."[7]

One of the roots of humor is the idea that "it's funny because it's true." The evangelical left's culture implicitly turns this maxim on its head and gives the impression that things are true because they're funny—which is not quite the same thing. As a result, rather than their ideas being explicitly and logically argued for, they are slipped into the zeitgeist through the use of humor, both in the positive sense and in the snide, sarcastic sense. This cynical "It's just a joke!" façade is a convenient mask for an ideology that dare not expose itself completely. Behind closed doors Parker made her real worldview plain, claiming that "people don't *know* what they want until you *give* it to them."

It's no surprise that Parker was best friends with playwright Lillian Hellman, remembered as much for her writing as for her fondness for Stalin and her lifetime of dissembling ("Every word she writes is a lie, including 'and' and 'the.'"). And it should be no surprise either that, with typical leftist earnestness, Parker willed her estate to Martin Luther King despite never having met him or even having any interaction with him whatsoever.

After being discovered by the worst of the web, Ben Garrison ended up embracing his bad luck. He began to draw cartoons with New Right ideas, earning him acclaim and acceptance. There are far fewer Photoshops of his more recent work, and it's now become clear that Garrison is no hatemonger. Furie has tried the opposite tack, and it looks unlikely to be an effective one. His belief that he had some form of effective ownership over Pepe the frog was quickly put to the test in May 2017. Furie "killed" Pepe the frog in a strip and even drew the funeral in a frankly delusional attempt to strike the character from popular consciousness. It didn't even take hours for internet provocateurs to then appropriate Furie's other cartoon characters and make them even more explicit symbols of and advocates for literal Nazism. Landwolf's first name was declared to be Heinrich, for instance, and the squiggly lines in his sunglasses edited into a highly-stylized SS logo. Pepe himself was depicted to be resurrected à la the risen Christ.

Just as with Campbell's and Warhol, Furie created Pepe but someone else gave him meaning. "Reclaiming" him would be akin to Campbell's insisting . . . actually there could be no equivalent since the concept is absurd. It is literally impossible to remove the connotations and symbolism that an image has accumulated over time. New meanings may emerge, but past references will always be lingering in the background. Yet this desire to decree universal meaning is, again, a testament to the evangelical left's demand to maintain total control of discourse and even thought.

5

*

AIRTIGHT

> When we win, do not forget that these people want you
> broke, dead, your kids raped and brainwashed, and
> they think it's funny.
>
> —SAM HYDE

I still remember being taken aback when I read an article in
TV Guide in 1995 where the author was giddy that we would
"finally" get to see a black Vulcan. The idea that humanoid races
would evolve identically and independently on other worlds
is insane even by sci-fi standards, but if we had "white" Vulcans then surely there must be VOC—Vulcans of Color—as well.
As far back as 1997, *Vibe* magazine used typical progressive
tactics to dismiss such an obvious criticism: "Every once in a
while you get people who still can't accept a black Vulcan," the
actor who played Tuvok pointed out. The author of the article
reached the inevitable conclusion: *"white supremacist Trekkies?"*
(emphasis in original). It's unclear which is more dimwitted:
the idea that the only possible opposition for extraterrestrial
diversity hires is white supremacy or that white supremacists
are somehow incapable of enjoying *Star Trek*.

In other words, even imaginary worlds that literally don't exist must still be remade to fall in line with the edicts of evangelical progressivism. Not only is there nowhere on earth to escape it, but adherents to the creed insist upon controlling the worlds people go to escape the earth. Whether sci-fi, fantasy, or some video games, it doesn't matter.

The video game subculture, as with other "nerd" subcultures like comic books and sci-fi television, has always been heavily male dominated. That's not to say women aren't made to feel welcome; most nerds would gladly give their ten-sided dice to be able to play an RPG with a girl. But such males are relatively low status, and associating with them—especially at a young age—is socially costly to females. That's the argument, anyway.

Let's take a role-playing video game like *Super Mario Bros.* (Yes, I know it's not an RPG; I just wanted to give the gamers reading this a momentary spike of rage.) As Mario and Luigi make their way across the levels, they encounter an array of enemies whose only purpose is to keep the player from achieving his goals by destroying him. Each enemy has different properties and must be dealt with accordingly. The little mushroom Goombas can either be stomped on or shot with fireballs. The hard-shelled Buzzy Beetles are fireproof but can be stomped on, while our heroes can use fire against the aptly named Spiny but can't stomp on one for obvious reasons.

When navigating such a game, therefore, players dedicate a large portion of time to figuring out how a given enemy operates and what tactics are the most effective at defeating it. To consider what a Goomba "wants" or why it acts the way it does is nonsensical in this context. Or rather, the clear answer to why a Goomba is doing what it's doing is because it's been programmed to act that way. Reverse-engineering its programming is therefore a useful technique to figuring out how to advance in the game.

The story of Gamergate has been told ad infinitum. As briefly as possible, it started with allegations from her boyfriend that a game developer named Zoë Quinn was trading sexual favors for positive attention in the gamer press. It was this spark that exploded into Gamergate and allowed Milo Yiannopoulos to make a name for himself. He consistently covered the story for Breitbart, reporting in September 2014,

> Several prominent gaming journalists across America are part of a secret [GameJournoPros] mailing list on which they discuss what to cover, what to ignore, and what approach their coverage should take to breaking news, Breitbart London can reveal.
>
> This revelation echoes the 2010 JournoList scandal, in which liberal reporters were caught colluding and smearing their ideological opponents in a private mailing list set up by Ezra Klein, now the editor-in-chief of Vox.com.

But unlike JournoList, which featured reporters who covered politics, the gaming community ostensibly had nothing to do with politics. Gaming is inherently an escape from serious issues. This was a crucial moment for many to realize how pervasive the evangelical left feels its reach needs to be.

"I'd say about 60 percent of people in Gamergate were far left to left-leaning," explains Breitbart tech reporter Charlie Nash. "It was gamers annoyed that reviewers were saying that something is a great game just because they were friends with a person involved. They then realized that these same journalists and industry officials were using their shadow cabal to punish people for having the wrong political opinion. Let's suppose someone had views that were, say, too conservative or thought there were only two biological genders. They would then plot to either ignore him, not get him a job, or get him out of the industry entirely. If you were a games journalist or a developer, if you showed any support for Gamergate, your career usually didn't last long because they had all the contexts in the industry."

In terms of gaming, the outcome was hardly victorious. "They still have control," Nash said. "Nothing's changed because they've purged everyone who disagreed with them. Since then, people have started their own review websites but they're just blogs." In February 2018, *Subnautica* sound designer Simon Chylinski was publicly fired because of old tweets that were uncovered, such as his claim that "importing random ppl from the 3rd world is also importing 3rd world tier crime rates and IQ" and telling author Richard Dawkins that "All the former british colonies r now some of the best places in the world. Brits dont need to feel bad about this. U guys did well."

But Gamergate was an important moment in proving the existence of the Cathedral, the idea that what is being presented as fact is actually a carefully coordinated movement by elites to establish and impose their view of what reality is and how it should be. The GameJournoPros list created the appearance that different outlets were independently coming to the same conclusions, even though it was quite coordinated.

This is how the gamers came to see what conservatives are often loath to say: the evangelical left is an army of programmed enemies with whom discourse is quite literally pointless and whose only role is to destroy the heroes (or, as leftists would say, "protagonists," because "hero" is a problematic term). Yes, they are "part of the game" in the same way that the left is part of the country, the system, and the government. But their desire is to eradicate their opponents, not to coexist with them. They are the Goombas.

In gaming there is something called an "exploit," an action

that's against the spirit of the game but technically doable and therefore acceptable in some sense. A quintessential exploit works as follows: Many games have stores within their worlds where the players can sell back unwanted items in exchange for money. These items will *not* become available for repurchase and will effectively cease to exist, since stores are programmed to only sell certain specific, fixed inventory. That way, as the game advances, players can buy increasingly stronger weapons and armor but can only do so at the appropriate points in the game lest they get an unfair advantage early on.

Many games also have quest items, unique items that are necessary to complete the game. For example, there might be a silver key without which the player can't access a certain important castle. Well, what happens if the player decided to sell that key? Selling a quest item to a store and then being unable to buy it back would effectively render the game dead. Within the context of the game, the key is permanently inaccessible and the player will never be able to proceed to that castle.

This type of scenario provides a problem for game programmers. Many get around this by making all quest items unsalable. One simply can't sell them at the stores in the game at any price. Other games are programmed differently: as soon as the quest item is sold, it instantly reappears where it was first found. Meaning, there are now effectively infinite keys teleporting into existence. Whether this is an overlooked mistake in programming or a necessity based on how the game was written is somewhat irrelevant. It certainly doesn't make actual sense within the world of the game.

So what some players do is obvious: get the key; sell it; return to where it reappears; get it again; sell it again; repeat as needed. They are exploiting the programming of the game and earning their character unlimited funds in the process. One can see why some consider this cheating, even though the player isn't necessarily competing with another person but only trying to finish the game.

What this illustrates is how gamers think. Their hobby—not their job, but what they do for *fun*—consists of living in worlds created by others, figuring out the rules those worlds operate under, and then bending or even breaking those rules to get the result that they want. They also have an enormous amount of spare time and are quite prone to thinking logically and systematically when it comes to achieving their goals.

This is who the evangelical left chose to pick a fight with.

Gamergate was the probably the first time the evangelical left came up against an enemy who was completely focused on tactics and completely uninterested in how or why they were saying what they were saying. The goal was to clear the playing field of the enemy, and to do that one needed to understand the programming. In fact, gamers have no choice but to learn which weapons work against which opponents. The more powerful the enemy, the more specific the weapon used against them usually needs to be. Bombs are needed to defeat the triceratops-like Dodongo in *The Legend of Zelda*, and the final enemy Ganon can be felled with the silver arrow and only the silver arrow. As these combinations are sometimes hard to figure out, it is the norm in gaming culture for such techniques to become widely disseminated.

As such, a list of various types of leftists, their attacks, and their vulnerabilities was quickly drawn up and distributed online. By having such a reference guide handy—and having a movement populated by gamers who understand strategy—responses to progressives became uniform and independent without any sort of leader issuing orders. Further, there was constant in-field testing and feedback as to what worked and what didn't. The leftists were unable or unwilling to change their tactic of crying "racism." The gamers, on the other hand, were trying every weapon until they found what worked—and they found the weapons that they needed.

One type of foe that became identified was the False Flag, a poorly disguised progressive who, say, suggests flooding an enemy's Twitter account in order to cause psychological stress. Knowing that the corporate press would be more than happy to exploit a toxic individual to paint an entire group with the same brush, the response to this type was obvious: "Condemn. Reply and clearly state that you do not agree with the shill. Report on sight."

Whatever the technique, a counterstrategy was developed—and gamers and trolls had fun doing it. Reality competition shows like *Project Runway* and *Top Chef* thrive on television. Rather than casting exhibitionistic lunatics like other series, the shows are populated by talented people being forced to be creative under artificial constraints: Make a dress out of things found in the supermarket. Cook a monkfish dish that children would enjoy. The interest comes in watching the designers and chefs navigate their skills to meet these difficult, often arbitrary limitations. It's the same scenario when certain words are banned by a given social media platform. New funny euphemisms are developed. Because they are clever and original, they spread and have even more power than that which they are meant to replace. What can be done when a community, merely out of spite, starts to refer to African Americans as (literally) "n words" or "outdated farm equipment"? Is this less hurtful and hateful at all?

In September 2016, YouTube started a new campaign to more closely suppress racist hate speech on the site. On September 21, a /pol/ user asked, "All it would take would be for internet arseholes to use a common word in place of something racist, like if they started using 'google' instead of 'nigger' what the fuck are they going to do then?" Thus, "Operation Google" was launched. It was a call to refer to blacks as "googles" and Jews as "skypes" in order to make banning the "slurs" technically impossible. The call to arms also included a photograph of a lynching labeled "Google hangout" and a looting entitled "Google shopping."

Of course the progressive entertainment wing took aim at Gamergate as well. The popular teen drama *Degrassi* had the gamer kid bringing a gun to school. The same progressives who had a years-long campaign against high school bullying now had no problem denouncing the nerds—the textbook bully targets, voted "most likely to be shoved into a locker"—as racist pre-murderers. What had changed? The nerds were no longer bowing down to progressive domination and were therefore fair game (pun unavoidable). This comes as no surprise: the basis for many religions is belief in the creed or at the very least deference to its edicts. As members of the New Right enjoy pointing out, the word "Islam" literally means submission.

Far from merely defeating the enemy, Gamergate led to a discussion about how to keep the enemy from "respawning" (i.e., reappearing despite its ostensible defeat). How do progressives manage to get a foothold, and how can they be prevented from doing so? The Alt-Right blog SocialMatter.net had a 2014 article that offered a blunt assessment of how entryism works, and how and why it should be opposed. "Female groups are of little civilizational import and are largely inconsequential," author Paul Tissot states flatly. On the other hand, because "[f]emales are very interested in colonizing high-value male spaces," "[m]ale groups are subverted and redirected to femcentric goals/visions if women are present and not managed with an iron fist."[1]

According to this thinking, patriarchal culture (i.e., the only culture of value) operates like a cuckoo. Women glom on to male subcultures and reorient them to their own values much like a cuckoo parasitically tricks other birds into raising her young at the expense of their own. How this occurs is via that one female who would join a group. Because she wants to join a predominantly or exclusively male-oriented scene, she is by definition "not like other girls." But psychologically she is *exactly* like every other female, and necessarily so. She thinks she's a roommate when she's actually a houseguest. Soon she will be making demands, and a certain percentage of weak males will appease her whether due to being conflict-averse or to trying to win her affections. Then it becomes a numbers game, and soon war until domination.

Entryism need not refer to men refusing to allow women in; it can be used in general to explain the need for some sort of (usually ideological) purity to maintain group cohesion. The term has roots that go back decades, but the New Right has revived it as a weapon against conservatives and Republicans who thoroughly embrace inclusionism, diversity, "diversity," and the Big Tent approach to elections and governing.

As Gamergate proceeded, the counterrevolution grew. Online trolling has a strong overlap with video game culture, and the two formed quite a natural alliance. As such, any systemic attempt to ban "hate speech" or "racism" in an online context was analyzed in a similar way by gamers and trolls alike. The goal became: given the barriers in place, how can one still achieve an outcome that has been decreed as not only undesirable but forbidden?

This is why the term "weaponized autism" is such a frequent online joke ("joke"?). In his book *The Science of Evil* Simon Baron-Cohen discussed how autism and sociopathy are very closely related psychologically. An autistic person might tell someone that, yes, that dress does make her look fat. He does this not to be hurtful but because his literalism renders him incapable of understanding that the question is not to be taken at face value and is actually a demand for validation instead of a genuine inquiry.

A sociopath might have the same verbatim response, but in his case it would either stem from an indifference to causing harm or even from a desire to do so. Interestingly, people with autism are very much the subjects of sympathy while sociopaths never are, despite both having inalterable legitimate neurological conditions that neither has chosen. So regardless of whether some gamers and trolls are autistic or sociopaths or both, they showed no mercy and did not regard their foes as fully human. The goal became finding the workaround to an arbitrary edict and not worrying about the feelings of others.

For many people, the question then became why would anyone *want* to engage in hate speech or racist talk in the first place? The answers are varied. They could have a genuine desire to engage in discussion or dialogue about taboo issues without fear of censure. It could stem from a sense of power in upsetting others (especially one's enemies) or in subverting banality to humorous ends. It could be a simple "because I feel like it and don't have to explain myself to you." Even Lisa Simpson—literally a cartoon caricature of progressivism—couldn't help but sigh with longing upon hearing bully Jimbo Jones described as "a good-looking rebel who plays by his own rules."

Because the evangelical left—like most human beings—is highly lacking in empathy and unable to perceive other points of view, its members tend to equate their perspective with universally perceived truth. A reaction to a joke or a meme takes no thought whatsoever. It is visceral and it is immediate. Therefore, it follows that one's reaction must be true and *obviously* so, since we know things are obvious when they are immediately understandable. The fact that these immediate, visceral reactions are a function of the individual's psyche and values and not akin to seeing and identifying, say, an apple on a table is something most people would never even consider.

As such, what is "obviously" hate speech or racism is sometimes more of a gray area or not even hate speech at all. In the movie *Ghost World*, Enid's art teacher is forced to give her a failing grade for reappropriating past racist commercial iconography. While the painting is intended as a condemnation of racism and an analysis of the sort of imagery that was once taken for granted but is now considered unconscionable, the teacher nevertheless has no choice but to give her an F—those are the rules. The revisionist attempts to strike the n-word from Mark Twain books—crucial historical proof of America's racist history—represent another example of progressive social domination taking precedence over context.

Bristling at any sort of restrictions on speech can therefore be seen as resentment at both being told what to say and at being classified as something one isn't. The evangelical left is very big on respecting someone's chosen identity in terms of issues such as gender and sexuality. Yet when it comes to being a racist or the phobe du jour, any progressive feels quite comfortable labeling another person as such. That's because being a racist is one's default spiritual condition. It is only via the saving grace of progressivism that a human being is able to escape that fallen state.

Thus, the overwhelming focus of New Right thinking and activism isn't about fighting a specific bill or arguing with the left issue by issue. Conservatives could and did make the fair and honest case that the way Obamacare was passed was legally obscene. The Democrats took an unrelated bill that had a majority, deleted the entire text, and inserted the text for Obamacare instead. Then, they passed the entirety through reconciliation, which does not require a filibuster-proof majority but is explicitly meant to be used exclusively for budgetary issues, not legislation. The conservative criticism was true and accurate—and pointless. It had literally zero impact on stopping the bill's passage.

But, as with the individual mandate, the conservative fixation with Obama himself was straight out of the Heritage Foundation. For New Right adherents, the key is to identify leftist techniques and call them out when they are being used, and to make certain they are being stripped of their efficacy whenever possible. There will always be another Obama. One can argue all day long about whether *Roe v. Wade* is justified by the Constitution, but having five Supreme Court justices who say "no" would be far more important to pro-lifers than winning said argument. And since the New Right is far more focused on culture than politics, the strategies are far different.

The mother of all New Right techniques is that of the red pill, or variants thereof like "red-pilling" or "becoming red-pilled." The term comes directly from the film *The Matrix*. In the movie, everything that the vast majority of mankind sees is actually a lie, a false reality constructed for their benefit and comfort by a secret ruling cabal. Morpheus (played by Laurence Fishburne) offers Neo (Keanu Reeves) a choice of two pills. "You take the blue pill," he explains, "the story ends. You wake up in your bed and believe whatever you want to believe. You take the red pill, you stay in Wonderland, and I show you how deep the rabbit hole goes."

The film's concept is virtually identical to how red-pilling is evoked in New Right and broader internet circles. Namely, demonstrating to someone that what is presented as fact by the corporate press and entertainment industries is only (at best) a shadow of what is real, that this supposed reality is in fact a carefully constructed narrative intentionally designed to keep some very unpleasant people in power and to keep everyone else tame and submissive.

Obviously, as in the film, the powers that be are desperate to ensure that such things never happen. As a result, any attempts at red-pilling are preemptively dismissed by such terms as "conspiracy theory," which is made synonymous with lunacy and idiocy. That the CIA is quite literally a conspiracy—a secretive organization designed to spy—is something most people can accept as factually true yet still find emotionally hard to express.

For most people, it is enough to hear the word "conspiracy" for it to force all further interest to vanish like a magic spell. To them, the idea that things aren't largely what we're told is simply absurd and not worth further investigation. It is a position held by the vast majority of human beings, and this near universal consensus understandably gives them comfort. But it can't really be said to give them truth.

One hundred people watching the same television show and agreeing with what that show presented have no independent claim to truth whatsoever; they are only taking what has been shown to them at face value. It is certainly possible that everything the corporate media puts forward as truth is, in fact, true. But there also exists the possibility that corporations, naturally, act out of self-interest and the need to seek and maintain power, and that the presentation of truth is only useful insofar as it serves that goal (assuming they are even capable of perceiving said truth correctly to begin with).

In several interviews, I have had to make the point that you're supposed to take one red pill, not the whole bottle. Once someone accepts that the media constructs a story of its own, the revulsion can lead to an equally absurd world where literally everything is a lie and everyone is consciously and actively in cahoots all the time. This leads to thinking that progressivism is a conscious and intentional scheme to destroy the West via whichever nefarious group one latches on to.

The idea that the media is downright nefarious is not something that was part of political discourse until quite recently. What Mackinac Center vice president Joseph Overton codified is the idea that, at any given time, there is only a certain range of discourse that is considered publicly acceptable. In the 1840s slavery was widely defended and even lauded. The "peculiar institution" has no advocates today—and not only are there no advocates, but anyone who dared to advocate such a thing would suffer severe social, personal, and professional consequences. This respectable range is known as the Overton Window, and Trump's moving of the Overton Window was the argument for a Trump presidency that had some of the broadest support across the entire New Right.

The left's exploitation of the Overton Window is a major explanation for how progressivism increased its control over society despite ostensible conservative opposition. Imagine a scale from one to ten. The progressive wants to move it to ten, the conservative stands athwart history, yelling stop—and compromises at five. The next political cycle now starts with the scale from five to fifteen, including things that would have been unthinkable last time. So the entire political discussion creeps ever closer to progressive fundamentalism.

Trump, however, yanked the window very heavily to the right. Things that conservatives found unacceptable to even discuss, let alone advocate, he proclaimed loudly and proudly. This forced the left to move with him in terms of issues, if only to counter his rhetoric and shoot it down. A search for "I can't believe we're having this conversation!" on Twitter or Facebook would yield so many results that it would take a supercomputer the size of Trump Tower to tally them all. One interesting side question is whether Trump has actually moved the Overton Window or if, in my view, he is simply creating a second window parallel to progressive discourse. There are many indicators that Americans are literally beginning to speak, if not different languages, at least different *dialects* when it comes to politics and culture. Terms such as "illegal alien" vs. "undocumented immigrant," "tax increases" vs. "revenue generation," or even simply what pronoun to use when discussing transgender people are all demonstrations of the fact that both political sides are attempting to control thought by controlling language—as well as using language to demonstrate one's political allegiances.

Here conservatives miss the mark. They do understand that, for progressives, language is not merely used to communicate ideas but to control, among other purposes. As such, conservatives have argued about "political correctness" for years, but in this they are hypocritical. The idea that "political correctness" is a uniquely left-wing phenomenon is simply untrue. There is a left-wing iteration of conversational policing, but this is in no sense unique to the left. There are many subjects to which people who are right of center react with the same umbrage that a liberal would in a parallel situation. Speaking with a conservative about the police or the military is exactly like speaking with a progressive about people of color. The immediate instinct is to defend the group from any criticism. A calm, reasonable discussion of the subject is the aberration rather than the norm. Speaking of black crime is racist; speaking of American war crimes is also "racist" (in the sense that "racist" simply means "that which I'm against").

In 1981, for example, the first season of *Dynasty* had Jeff Colby cracking jokes with elder patriarch Blake Carrington about smoking marijuana as they dined in their opulent mansion—hardly two archetypical hippies. Not long after that came Nancy Reagan's "Just Say No" campaign, and the idea that illegal drug use of any kind could be shown in a positive or even neutral light on television fell by the wayside.

Most conservatives are also averse to calm discussions of

children and sexuality. And for some sects of conservatism, the idea of "the Constitution" is fetishized far more than the actual document should be. Such types do not react well to being reminded that the best part of the Constitution, namely the Bill of Rights, were edits to the original document. My personal favorite is trolling conservatives with the indisputable fact that "more voters wanted Hillary Clinton to be president than Donald Trump." Despite themselves, they then launch into their best "What difference does it make?" Benghazi-hearing impression. It's hysterical, in both senses of the term.

For progressives especially, language is used as "in-group signaling," a cue that one is on the correct team. Many have made the observation that the term "African American" is grossly imprecise. The phrase is now frequently used to describe Caribbean Americans as well as non-American Africans. In practice, "African American" is simply a euphemistic way of saying "black." In other words, "African American" is literally wrong but functionally appropriate—because the function of a euphemism is to reference something without actually saying it.

Most Americans don't know that referring to "Eskimos" is forbidden north of the border, with the preferred term being "Inuit." Much as with "African Americans," however, there are people-formerly-known-as-Eskimos whose tribes *aren't* Inuit. Yet the term is in use because it serves its purpose: it demonstrates that the speaker is trying to be sensitive and is with the program. The terms are used to identify the *speaker* as much as the *subject*. Like the password to some underground club, the right cue is more important than the literal accuracy of what is actually being said. The doorman waves patrons in regardless of whether or not the crow actually flies at midnight.

We are social animals, and as such the vast majority of human beings prefer to be part of the in-group (which for many, especially in urban areas, means the progressive milieu). This makes perfect sense. The right positioning helps a person with everything from getting a job to getting laid. As a consequence of this psychology, progressives are left with a problem. It costs nothing for someone to adopt the correct term in their speech. So as a "proper" term becomes popularized and pervasive, it inevitably loses its function of distinguishing "good" people from the bad due to those who are simply trying to pass as "good."

The progressive solution to this problem is to constantly change language in order to maintain some semblance of verbal social cues. "Black" became "colored" became "Negro" became "Afro-American" became "African American." There are few things that progressives like more than presenting the appearance of being on the cutting edge of social thought. (What, you don't subscribe to the *New Yorker*? You really should be reading it.) Conversely, someone using the wrong term is "obviously" using outdated speech and therefore can be dismissed as having outdated thoughts.

Alongside in-group signaling is virtue signaling, an extremely common if not universal aspect of evangelical progressive culture. Since the progressive religion is based on salvation through faith and not via works, there are often no positive achievements to demonstrate one's salvation—either to others or even to oneself. Progressives are thereby forced to "do something" without actually *doing* anything. We've seen this in Hollywood during the AIDS crisis, where a red ribbon was worn both by those actively fundraising to fight the disease and those who simply wanted to stick something on their lapel to show that they were one of the good guys. Unlike the deadly disease, those ribbons came and went fairly quickly.

More recently, virtue signaling was seen with the meme of people posting photos of themselves holding up a sign that read "Bring back our girls" after almost three hundred female students were kidnapped by Boko Haram in Nigeria. The nadir of this was when First Lady Michelle Obama got in on the action, dour look and all (so serious!). Boko Haram is an Arabic-speaking organization, and it's doubtful that Mrs. Obama's forlorn expression would have caused the radicals to feel pity as opposed to glee for causing their enemies such distress. But this picture was done as a signal to Mrs. Obama's group, not as an actual message to the kidnappers.

Now, thanks to Facebook, anyone can easily put a filter over their profile photo the next time a radical Islamist commits mass murder in some country that we ostensibly care about. Note that the tagline was "Je suis Charlie" after the Charlie Hebdo killings and not "Nous somme Charlie." *I* am Charlie, not *we* are Charlie, because this is a social proclamation of one's claim to goodness.

Yet these cases are somewhat mitigated; both are examples where most people (correctly) felt helpless about effecting change regarding a tragedy and yet still desperately wanted to (appear to) do something about the events. The purest of virtue signaling can be seen in the likes of what was found on actor James Franco's now-deleted Instagram page. Franco's brief bio included the caveat "if you're racist, sexist, or homophobic, get the f*** out of here." It takes courage to stand up to "racists," but writing out the F-word is a bridge too far, apparently.

The idea that Franco's disclaimer would give anyone pause is absurd—not to mention the fact that very many racists, sexists, and homophobes would be the first to deny that they're those things (and possibly even delude themselves accordingly). The actual purpose, then, was for Franco to signal to his tribe that he is a good, moral person fighting against heresies.

One ancillary to virtue signaling is "white knighting," a largely online phenomenon wherein a male rushes to the defense of a female he doesn't even know in hopes of proving what a great person he is. This often results in him getting rebuked and being told that "she's not going to fuck you, bro." The opposite of this behavior is "black knighting," where males attack females out of proportion in hamfisted attempts to demonstrate their supposed masculinity.

One of the major recruiting aspects of New Right culture is its ability to identify and weaponize such psychological effects, especially against ostensibly educated people who are convinced that "racists" are all mouth-breathing inbreds. By far the most central prism through which their foes are analyzed by the New Right is the intellectual phenomenon known as the Dunning-Kruger effect. Psychologists Dunning and Kruger gave students exams and then graded them. Then they asked the students how they thought that they had done on the tests. What they found was that those who did the poorest were also the worst when it came to judging their performance relative to others. As one acquaintance of mine put it, stupid people don't know that they're stupid.

Given that college graduates and those with higher degrees thereby have "proof" that they are bright—and to equate "bright" with "brilliant" is not psychologically difficult to do—we are left with an entire population of people who aren't exceptionally smart but are certain that they are. One university study had over *90 percent* of faculty regard themselves as "above average." This was not in comparison to the average person, but to their colleagues. In other words, the vast majority of academics think they are better than average at their job. The implications of this are obvious (though not, perhaps, to these self-assessed brainiacs).

This manifests as a phenomenon that Alt-Right writer Vox Day refers to as "mid-wits." It is true that poor spelling correlates with lower intelligence and lower education levels especially.

But the inverse is not true at all; having good spelling does not make one particularly bright. Knowing the distinction between "your" and "you're" is possessing the knowledge of a second grader, yet a mid-wit would take this as evidence of their own intelligence if not genius.

Equating education with intelligence is like equating money with class. As Day puts it, "Those who possess above-average intelligence and trouble to occasionally read newspapers and magazines tend to genuinely be under the erroneous impression that they possess superlative intelligence. [. . .] The mid-witted individual tends to compare himself to those below the average and concludes that because he isn't like them, he must be a genius."

It is the difference between the relative and the absolute. The tallest person in a given group might not, in fact, actually be tall if the group consisted entirely of short people. Similarly, genuinely intelligent people tend to focus far more on the other party's ideas when it comes to discussions rather than looking for signifiers of intellect, verbal cues, or relative levels of social credibility.

Having a Harvard or Yale degree does not even imply that one is smarter than everyone who graduated from every inferior school (not to mention those who didn't attend college at all). Further, being smarter than another person doesn't imply that one will outthink them on every issue, especially given different bases of knowledge, expertise, and experience. One can easily imagine Barack Obama being smarter than everyone in his cabinet. Yet it's absurd to posit that he knew more than every one of them when it came to their own departments. The smartest, most informed person on earth will still be ignorant of over 99 percent of human knowledge.

In addition to delusions, there are intellectually dishonest techniques, such as motte and bailey. As explained on the Slate

Star Codex blog, motte and bailey is an intellectual form of bait-and-switch. As the blogger explains it, there's a tower (the motte) surrounded by a field (the bailey). The field is used for production of food, the tower for defense. In discussion the concept refers to the tendency of people to make a spurious claim, retreat to the tower of indisputable truth when challenged, and then return back to making the claim as if it had been proven. As in:

CLAIM: All white people are the inherent beneficiaries of racism.

CHALLENGE: What about poor whites living, say, in Appalachia?

CLAIM: Are you really saying that racism hasn't historically and to this day been a strong force in our culture?

CHALLENGE: Of course not.

CLAIM: Right. All white people are the inherent beneficiaries of racism.

This toggling is by no means unique to progressives or even people on the left. The Alt-Right version is to recognize that the number of Jewish people in media is out of proportion to our percentage of the population. Therefore, they claim, we have sinister, nefarious aims. When challenged on the latter (as if progressive WASPs in the media don't have the same precise biases and worldview), they respond by reiterating the numbers of Jews—a numerical data point that was never in contention to begin with.

Given all this, rather than fighting the left, many members of the New Right argue for using what they call "agree, amplify, and accelerate." In other words, since evangelical progressivism is in defiance of reality, hastening its collapse by encouraging its purest strains is arguably easier (and certainly more fun) than actually fighting it—another strategy that is anathema to most conservatives.

The "agree, amplify, and accelerate" strategy has started creeping into mainstream right-wing ideology, the smarter adherents of which can't help but notice that the New Right is more effective at many things than they had been. Hence Kurt Schlichter's May 2017 TownHall.com article "Liberals Are an Inferno of Flaming Crazy and We Should Pour Gasoline on the Fire." Though it's a toned-down version of the AAA approach—and the necessary insistence that "Alt-Right weirdos" "don't count" (bless your heart, Kurt)—Schlichter recognizes the appeal of the strategy on some level.

These concepts are widely discussed in online forums and on social media. Yet there is no real text that codifies New Right analysis, for several reasons. First, there really isn't anyone in a position to write it. Second, the material would be considered quite niche. Yes, there aren't that many members of the New Right—but there are just over five hundred members of Congress, and they carry enormous influence. It's not a numbers game in terms of political warfare, but it certainly is in terms of publishing. Finally, the tactics and analyses are dynamic, responses to ever-changing real-time operations, both from and against the left. That's simply the nature of warfare.

The closest thing to a manual for fighting the evangelical left comes from Alt-Right sci-fi author Vox Day. Years ago, Day used to be colleagues with Ben Shapiro at the heretical right-wing website WND. Day wrote:

> We corresponded a few times and were on friendly, if distant, terms. I mean, what do you talk about with a little kid whose idea of a good time is launching obvious rhetorical attacks at liberals? As he matured, he

gradually began to question the ideas he was parroting, and reached the point where he considered quit-
ting the media game.

I'll have to dig out the emails to figure out exactly
what I told him, but if I recall correctly, I encouraged
him to resist the temptation to become a media whore.
I understood the allure, as it was a poisoned apple that
was also offered to me, but perhaps it was easier for me
to turn it down since I was living in Europe and already established in the game development world.

Ben, unfortunately, couldn't resist the apple, or the
easy way forward, writing whatever his backers told
him to write. I haven't read him much since he wrote
those dreadful, chickenshit columns in 2005 [i.e.,
Shapiro's two "Why 'ChickenHawk' Argument is Un-
American" pieces], so I don't know how much of what
he writes he genuinely believes now and how much
he is still parroting. Of course, the human mind being
the incredible rationalizing machine that it is, it's entirely possible that he has come to believe what he's
been told to say.[2]

As is so often the case with the New Right, Day's contempt
is as great for the conservative Shapiro as it is for the left. In
2016 Day wrote that Shapiro is "not pro-American, he's not a
nationalist, he's just another nominal Jewish 'conservative'
who is a professional member of the mainstream media's Po-
temkin opposition and more devoted to fighting racism than
big government."[3]

Day's 2015 book *SJWs Always Lie* is presented as a how-to
guide to deal with the members of the evangelical left, specifically referring to their "Social Justice Warriors," or SJWs. Here

he presents the New Right worldview in concise, pithy form: "The most important thing is to grasp the fact that you are never safe in the vicinity of SJWs. [. . .]Attempting to mollify, appease, or otherwise accommodate the SJWs around you will not put you at any less risk but tends to make you more vulnerable to their attacks in the long run. [. . .] This is true even if you are sympathetic to some of the ideas that SJWs claim are their goals, such as equality, diversity, respect, feminism, income equality, fat acceptance, gay 'marriage,' transgender acceptance, vegetarianism, religious ecumenicism, and atheism. In fact, this is particularly true if you are sympathetic to any of their objectives, as you are more easily pressured and policed."[4]

This is not a subculture that looks fondly upon the days when Ronald Reagan and Tip O'Neill shook hands and came to a bipartisan consensus. For Day and others on the New Right, the progressives are the enemy—unsalvageable, evil, and inherently damaged. In contrast to Shapiro's *How to Debate Leftists and Destroy Them: 11 Rules for Winning the Argument*, Day is not interested in debate. "The most important thing to accept here," Day says, "is the complete impossibility of compromise or even meaningful communication with your attackers. SJWs do not engage in rational debate because they are not rational and they do not engage in honest discourse because they do not believe in objective truth. [. . .] A large percentage of SJWs are prone to various forms of mental illness; being competitive with regards to their victimhood, it is not at all uncommon for them to openly brag about being on various antidepressants and other psychiatric medications."[5]

Day's solution comes in several steps, including building alternative institutions, rejecting their ideals, defunding and destroying their propaganda centers, and explicitly denying them employment. In many ways this precisely mirrors the progressive view of how the New Right should be treated, as evil hatemongers who should not be given a platform to express their views and most certainly should not be hired by reputable companies. The so-called Era of Good Feelings ended in the early nineteenth century. For the New Right, we are in the Era of Ill Will, and it is difficult to see how it will draw to a close in the near future.

6

★

THE CASE AGAINST DEMOCRACY

> You have the courage to tell the masses what no poli-
> tician told them: you are inferior and all the improve-
> ments in your conditions which you simply take for
> granted you owe to the effort of men who are better
> than you.
>
> —Ludwig von Mises

On March 18, 2014, the Reason Foundation hosted an event to discuss *Dear Reader*, my book on north Korea. I was interviewed by John Tierney of the not-yet-failing *New York Times* in the basement of the Museum of Sex. After I discussed things such as why Kim Jong Il claimed to hate the *Mona Lisa* and what he meant by "Juche gymnastics," I stuck around to sign books for those interested in such a thing.

A tall man with very dark eyebrows and a full head of gray hair approached me with his Korean girlfriend. It was Jonathan Haidt, and I was pretty much beside myself that someone of his stature (as in acclaim, not as in height) would come to my talk.

"Oh wow," I sputtered. "I can't believe Jonathan Haidt is here."

"It's pronounced *height*," he said, in a friendly manner.

"Not tonight. Tonight it's Hate and Malice."

Haidt is soft-spoken but not meek. His words are measured, and when he listens he is one of the few people I've ever met who actually stops to consider everything that he is being told. He presents his response not just by discussing what he thinks but by describing what evidence brought him to that conclusion, both pro and con. He is clearly and unambiguously bright. Yet he is so matter-of-fact in his approach that one would never guess that he is one of the most important political thinkers on earth today.

In no sense is Haidt a member of the New Right. He identifies as "a centrist who sides with the Democratic Party on the great majority of issues" and who has never "voted for a Republican for Congress or the presidency," though he "has learned a lot from the writings of conservative intellectuals."[1] The issue Haidt is most passionate and vocal about is fighting the intellectual hegemony found on college campuses. He stresses in many ways the need for greater intellectual diversity in all spheres of thought, pointing out the many very well-known negative consequences of having a setting devoted to thought wherein everyone is already in some form of agreement . . . *or else.*

His wife Jayne Riew has a site called TheInvisibleMonth .com, detailing "how hormonal effects fly under the radar of consciousness." In this sense both partners deal with an essential element of New Right thought: that politics is largely irrational or non-rational and we don't even realize it. No one has brought this idea more to public consciousness than Haidt.

In a show of how bizarre a Venn diagram the New Right subculture is, Haidt's thinking parallels very closely that of a group with far less prestige: the Pick-Up Artist community. There is a tangential relationship between PUAs and the New Right, just as there is with Men Going Their Own Way (MGTOW). This latter scene is not just antifeminist but antiwoman, and it advocates for male self-improvement and integrity as opposed to what is perceived to be the cultural and personal subordination of men and male values to those of women.

The most famous of PUAs is Neil Strauss, whose book *The Game* was a memoir of entering PUA subculture and being mentored by Mystery, the best pick-up artist in the world. Like an actual social scientist, Mystery had broken down the dynamics between male and female courtship almost into a flow chart. One of his most important insights was that attraction is not a choice but a visceral response, and one that can be, if not "forced," then certainly "induced." His ideas provoke intense hatred from feminists, who insist that these techniques are absurd, ridiculous, and never work on anyone while simultaneously arguing that they are so effective that they manipulate women into unknowingly giving up their autonomy.

Mystery's techniques are translated into the most basic elements possible. For example, how does a man know when to make a move? PUA teaches "kino escalation," a gradual increase in physicality from touching hands for stupid reasons all the way up until the first kiss. Now, reaching first base is the organic conclusion to a series of moves instead of an awkward gamble at the end of the date. A "kiss close" to an encounter is certainly far better than a "number close," the fairly easy (and now somewhat dated) achievement of getting a girl's phone number.

The most notorious and misunderstood PUA technique is "negging," which from the name implies going up to a girl and insulting her. But as Strauss's editor Jeremie Ruby-Strauss pointed out to me, "You only neg 9s or 10s. The rest have been negged by life already." In other words, the odds are extremely high that any woman complaining about negging is someone who shouldn't be negged to begin with. Negging females of the highest status is supposedly necessary in order both to demonstrate that one isn't simply part of the unwashed sea of horny men desperately seeking their attention and to get them to drop their guard (their needed shield against said unwashed sea).

A neg is a comment that is ambiguous and designed to force a response, *not* one that is simply curt and dismissive. The example Strauss used was to ask a woman, "Are those nails fake? I think they're cool." It also gave him the opportunity to unobtrusively take her hand, thus breaking the physical contact barrier. The one I personally use in dating apps—with close to a 100 percent response rate—is, "Not much of a talker, I see. I like that in a woman."

The broader point is that the female is unaware that these techniques are being used and finds herself intrigued and eventually attracted to the man. Yet if she were asked *why* she was attracted to him, she would never say, "Because he commented on my nails." She would, however, glom on to his positive attributes, confuse correlation with causation, and (incorrectly) think that those attributes were the ones that brought about the attraction. That's not what had actually happened, but because she was oblivious to the PUA techniques she mentally constructed a coherent narrative that made sense. Attraction first, explanation later. That's why PUAs insist that men ask other men for help in picking up women, as opposed to their female friends. One doesn't ask a deer how to catch a deer; one asks a hunter.

Although he would probably bristle at such a gauche comparison, Haidt's work provides similar insights when it comes to morality and one's political views. What Haidt discovered through his research is that ethical thought is not only nonrational (though not necessarily irrational) but that it can rewrite facts and reality in order to force desired outcomes—and a person doesn't even realize that that's what's happening.

What Haidt did was to pose hypothetical ethical situations to people and then ask them for their moral response. Then he further challenged them to explain why they had the response that they had. The important thing was to ask questions in such a way that there was some moral ambiguity—situations could have moral transgressions but without anyone being transgressed against. As he put it, "My idea was to give adults and children stories that pitted gut feelings about important cultural norms against reasoning about harmlessness, and then see which force was stronger."

One scenario Haidt posited was of a pair of siblings that decided to have a one-off sexual encounter, with her being on birth control and him using a condom. They enjoy the act but never repeat it and grow closer having this secret between them. Another scenario has a girl with access to a cadaver that is about to be incinerated. Rather than waste meat, she cuts some of the flesh off and eats it. Then there's the one about the woman who had nothing to clean her toilet with, so she cut up an old American flag and used it as cloth.

What the research found is that though many people had an opinion, few had a *reason* for said opinion—certainly not an immediate one at hand. Worse, when challenged to justify their perspective, *they would even resort to rewriting the very premise itself,* violating very basic logical principles in the process. For example, one subject brought up the fact that inbreeding leads to deformed children, even though the incest scenario clearly stated that pregnancy could not ensue. "Well, we don't know if the condom broke" is not a response to a constructed hypothetical. We know *everything* that happened, because the entire scenario was made up.

Through further research, Haidt deduced that there are certain axes upon which we make moral and thereby political judgments: Care/Harm, Fairness/Cheating, Loyalty/Betrayal, Authority/Subversion, and Sanctity/Degradation. The weight a person gives each axis informs their political stance. Those who care strongly about authority end up as conservatives, while those who emphasize fairness end up as liberals.

What this means is that though our political views follow logically from basic principles, they are basically *non-rational*. But whether those principles are the correct ones in a given context is harder to say. We will always have a reaction, but we might not always have a reason for that reaction—and even rarer will we have a *rational* reason for that reaction.

The metaphor Haidt uses to describe how we engage in moral reasoning is that of a rider on an elephant. You can steer the elephant one way or another, often with great difficulty. But the elephant has an enormous amount of momentum, and it takes concentration and focus to budge it in any other direction—and one can only budge it so far. An implication that Haidt is not a fan of—but is essential to New Right thought—is that rational civil discourse is not only difficult, it is by and large *impossible*.

The idea that political views are determined by rational discussion and thought can be disproven by a glance at a map. Voters of one type tend to be clustered in certain areas, while different types appear elsewhere. If rationality determined ideology, we would expect to see a fairly even distribution of worldviews across the country. Instead what we see are pockets segregated by thought.

In fact it's easy to demonstrate how this plays out on an individual level. I call this basic scenario the Daedalus Dilemma. The Greek myth of Daedalus is a familiar one: Imprisoned in a tower, Daedalus and his son Icarus strive for a means of escape. Clever Daedalus fashions makeshift wings out of feathers and wax. As they depart for freedom, Daedalus warns Icarus not to fly too closely to the sun lest the wax melt. Icarus ignores his father's words and does precisely what he was warned against. His wings melt away, and he drowns while Daedalus flies to safety.

Now suppose we took Rachel the right-winger and Larry the leftist and locked them in a tower with wax and feathers. Let us also suppose that the only way they could act is if both parties reached some agreement on a course of action. How it would play out, given their thought processes, would look a little like this:

Larry would immediately begin to fashion wings to further their escape.

"What are you doing?" Rachel would ask. "If we try to fly out of here, one of us will die."

"That's absurd," Larry would reply. "We know what to avoid, so both of us will fly to safety."

"But Daedalus and Icarus knew what to avoid, and one of them died."

"It's simple: we won't repeat their mistakes. That's how progress works."

"If it were only that simple," Rachel would point out, "Icarus himself wouldn't have done it. The mistakes of the past are warnings for the present."

"Fine," Larry would say, exasperated. "But if we can't agree to leave, then you're condemning us to remain in prison! Inactivity is not an option."

"I'd rather be in prison," Rachel would reply, "than dead. Sometimes the best choice is still a bad one."

Both parties are arguing for what they regard as the obvious, best course of action. Yet both—acting logically and truthfully, *with access to the exact same data*—have reached entirely opposing conclusions. And so we leave them, unable to understand each other, angry and frustrated, in a prison neither of their own making nor of their own choosing—but a prison nonetheless.

We all tend to dismiss data that goes against our convictions while accepting that which reaffirms what we believe. And if the human mind is perfectly capable of ignoring and rewriting the bases for Haidt's moral scenarios, the idea that charts and graphs will change minds becomes downright absurd. To show how deeply irrational our moral reasoning can be, let's take another of Haidt's examples. He asked, "Which job would you rather have: one where you earn $90,000 a year while your co-workers earn on average $70,000, or one where you earn $100,000 but your co-workers earn on average $150,000?" To the astonishment of right-thinkers, Haidt learned that a great number preferred the first choice. There are people who explicitly and genuinely would prefer to have *everyone* worse off. It is very rare to see a conservative acknowledge the possibility that the left intentionally prefers what's worse for everyone in service to some higher ideal.

This is also a big difference between everyday leftists and the evangelical left. Leftists, broadly speaking, feel that a safety net is necessary and that we shouldn't have a society where people are sick, starving, and left to die on the streets—especially if those circumstances are due to no fault of their own. They freely admit that we need a balance between spending and taxation, and they understand that having a welfare state that is too generous might discourage some from working.

With the evangelical left, it comes down to ideology. When asked if he would raise the capital gains tax even if it meant decreasing revenue, candidate Obama said, "I would look at raising the capital gains tax for purposes of fairness." "Fairness" simply means "what I approve of," a subjective term that seems objective but has no actual inherent meaning. In other words, even if *everyone* were hurt—those paying capital gains and those who depend on the programs partly funded by capital gains taxes—Barack Obama still would consider raising the tax. This is not someone that people on the right are capable of having discourse with. If "that's not fair" is one's argument, one isn't really making an argument at all but an assertion. And to take the route of saying "why yes, that *is* fair" is to accept the premise that "fairness"—a thoroughly leftist term—should be the basis of discussion.

Even worse, to get a Barack Obama to recognize that this is what is happening in his mental processes would also be a Herculean endeavor. Here we have what I call the Pistachio Paradox. Let's suppose another progressive, say Nancy Pelosi, was asked to name her favorite flavors of ice cream. In response, let's pretend she listed (in order): chocolate, vanilla, strawberry, and pistachio. Let's further suppose that about two-thirds of the time she eats her favorite flavor, chocolate. Then, two-thirds of the other time she eats vanilla. Then, two-thirds of the remaining time she eats strawberry. This means that she would actually only choose pistachio 0.27 percent of the time. If she ate ice cream every day of the year, she would only end up choosing pistachio *once*. Yet Pelosi could still claim, legitimately and honestly, that pistachio is one of her top choices when it comes to ice cream.

This paradox is precisely the same when it comes to political choices. A leftist can genuinely believe in things like the Constitution, property rights, and national sovereignty. However, even if those are their fourth priorities—hardly low on a list—other considerations will come first *over 99 percent of the time*. If confronted by their apparent disregard of these values, their reaction will be based on confusion if not downright anger—and logically so. "What do you mean I don't value that? It's one of my top four priorities!" Conservatives are the same way. They claim to be for small government but spending still increases every single year, above the rate of inflation, under Republican presidents. So yes, they believe in it—but they will always choose another flavor first.

All of this feeds into an extremely strong skepticism of democracy among the New Right, if not downright apathy or opposition. In this they are not alone. Leftists inevitably froth at the mouth when I point out that the right to bear arms is more central to the American legal system than the right to vote. This should be of no surprise, since their creation myth is so heavily tied in with extending the voting franchise. As such, they do tend to see any attacks on democracy and voting as thinly disguised attempts to roll back the Voting Rights Act.

Yet being skeptical of mass voting can be traced back to the time before America even existed. Restrictions on voting have been based upon gender, race, citizenship status, criminal record, demonstrations of intelligence, age, and property holding. The Founding Fathers certainly did not believe that everyone should be voting. It was as recently as 1971 that the Constitution was amended to lower the voting age to those who are eighteen. When I walk into a room and flick a switch, I expect the lights to turn on, not to be provided with free dental coverage. Why should flicking a switch in a voting booth be any different? Is it all that surprising or unfair that people who bring nothing to the table should have problems putting food on it?

The model that we are taught in our largely government-run school system is this: Issues arise in a democracy (technically a democratic republic). "Both" sides, through public discourse, put forth their points of view. Politicians campaign and make speeches, while the media educates the public and makes reasoned arguments for each perspective while respecting all sides of the argument. Then the citizenry makes an informed, reasoned decision, balancing both sides of all the issues, and votes for the (one of two) politicians who best represent their personal point of view. This is why it's so important for everyone to keep up on current events, because the basis of our system is an informed citizenry. Otherwise, all sorts of bad things will happen.

So what is the alternative? We're frequently told that those opposed to democracy are "fascists." In some sense that is true, though the term is misleading because "fascism" has such understandably negative connotations. "Corporatist" might be a euphemism but would still be just that, a euphemism that obscures the actual state of affairs. So when using the term "fascist" I use it not as a term of condemnation per se but as one of classification—just as so many college professors speak of Marxism as completely detached from the connotations of Stalinism.

John P. Diggins's *Mussolini and Fascism: The View from America* extensively details the love affair America and her intellectuals had with Mussolini's experiment. What is completely glossed over in our history books is just how respected he was. There are two reasons for this omission: The first is the lingering effects of World War II anti-Axis propaganda (which is part of the reason why Stalin is nowhere near as vilified as much as he should be). Second, of course, is due to the fact that Mussolini hitched his wagon to one of the most evil dictators in human history and pretty much destroyed his country in the process.

Condemning Mussolini for allying with Hitler is in some ways like condemning the United States for allying with Stalin to fight the Axis. Obviously the U.S./Stalin relationship ended (especially during the Korean War), while Mussolini followed Hitler to disgrace and the grave. But to regard one partner as effectively synonymous with the other—even if true from a moral perspective—is not accurate historically or philosophically.

After the 1929 market crash, it was a given among all right-thinking people that pure capitalism was not practicable.

Though many were enthralled by the Soviets, others were either skeptical or knew that such a scheme could never come to pass in the United States. Along came the Mussolini model, which was seen as the middle ground between the two extremes of capitalism and communism. His fascism was the "third way," a system that allegedly preserved the best of free markets with the best of socialism. As such, many of the New Right can be described as "pre-fascist." And just as Mussolini did back then, this can lead to members of the New Right allying with racists and anti-Semites now.

In 2013 I spoke at a seminar discussing politics and culture. At one point all the speakers assembled on the stage for questions from the audience. I decided to take advantage of a lull in the discussion and asked my fellow lecturers what one book they would recommend to everyone. Unbeknownst to me, the one I myself chose was precisely the book Mencius Moldbug recommends above all others: *The Machiavellians* by James Burnham.

Long out of print and difficult to find (as of this writing the cheapest copy on Amazon is $230), *The Machiavellians* provides the grounding for much of the New Right's views on politics. As Moldbug put it, *The Machiavellians* is the book to read "if you want to learn the more general art of thinking about politics in terms of realities, rather than in terms of symbols."[2] The text is amoral—which is often incorrectly equated with immoral—in its description of the political process. "Why not evaluate this philosophy objectively by its results—not by its ideas or by its objectives, which don't matter, but by its actual impact on physical reality, which does? [. . .] Suppose our 'classical Enlightenment liberalism' is a drug, applying for FDA approval. If it fails this approval, why convince anyone to believe it?" For Moldbug, *The Machiavellians* is "the #1 resource for learning to think in this way."[3]

Its author, James Burnham, like his book has become somewhat obscure over the years but still occupies an extremely pivotal position in American right-wing thought. Burnham can reasonably be seen as the missing link between modern-day conservatives and the New Right, with his thinking being the most recent philosophical point where members of both groups can come together in full (or at least very strong) agreement. Politically, both groups would most recently agree on Reagan or perhaps Goldwater, but each side would dismiss many aspects of Reaganism or Goldwaterism as not "really" reflecting the man. With Burnham it's different. Both sides would accept nearly his entire intellectual framework and method of analysis.

Like many others who would later join *National Review*, Burnham came from a communist background. In his case he was a Trotskyist, to the point where he was actually friends with Trotsky himself. But Burnham soured on communism, especially as practiced in the USSR, and drifted to the right. His 1941 book *The Managerial Revolution* touches on a theme that would be expounded on in *The Machiavellians* and then diffused throughout New Right thinking: namely, that what we see as our democratic society is but a façade to obscure rule and control by an unelected and often hidden elite.

The Machiavellians is unusual (or perhaps banal) in its structure, in that Burnham declares four thinkers to be "Machiavellians" and then discusses the nature of their ideas. It almost reads like a book from Buzzfeed: *Four thinkers who reject democratic equality: #3 will surprise you!* Three of the four are almost completely forgotten today: Gaetano Mosca; Georges Sorel; and Robert Michels. The fourth, Vilfredo Pareto, is an extremely important economist who lent his name to such concepts as the Pareto distribution, Pareto efficiency, and Pareto analysis—all of which are still used and taught even in basic economic courses. Yet Pareto's political thought, discussed by Burnham, holds nowhere near the gravitas as his economic work. What these Machiavellians have in common, according to Burnham, is "their refusal to take at face value the words and beliefs and ideals of men."[4]

What Robert Michels brings to the table is what he calls "the Iron Law of Oligarchy." In the same way that many argue that communism "works in theory but not in practice," Michels claims that it is *democracy* that doesn't work in practice. In fact, as he frames it, it might be one of the few things that doesn't even work *in theory*. Meaning, it is impossible to even imagine a scenario where democracy works as democracy.

The claim of democracy and even our representative democracy is that as more people participate, the more inclusive it becomes, and the more legitimate the outcome is. The greater the voter turnout, the better. These are two separate claims, however, that are often equated. Increased voter participation rates might certainly be a good thing, but there is no point past which the system can be regarded as legitimate. It's either legitimate for the 60 percent who voted to speak for the other 40 percent of the population or it is not. It is either legitimate for the 35 percent of people who voted to speak for the 65 percent of non-voters or it is not.

Breaking this down, we see a very common left-wing technique, one used by other political groups as well. First, posit an unworkable ideal (in this case, 100 percent democratic participation). Next, convince others that it is in fact an ideal, and then acknowledge that said ideal is impracticable. Finally, redefine the ideal as a mere goal and claim that progress toward that goal is therefore good. This is all based on the assumption that morality is a continuum as opposed to a binary proposition—both of which are plausible positions to take. *Reductio ad absurdum*, one can say that never killing anyone is an impracticable ideal and therefore someone is still a good person if they're not murdering 99 percent of the time—or if their rate of murdering others has been decreasing, hence "progress."

Some would argue that a majority has the right to speak for the minority, that once voter participation reaches 50 percent, then the outcome can be considered legitimate. And here is precisely Michels's principle put into action: even theoretically, in a democracy someone is setting the guidelines for everyone else. *Elitist rule is inevitable.*

The purest example of democracy is the town hall. Of course, everyone speaking at once would make for a pointless cacophony. If they took turns, everyone saying whatever they wanted to about everything that they cared about would be interminable. So even in this most democratic of settings, someone must necessarily set the agenda for what is being discussed, who can speak at a given time, and how the questions are to be framed. An entity that sets the agenda for discussion, recognizes individual speakers, and frames questions for everyone else is an elite.

The New Right holds to the idea that aspiring to the literally impossible (i.e., pure democracy) is insane, dangerous, and almost inevitably counterproductive. Democracy should thus be regarded not as an ideal but as a bait-and-switch used by the left to foster their own elite—one that is allegedly in the service of everyone. It is one of the left's myriad excuses to claim for themselves the right to set the agenda, to recognize who can speak, and to frame the questions of the day. As Michels further claims, it is inevitable that the more "democratic" a party or nation claims to be, the more rigid the hierarchy becomes in practice. It's no coincidence that the official name of north Korea is the Democratic People's Republic of Korea.

But even if oligarchy is inevitable, social change still occurs. The French Revolution was more democratic than the monar-chy. The federal government was different from the Articles of Confederation, which were in turn a departure from the period when what became the United States were thirteen British colonies. Here is where we come to Vilfredo Pareto.

Pareto argued that the way societies move is via the circulation of elites. Every society has some elite (or ruling class) or another. Access to the elite might be more open or closed. In an aristocracy, where admission to the elite is via birth, it is largely closed. A closed elite is dangerous in the long term, since it is socially disadvantageous for the best and the brightest to not be allowed entrée. In the elitist sense, then, Hillary Clinton will always have far more in common with (either) George Bush than she would with a union janitor who (unlike her) voted for the Democratic Party his entire life. It's the sort of observation that seems obvious to virtually everyone but swiftly goes out the window when discussing politics.

The idea that the health of the elites means the health of a society is diametrically opposed to the leftist insistence that, as Gandhi put it, "A nation's greatness is measured by how it treats its weakest members." The Bible agrees. Matthew 20:16 states the goal that "the last will be first, and the first will be last." In a New Right context it is the elites who determine how the weakest are treated, and the health and prosperity of the weakest is due largely or even exclusively to their superiors. The fact that such a statement sounds downright repugnant to most readers and novel in the sense that it's never part of common American parlance—can be taken as evidence of the complete dominance by the Cathedral of popular discourse.

This brings us to Georges Sorel. Sorel is in many ways still admired by erudite and heretical thinkers on the far left. He is closely associated with syndicalism, which basically posits a political economy run entirely by unions. In one sense this might be regarded as anarchist, since there is no distinction between workplace and government—and Sorel very much fits in perfectly with many in the Occupy crowd. In another sense syndicalism can be regarded as totalitarian, in that every individual is subsumed into one group or another.

Sorel is best known for his 1906 book *Reflections on Violence*. In this he takes on some of the more spurious claims that law-and-order types need to hold true. For example, many conservatives claim that "terrorism doesn't work." However it is certainly true that after a certain point terrorism does work in *some* sense. The attacking of Hiroshima and Nagasaki, civilian centers, can be described as terrorist behavior, though most Americans would bristle at saying so. The logic goes as follows: terrorism is bad; the Japan bombings were justified and therefore good; the Japan bombings weren't terrorism. Yet the bombings were in fact meant as demonstrations of strength meant to force a political outcome, in this case complete and utter submission from the Japanese government (i.e., the "unconditional surrender" that they did in fact secure).

One might say that "terrorism doesn't work the way it's supposed to." But to assert that "terrorism doesn't work" in the sense of "terrorism doesn't effect change" is transparently false. "That's what the terrorists want!" is often used as an argument both for *and* against increasing our foreign presence. Since aggression and retreat have *both* been responses to terrorism by different political actors over the years, it's therefore true that terrorism must in fact work *some* of the time, regardless of whether one thinks it works to induce more violence or that it works to cause retreat.

Sorel also insisted on the use of non-rational motivations to mobilize large numbers of people. Specifically he advocated what he called the myth of the general strike, and he used the word "myth" quite intentionally. It's a similar conceptualization to how the New Right identifies and attacks the pervasive

Narrative in media and entertainment. Here again is why conservative arguments about marginal income tax rates are so laughable; they are competing against an ideology that triggers the same parts of the brain as a biblical parable.

That the masses would even be motivated by principle—or even be able to fully comprehend a principle and its applications—is hard to stomach. As in *Brave New World*, the democratic process allows the masses to be given a veneer of choice at the cost of any sense of individuality and freedom. It's the proverbial iron fist in a velvet glove delivering the greatest handjob in history. Yet this sacrifice is one that many humans are more than happy to make. As cynic H. L. Mencken once pointed out, "The average man does not want to be free. He simply wants to be safe."

Those who need leaders are not qualified to choose them. In a sense, asking people to make political decisions is like asking them to forecast the weather. They're not in a position to do so, and it is silly to expect them to. Democracy entails people who run their businesses well being forced to run their businesses poorly by people who can't run businesses at all.

There is another thinker who Burnham does not discuss but is yet still part of his so-called Machiavellian milieu: Gustave Le Bon. Le Bon's 1895 book *The Crowd* might be one of the most influential in history—not because of how many read it, but because of *who* read it. Hitler, Lenin, and especially Mussolini were all heavily influenced by his study of mass psychology, explicitly so. Indeed, it seems almost impossible to conceive of a totalitarian government without also assuming a heavy element of propaganda and thought control.

Though his main concept is widely accepted and understood now, Le Bon argued that human psychology differs enormously when in a crowd situation. He put forth the idea that crowd behavior is not at all akin to that of a group of individuals each acting in accord with right reason, and that crowds ("mobs" might be a better term) act in certain ways that none of its given members would if separate from the collective.

There has been much digital ink spilled over so-called Twitter mobs and how social media brings out the worst in us, thanks to things like tribalism and the anonymity of the internet. Most if not all of these premises are present in Le Bon's thought, which validates another right-wing precept: despite unthinkable advances in technology, human nature is virtually immutable. We are the same people that we were even a couple of thousand years ago. This undermines a central tenet of progressivism, that now we're all smart but before everyone used to be dumb (how convenient for us!). Some on the New Right would posit that we were smart *then* and that we've being going down the wrong road for quite a long time.

Then there's the other antidemocratic view, one which sees technology as the solution. For such members of the New Right, government is merely a technical issue to work around, a programming virus incarnate and nothing more. From this perspective, what the masses think is of no consequence; all that matters is ensuring that they are made powerless to impose their desires on others.

These types are very bullish on Bitcoin and other cryptocurrencies, jokingly referred to as "magic internet money." Bitcoin uses encryption to both ensure anonymity and keep the virtual currency secure. When alleged Silk Road operator Ross Ulbricht was accused by the government of (among other things) using Bitcoin to hire hit men, even the FBI couldn't access the Bitcoins Ulbricht had in his online wallet.

This segment of the New Right notes that one doesn't need to persuade the common man that private roads are an improvement over public ones. All that matters is that a given driver has an EZ-pass that deducts tolls correctly—and that the tolls for free-market-built roads would be cheaper and the roads themselves better maintained. A theory of the proper role of the state isn't necessary to compare UPS, DHL, and FedEx to the post office, or to know that the latter is run by the government. In this perspective, not only will the market replace government *ends*, it will also replace the government *means* of democracy. As Peter Thiel flatly put it, "I no longer believe that freedom and democracy are compatible."[5]

7

★

PENTHOUSE LEGEND

I'm constantly bemused with how much shit-talking
and moral finger-pointing that white people from, say,
an "enlightened" town such as Seattle do about those
horrible "racist" white Southerners. But Seattle is only
8% black; Mississippi is 37% black. Historically, the
South has always been the blackest part of the United
States. More than half of black Americans still live in
the South. So who really has had more contact with
black people—snooty white progs in Seattle, or those
perpetually demonized Southern rednecks? Who truly
is prejudging here?

—JIM GOAD

In 2014 I was offered a freelance position at the personal-essay
website Thought Catalog. Chris Lavergne, the site's founder,
emailed me to connect with the man who would be my editor:
Jim Goad. "Jim Goad," I replied, "needs no introduction!!!"
While this may be true in New Right circles, Jim Goad is not a
household name when it comes to the mainstream.

I first learned of Goad in 2006, when a punk friend of mine
couldn't stop raving about him and his work. He is a litmus test
of sorts; knowing his name means one has spent time consum-

ing alternative forms of media. The corporate press has an in-sistence on finding leaders and figureheads in the New Right, but this is not an organic approach. A parallel can be found in the Tea Party. Sarah Palin, for example, might be regarded as "Tea Party aligned," but she was not involved in organizing the movement. There are no Tea Party leaders that are household names. An even stronger parallel would be Occupy Wall Street, where no one can be thought of as really representing the scene. But if Iggy Pop is considered the Godfather of Punk, Jim Goad is the Godfather of the New Right.

Like many members of the New Right, Goad disavows any such affiliation. "I do not and have never identified as 'right wing,'" he insisted to me. "The political binary is the dumbest of all. It's based on the seating system in the old French legisla-ture, and I refuse to base my life on anything French." This is the philosophical equivalent of denying the gender binary. So odious is the right wing in America that Goad would apparently prefer to think of himself as polifluid or poliqueer. (Which is, after all, his right to do.) I didn't bother to ask his preferred pro-nouns, but I'm assuming he's fine with "he." But despite his protestations to the contrary, other than right wing or left wing, there's really nowhere else to go on the axis.

What makes Goad the prototypical New Right personality is the fact that he combines three elements that make up the subculture. First, biography and demographics. Members of the New Right are ostensibly privileged due to their demographics, but they perceive themselves as (and usually are) far more mar-ginalized than those in the mainstream. Second, a contempt bordering on disgust for elites and those who would delineate the boundaries of acceptable public discourse. Third, the use of nontraditional methods to disseminate one's ideas. All these combined for the first time in Jim Goad and his work.

James Thaddeus Goad grew up near Philadelphia in a family

that was not exactly the Brady Bunch. As he recounts in his autobiography *Shit Magnet: One Man's Miraculous Ability to Absorb the World's Guilt*, "Early on I learn that families are groups of humans who bruise each other and draw blood from each other and scream like foamy-mouthed dogs at each other.[1] [. . .] I hit them back when I became strong enough to do so."[2] With Mom it was age twelve, with Dad having to wait until seventeen.

Here we see an idea essential to the New Right: the concept that civilization is merely a thin veneer, that within man lives a savage barely disguised and liable to be exposed at any given moment. For the evangelical left, violence is a personal or social aberration that needs to be explained. For the New Right, what needs explaining is how violence has managed to decrease over time given just how violent Mother Nature really is.

Goad was a college graduate, majoring in journalism, but he always lived a marginal life in "up-and-coming" neighborhoods. As a consequence, he had far more firsthand experience with the poor and with minorities than do most urban elites. His writings are therefore focused on classism rather than racism as being the quintessential American divide.

In the 1980s and through the mid-1990s, zines were an influential underground way for people with niche interests to communicate and stay in touch. Handmade and with varying degrees of professionalism, they were almost always xeroxed, folded in half, and stapled together. As a result, the typical zine looked more like a long ransom note than any actual magazine.

Produced with his wife Debbie, the Goads' zine *ANSWER Me!* was of a higher caliber. It featured black ink with two-spot-color covers for issues 1 and 2 (the murder issue), and full-color covers for issue 3 (the one with Hitler) and the final issue (the rape issue). From the beginning, Goad shed his light on people who were not members of polite society. Issue 1 included interviews with transgender Warhol superstar Holly Woodlawn (whose memoir was called *A Low Life in High Heels*) and *Pimp* author Iceberg Slim, as well as essays on masturbation and twelve-step groups. Issue 2 had Goad speaking with Church of Satan founder Anton LaVey, Klansman David Duke, and pornographer Al Goldstein—surely the only publication on earth to feature the three. The articles included essays urging the reader to "Kill your mom and dad. Feel good about it" and a rundown of "the hundred most fabulous killers of our time." By issue 3 Goad was talking to assisted-suicide advocate Jack Kevorkian and Reverend Al Sharpton, and offering "one hundred reasons to commit suicide." The final issue—which was not included in the original collected edition—ran the gamut from "Let's hear it for violence against women" to "Rape is love" and "Fucking Andrea Dworkin."

The more recent collected edition includes a very unsubtle photo of Goad with a German moustache alongside his wife, who is brandishing a pistol. Goad's T-shirt says "RAPE" and hung on the wall behind them is a flag with both a swastika *and* an Iron Cross. That the Mrs. was Jewish and the photographer Israeli are both facts irrelevant to interpreting the picture. For some, it's silly and juvenile; for others, it's silly and juvenile and obscene.

The publishing history of *ANSWER Me!* is not a pleasant one, and it illustrates not only the intransigence of the left but also how much their fortress has been weakened in the ensuing decades. "The magazine gets banned in England," Goad recounts. "Customs officials seize it in Canada and Australia." While this sort of thing might have worked in the 1940s, it certainly had the unintended consequence of drawing attention to the taboo by the 1990s. But then as now, rape was a touchy subject. Goad had been corresponding for a while with Richard Ramirez, who as the "Night Stalker" was responsible for killing over a dozen people. "After I sent him the Rape issue, his letters stopped," recalls Goad. "One of Ramirez's pen pals later informed me that Ricky had asked him, 'Don't you think that issue went a little too *far*?'"

In an anecdote that anticipates the current cultural situation perfectly, a nineteen-year-old feminist demanded that her Bellingham, Washington, newsstand pull the zine from the shelves. When the newsstand refused, she complained to her boyfriend. Cleverly, he took the zine to the local rape crisis center, which then took it to the district attorney. When the newsstand again refused to pull the zine, the DA charged them with Felony Promotion of Pornography.

Goad viewed it as a first amendment issue, quipping that "there were certainly more ideas bandied about in *ANSWER Me!* #4 than in *People* or *Reader's Digest*." The store was acquitted, but that's only part of the story. If there had been an issue 5, how many outlets would have chosen to carry it? It would have been akin to playing Russian roulette, wondering if trying to sell a product would bring them needless financial and emotional costs—not to mention negative publicity. Threats of censorship by the government lead to self-censorship by the market.

Then, in yet another storyline that could be told today, in September 1994 a lunatic shot the White House twenty-nine times with an assault rifle, harming no one before being tackled by Secret Service agents. In March 1995, Jim was being partially held responsible in the media. Mark David Chapman had explicitly claimed that *The Catcher in the Rye* inspired him, writing "This is my statement" in the copy of the book he bought on the day he shot John Lennon. No one credited J. D. Salinger for Chapman's actions, but Goad was an easy target.

With this as the backdrop, Goad can also be seen as akin to Larry Flynt. And just like Flynt, Goad's relationship with women can be described as "complicated." During his marriage to Debbie, Goad began an affair with a uniquely unhinged woman named Anne. In his memoir he documents his relationship with her in excruciating detail. It is excruciating not in the sense of minutiae but in the sense of constant cringeworthy pain. To call their interactions toxic would be an understatement since toxins at least serve a natural purpose.

Between the two of them there were multiple restraining orders and constant drinking and violence. At one point Debbie got terminal cancer and befriended Anne. The police were involved more times than should be permissible by law. Finally, Goad and Anne were driving one day and she began hitting him. Having had enough, he hit her back—and went to jail for it. For most people, this is enough to read Goad out of polite society (even though he had never really been a part of anything remotely close to polite society to begin with).

Goad and I met in person when he came to Brooklyn for Thought Catalog's holiday party. I made sure to get a photo of him, myself, and Ryan Holiday (author of *Trust Me, I'm Lying*) eating cotton candy as supervillains are wont to do. The thing with meeting provocateurs is that it is never clear just what they're like in real life. As I made plans to get dinner with Goad, I kept wondering if he was actually "like that."

In true Goad fashion, he'd recently gotten a titanium plate implanted in his skull after a plum-sized tumor was removed but the bone had failed to heal correctly. As a consequence, Goad had to wear one of those big (faux?) fur hats so beloved in my Motherland. The two of us met at the Meatball Shop in Williamsburg. The menu there is mildly counterintuitive. You have to choose what kind of meatball you want; which sauce; and how you want them served (i.e., as sliders or in a bowl).

It took seconds for Goad to begin eviscerating the waitress as she explained the process. "You know," he said calmly but scarily, "you don't have to talk to me like I'm in kindergarten."

"I'm not?" she replied, confused.

"Yeah, ya are. I know how to read."

So he *was* "like that," at least sometimes. On the other hand, I've had many conversations with him where he could not have been more amiable and downright humble, speaking freely of past mistakes and current insecurities. For those who want to dismiss him, it's hard to dismiss his body of work, much of which is now receiving mainstream credence via the New Right and especially following Trump's election.

Goad's *Redneck Manifesto* was published in 1997. It's far more erudite and scholarly than *ANSWER Me!* ever was. Avoiding what often could have been seen as provocation for its own sake, *Redneck Manifesto*'s main theme is that what is known as racism in this country is far more akin to classism. Goad's first target is the biggest atrocity in American history: slavery. "Most who specialize in researching indentured servitude agree that at least half, and possibly as many as two-thirds, of *all* white colonial immigrants arrived in chains,"[3] writes Goad. "To attract new 'volunteers,' the colonies had passed laws protecting white servants' rights. The plan backfired, as it rendered their upkeep more expensive. The supply of white servants diminished as more black markets opened up, cementing the shift toward black slavery."[4]

As most anti-racists are quick to point out, it is *whites* who have a long history of rioting in America. Hell, the foundational act that made America what it is was rioting in Boston. As one can expect, this led to precisely the same stereotypes as people have nowadays: "Planters were also said to have perceived blacks as less criminal and more docile than their hellstompin' white-trash co-slaves. A final reason for the transition from white slavery to black is so nose-crushingly obvious that it's often overlooked: blacks were visually identifiable by their skin color. They weren't so much *hated* for it as they were *identified* by it."[5]

Thanks to the bestselling *Hillbilly Elegy*, there was a brief moment where the left took stock and realized just how vitriolic and explicit their contempt for "white trash" America had become. It's unfortunate that it took an electoral loss to force a bit of—but not *too* much—soul-searching. In the 1972 presidential election Richard Nixon won over 60 percent of the popular vote, carrying forty-nine states (including his opponent George McGovern's home state of South Dakota). That year, *New Yorker* film critic Pauline Kael was widely miscredited with saying that she couldn't believe Richard Nixon won because no one she knew voted for him. In actuality the quote was more self-aware but also more vile: "I live in a rather special world. I only know one person who voted for Nixon. Where they are I don't know. They're outside my ken. But sometimes when I'm in a theater I can feel them."[6] The sense of contempt and revulsion at *them* could hardly be more clear. The left loves to complain about "otherizing" different groups but has no qualms about doing so when it comes to their preferred version of untouchables.

For Goad, this has been a concern for decades: "The Dumb White Bumpkin has always been a stock figure in the American dramatis personae. [. . .] A whole vein of human experience, of potential literature, is dismissed as a joke, much as America's popular notions of black culture were relegated to lawn jockeys and Sambo caricatures a generation or two ago. The redneck is the only cardboard figure left standing in our ethnic shooting gallery. [. . .] The trailer park has become the media's cultural toilet, the only acceptable place to dump one's racist inclinations.[7] [. . .] Dixie-hostile writers will often phoneticize Southern speech patterns when quoting some yokel they want you to perceive as ignorant—y'all know whut ah'm talkin' 'bout—

when to do the same with a black or Hispanic inflection would be considered an unbearable stereotype in these enlightened times."[8]

Because the vernacular is spoken by lower-class (i.e., "inferior") people, it is itself therefore assumed to be inferior. Racism and classism very closely overlap here as well. Queen of the Harlem Renaissance Zora Neale Hurston was condemned for accurately transcribing the accents of her fellow Southern blacks in her writing and research. But as linguist (and person of color) John McWhorter pointed out, there is no right or wrong English. Such dialects are perfectly valid and follow their own syntax. This confusion stems from an idea that the way whites speak is "correct" as opposed to "popular." As Goad insists, equating the two is a major flaw of leftist culture in America.

As most on the left are painfully aware in other circumstances, a lack of respect in popular consciousness can lead to profoundly negative effects in real life. When a population is regarded as a joke or as something less than, their suffering becomes not a source of empathy but a source of amusement or even contempt. "I started losing faith in liberalism," Goad recalls, "when I began noticing that every liberal who accused me of white privilege seemed to come from a more privileged socioeconomic background than I did. I got sick of their middle-class hypocrisy that shed tears for the black 'struggle' while laughing at my white-trash roots. If indigenous Amazonian tribes were subjected to acid rain, the liberals were emotionally devastated. But if a trailer park full of white trash across town all got cancer because they lived atop a toxic dump, it was a joke."[9]

With "white trash" being regarded as somehow inferior and condemned further as being the embodiment of everything wrong in racist, backward America, their lower social status was regarded as downright *just*: "White-trash pathologies are almost never seen as a response to environmental factors, while the behavior of impoverished non-Euros is always viewed this way. [. . .] To justify the ideological Anschluss against white trash, one would have to establish that hillbillies wield an unholy degree of power. As leftists have argued for years, the only true racists are people with the power systematically to oppress others. [. . .] They simultaneously depict white trash as dumb as oak sap, yet able to pull off an intercontinental conspiracy that enslaved most of the melanin-rich world. [. . .] Rednecks are portrayed as the embodiment of white power, when the only time they're likely to encounter a powerful white man is when the boss barks at them down at the factory."[10] When Democratic senator Harry Byrd said, "There are white niggers. I've seen a lot of white niggers in my time; I'm going to use that word," he was basically channeling Goad's worldview.

Goad's analysis of race and class in America broke through to academia, in Penn State professor Shannon Sullivan's superb 2014 book *Good White People: The Problem with Middle-Class White Anti-Racism*. Sullivan, who is very left wing, takes a scholarly approach to Goad's ideas and agrees with many of his conclusions.

"With their disdain, scorn, and even hatred of lower-class white people," Sullivan writes, "good white liberals often use their guilt and shame to exploit class differences among whites, which allows them to efface their own complicity in white racism and white domination" and "[W]hite trash share too many similarities of speech, behavior, diet, and lifestyle with black people. White trash are uncomfortably close to those whom they are supposed to be radically different from. Whether willfully or ignorantly, white trash fail to speak, eat, dress, and otherwise behave as proper (middle-class) white people are supposed to do, and their breach of white social etiquette threatens the boundary between white and nonwhite (especially black) people."[11]

Sullivan's evisceration of the holier-than-thou evangelical left could not be any more devastating and on point: "It's true that white supremacists, as well as white trash, sometimes and perhaps often think, say, and do viciously racist things. But so do good middle-class white people, and that is the point. There are no saints to be found here. White liberals are just better at pretending that there are."[12]

She also agrees with conservative Shelby Steele's assessment that the evangelical left regards blacks especially as a mechanism for spiritual salvation: "White guilt obligates white people to black people 'because they needed the moral authority only black people could bestow.' This obligation merely reverses the previous situation in which only white people could possess moral authority. While that reversal might seem like a good development from a perspective of racial justice, it tends to make black and other nonwhite people responsible for white redemption and deliverance from racism." She adds, "[T]he true, even if unconscious purpose of white charity is revealed. It has very little to do with genuinely increasing the flourishing of black people, and everything to do with covertly using black people to generate middle-class white people's moral sense of goodness."[13] Sullivan's book won the 2016 Society of Professors of Education Outstanding Book Award—proof that there is more to New Right ideology than simple bigotry and agita.

Most importantly, Goad independently came to the same conclusions regarding the Cathedral as Moldbug did. As he put it,

> The sacred secular script you follow—cultural progres-
> sivism, egalitarianism, social justice, or whatever the
> fuck you're calling it these days—is simply Christian-

ity with God removed. Your "God"—your untouchable premise—is the naively childish and entirely unscientific notion of innate human equality. The moralism and the sanctimony and the witch hunting and the baseless assumptions are exactly the same. Just because your philosophy is different doesn't mean your psychology is. Your self-righteous mob mentality and communal bloodlust to scapegoat all heretics and burn them at the stake is identical.

There is no rational—and definitely no scientific—basis or evidence for a belief that all humans, either as individuals or in terms of average group abilities, are equal. All of the evidence suggests precisely the opposite. Since there is not the slightest evidence for human equality, it is nothing more than a belief in a myth that sounds nice and appeals to juvenile emotions. This belief must be swallowed like an invisible Eucharist as an article of faith—and if you do not flow with the crowd and profess faith in that transparently ludicrous premise, you will face the same treatment that heretics have endured throughout history. Their reaction is so fierce and unhinged not because they are so convinced their beliefs are true—no one who's secure in their beliefs would throw such tantrums upon being challenged. Instead, their reactions are those of blind acolytes lashing out at those who question whether their God exists.[11]

8

*

THE VICES OF GAVIN MCINNES

I'd like to formally apologize to all the trannies threatening to kill my family and "eat me alive." You are NOT mentally ill.

—GAVIN MCINNES

One of my favorite internet videos is a seven-minute film released in 2008 called *Sophie Can Walk*. "On September 16, 2006," the video explains, "Sophie McInnes was born. Doctors said she wouldn't walk for at least a year." Proud papa Gavin McInnes proceeds to put his daughter into a tiny wheelchair and take her from doctor to doctor, trying to get her to walk. The doctors' responses are as expected. "I really feel like this pessimism of this hospital saying it's going to be a year is like almost anti-miracle," McInnes snaps. "It's like they hate miracles."

Eventually, McInnes puts up flyers in the then-cool neighborhood of Williamsburg with Sophie's picture, promoting an imaginary charity with funds going to help her walk. "Oh, you're born and you can't walk?" McInnes muses. "That doesn't make sense. And why are we listening to doctors? This is the same thing as circumcision. They used to think snails work.

'Oh, you put a snail on your arm and it'll eat your blood!' Why was that medicine? Now they believe in astrology. That's not medicine!" The short film is a perfect time capsule of where Brooklyn culture was during that era, the mix of the irreverent with the odd and original.

McInnes was one of the cofounders of *Vice* magazine, which originally was a small publication discussing things one shouldn't discuss in polite company. There had been a column called "Street Boners" where McInnes lambasted the fashion choices of random passers-by. Due to his outspoken beliefs, McInnes has over the years been called a "conservative." In a binary political sense that might perhaps be the necessary conclusion. Yet to lump McInnes in with conservatives is not a very cogent way of looking at things. In 2012, Scribner's published his collection of autobiographical essays, *How to Piss in Public* (rechristened *The Birth of Cool* in paperback), which recounts several misadventures that are not exactly Rick Santorum–friendly. "I hate it when magazines have an article about drugs and they use an obviously fake picture," he recounts. "So with a name like *Vice*, we weren't about to use cinnamon and oregano to illustrate our cover story about pot."

At one point McInnes forced an ex-junkie employee to score a bundle (that means ten small bags for all you squares) of heroin and then proceeded to intentionally spill some on the floor in front of both him and another former addict employee. "For years they'd been trained to worship every granule of this stuff, so their Pavlovian instinct was to yell '*No!*' and try to stop it from falling," he wrote. "As they clamored to protect it, I spread the powder all over the floor with my shoe while saying, 'Oooopsie!'" Gawker acknowledged *Vice*'s "'90s retro edgy *ANSWER Me!* ripoff tone," and McInnes freely admits his enormous debt to Goad for having paved the way for *Vice*: the breaking of taboo, often in a juvenile and gratuitous way; the treatment of "lowlifes" with the same lens as celebrities; the utter outsider-looking-in perspective.

Toward the end of his book McInnes discusses the story of his four-day-long stag party, which turned into an all-male bacchanal. "The second day got more intense. Nudity had become de rigueur and fag jokes were no longer kidding." The event ended with his father French kissing one of Gavin's friends while ten others popped into a clearing dressed as Klansmen, burning a fifteen-foot-high cross "as everyone yelled, 'Hooray!'" In other words, to use the term "conservative" to describe both McInnes and, say, Jeff Sessions is to miss the mark entirely. They are as culturally opposite as it gets, despite both being very right wing in their own respective ways.

McInnes's edgy personality carried over into politics. In 2003 the *New York Times* did a story on the *Vice* brand and put him directly in the crosshairs: "He actually leans much further to the right than the Republican Party. His views are closer to a white supremacist's. 'I love being white and I think it's something to be very proud of,' he said. 'I don't want our culture diluted. We need to close the borders now and let everyone assimilate to a Western, white, English-speaking way of life.'"[1]

Matters eventually came to a head as *Vice* grew in popularity and corporations came bidding to buy out the brand. McInnes and the two cofounders parted company, which led to the following email being sent to McInnes's friends:

> Date: Jan 23, 2008 9:42 AM
>
> Dear children of my corn,
> I no longer have anything to do with Vice or VBS or DOs & DON'Ts or any of that. It's a long story but we've all agreed to leave it at "creative differences," so please don't ask me about it.

I first ran into McInnes at a *Reason* magazine happy hour in early 2015. He had recently been fired from Thought Catalog for writing an inflammatory piece about transgender people entitled "Transphobia is Perfectly Natural." As he put it, "They are mentally ill gays who need help, and that help doesn't include being maimed by physicians. These aren't women trapped in a man's body. They are nuts trapped in a crazy person's body."[2]

In my view the article did not come from an informed place and certainly did not come from a place of sympathy or empathy. The word "crazy," like the word "racist," has many definitions. To equate every sense of the term is sloppy at best. A grandmother who doesn't want her grandkids dating a black person is not the same phenomenon as a Holocaust denier or a Klansman. The high levels of depression, self-harm, suicide, and drug abuse among transgender people are pointed out by the trans community itself, as they have been by the gay community. From their perspective, these characteristics are heavily exacerbated by the way their community is treated and perceived by the culture at large. Worse, to equate someone who is having issues with their gender identity with someone who thinks they are receiving secret coded messages via Twitter is unreasonable, though both can loosely be called "crazy" in McInnes's sense of the term.

On her reality show *I Am Cait*, Caitlyn Jenner was constantly harangued by her trans friends for her right-wing views. Though not particularly politically informed or articulate, Jenner put forth the fairly obvious argument that an issue with the welfare state is that it leads to moral hazard. Meaning, if welfare benefits are competitive with prevailing wages, many people would prefer to receive the welfare than to work—and why wouldn't they?

Yet because transgender men and women were in fashion on the left in 2015–16, virtually everyone on the right bought into the idea that to defend transgender human beings is to accept progressivism in some sense. Further, the general right-wing aversion to the stranger aspects of the human experience made many of their gestures of support come from an intellectual basis but not necessary an emotional one. As a result, Jenner was not championed by many on the right even if for purely strategic purposes. The idea that to support her would violate some universal conservative principle doesn't seem cogent, as universal conservative principles are very few (if they exist at all).

On the other hand, some of the New Right—especially the Alt-Right—focus much on "degeneracy," a term like "racist" or "unfair" often meaning "that which I dislike." The word is a reflection of the fact that in a society where people are free to make choices, others will sometimes unavoidably make choices that we ourselves wouldn't. Sometimes they will even make choices that we personally find unappealing and downright repulsive.

Then comes the argument that behavior x leads to genuinely unacceptable behavior y, while ignoring the fact that simply because x sometimes precedes y does not mean that x causes y or that x causes y universally. It's safe to say that virtually every heroin addict tried marijuana at some point. It is not safe to say that the latter "causes" the use of the former, or does so in a large percentage—let alone every instance of marijuana use.

Some on the New Right claim that the historical decadence (or extreme social tolerance, depending on one's point of view) of the Weimar Republic "caused" Nazi Germany. This is to rely on one historical series of events and insist that it can and will be replicated in much the same way. Caitlyn Jenner on television might fit in to the New Right idea of "degeneracy," but we've a ways to go before the hyperinflation hits as well.

Yet there is another sense in which the term degeneracy is used, and that is in the claim that the evangelical left is engaged in an active, covert (and not-so-covert) campaign to destroy the nuclear family and to render all humanity completely interchangeable, regardless of one's biology. As with the New Right, this controversy has roots that can be traced back to the 1992 presidential campaign.

On May 19, 1992, Vice President Dan Quayle made a plea both for the importance of fathers within the family and for the family unit to remain intact whenever possible. As he pointed out, "It doesn't help matters when prime-time TV has Murphy Brown, a character who supposedly epitomizes today's intelligent, highly paid professional woman, mocking the importance of fathers by bearing a child alone and calling it just another lifestyle choice."

Murphy Brown was not an assault on the nuclear family per se. It was clearly a defense of single mothers as not being somehow inferior either as parents or as human beings. It came off as if Quayle was denigrating single mothers, when his point was far more nuanced than that. Yet after the attacks and denigration faded it became quite obvious to every non-ideologue that parenting is not that simple, and that ideology doesn't trump biological or sociological reality. The star of the show herself came around: "Candice Bergen says Dan Quayle was right," reported *Entertainment Weekly*. "The former 'Murphy Brown' star says she agreed with the ex-vice president's contention that fathers are indispensable."[3] The *Washington Post* op-ed headline from May 25, 2012, was even more blunt: "20 years later, it turns out Dan Quayle was right about Murphy Brown and unmarried moms."[4]

Yet this is where the New Right and conservatives part company. Conservatives would regard all this as a knee-jerk overreaction from the left, one that they course-corrected. The New Right would say that this was part of a larger plan. Take the case of interracial dating and marriage. It went from a literal crime to a stigmatized choice to a rare but accepted option to a standard often promoted in the culture. The default setting on dating apps is for all races to be considered.

The tactic is a simple one: persuade people that a certain prejudice is unacceptable, and then redefine that prejudice to include any distinguishing negative behavior whatsoever. We are currently being told that not being bisexual is homophobic, that everyone is on a sexuality spectrum except for gay people who are born that way, and that to be averse to having sex with a transgender woman simply because she has a penis is transphobic.

The concept of "degeneracy" is heavily criticized by Arthur Herman in a book McInnes himself constantly recommends, *The Idea of Decline in Western History.* Herman finds a thread across political movements that insist that catastrophe is right around the corner—despite human beings living longer and better by nearly every single possible metric. From the Nazis and race mixing to environmentalists and the death of the earth, Herman reduces them all to the equivalent of the comic trope of the man with the sandwich board insisting "Repent: The End is Near!"

When we met, McInnes invited me to appear on his *Free Speech* podcast, which admittedly thrilled me to no end. A young woman I didn't recognize was exiting as I walked into the recording studio. Gavin shot me a look to play it cool. It's a look we Russians understand well, so I did my best to amiably chat her up as she blathered about white supremacy in terms so cliché I forgot them as soon as she uttered them. She handed me one of her stickers, which read "From one white person to another its [*sic*] on US to end White Supremacy #whitework."

Her name was Heather Marie Scholl, and McInnes's interview with her went so viral that it has more views than all of his other episodes combined (despite other guests including such heavy hitters as Tucker Carlson and Ann Coulter). Apparently McInnes met Scholl on the street and invited her on. As she later posted on Facebook, she did not research him before agreeing to appear on the show.

"We do not have the best system in the world," Scholl told McInnes.

"Who has a better system?"

"There are many European countries that are much better off than us."

"You mean European countries with a higher density of whites, like northern Europe."

"That's one way to phrase it, I guess."

"You don't mean Turkey."

"No."

"You don't mean Eastern Europe, with the Communists," he continued, effectively destroying his own argument (though she was too lacking in something to pick up on it). "So the only time you can come up with a system that's better than America, it's a country that's more white than America."

I walked in expecting to discuss my recent book on north Korea. After a few dismissive comments about the book being done (as we all remember, the north Korean situation had been resolved by 2015), the conversation became about "the Jews." I suspect that McInnes thought I would be taken aback by this approach.

Gavin was of the impression that Jews invented political correctness. Yet I pointed out that every culture has heresy and taboo. Jesus died for being politically incorrect, for example. Eugene V. Debs was jailed by President Woodrow Wilson for opposing World War I. The writer Paul Graham tackled this issue in an extremely insightful 2004 cultural essay titled "What You Can't Say." "In every period," Graham wrote, "people believed things that were just ridiculous, and believed them so strongly that you would have gotten in terrible trouble for saying otherwise."[5]

"Every culture is a culture of fear," I insisted. "When wasn't it a culture of fear, in your mind? In the '50s? In the '60s? In the '70s?"

"2000–2005 was the least—"

"Wait!" I interrupted. "After 9/11 it was not a culture of fear? You're literally saying this?"

"Yup."

At a certain point you realize there is no speaking further to the person. That is when I said to Gavin, "OK."

McInnes is one of the few on the New Right who tried to organize the movement. On September 15, 2016, he wrote an article for TakiMag wherein he officially announced that he had founded an organization that he called "The Proud Boys." The previous Sunday fifty or so of his male fans had gotten together at a bar, with "no women because women are not allowed." It's unclear whether Gavin chose to hold the event at the specific bar because of its name, but Gaslight has certainly become one of the buzzwords of the nascent Trump era.

The term comes from the 1944 film *Gaslight*, in which Charles Boyer plays a man who attempts to trick his wife, played by Ingrid Bergman, into thinking that she is going insane. Necessarily, to use the term "insane" to describe oneself is a tacit confession that one feels like they are crazy. In fact the claim that one is getting secret messages from the television and newspaper is the stereotypical mark in bad movies that someone is insane.

The popular argument used to be that mental illness is not something that should be stigmatized, and the case for that is fairly easy to make. That these arguments used to come from sites like Jezebel and xoJane.com thrilled antifeminists to no end. That studies have found correlations between mental illness and being female, single, urban-dwelling, and college-educated was frequently used as a knock against feminist ideology. Mirroring progressive arguments against the right, claiming "they're all crazy!" was and remains a convenient way to dismiss an entire school of thought. Yet by 2016 an idea was being promulgated on social media that Donald Trump and his crew were "gaslighting" people.

On July 11, 2017, Donald Trump Jr. released his entire correspondence regarding meeting with a Russian attorney. "This is the dumbest and biggest crime in the history of American politics," claimed journalist Jared Yates Sexton. "There's not even a close second." (Perhaps a *distant* second would be FDR's concentration camps, I suppose.) Sexton continued, "I . . . worked on this story for a year . . . and . . . he just . . . he tweeted it out. [. . .] I'm not entirely convinced I'm not having a break from reality."

Though the cause of gaslighting may be external—in Sexton's case, our dubiously sane president and his family—it is still a confession that the individual does not feel in control of his or her own rational mental capabilities and is trying to blame external forces for this state of mind. In any case, it is an unintentional step in the direction of the New Right perspective that contemporary feminism is merely insanity wrapped up in a Wellesley diploma, cartoon-colored hair, and pre-diabetic obesity. Alt-Right dating impresario Roosh V even has a sarcastic article about what he calls "Lindy West Disease," named after the feminist author of *Shrill: Notes from a Loud Woman*:

> The first universal symptom is a spontaneous hair color change to a neon purple, red, or orange, usually coinciding with an instinctual decision to get a bowl haircut. Large, obnoxious glasses are often added within one month of infection.
>
> I have identified a fantastical belief system that is

highly correlated to disease. If a female states she "strongly agrees" to at least four of the following six statements, which are nearly universally embraced on the Tumblr web site, she is certain to contract Lindy West Disease.

- There is an active rape culture in America that makes its universities more dangerous to women than a South African slum.
- There is a worldwide conspiracy by men to force women to stay home and cook healthy and hearty meals for the families they love.
- Homosexual and transsexual lifestyles offer undeniably powerful advantages over heterosexual lifestyles.
- There is absolutely nothing wrong if a woman experiments with 100 different penises before marriage.
- It's possible to be morbidly obese but still healthy as a racehorse in its prime.
- "I'm deathly afraid of being a mother and how it would limit my consumer freedom."[6]

"Though the exact details are kept secret," McInnes wrote in "Introducing: The Proud Boys," "the meetings usually consist of drinking, fighting, and reading aloud from Pat Buchanan's *Death of the West*." As he was writing about the second meeting, the word "usually" seems a bit odd here. He then proceeded to rattle off that there were several other chapters throughout the country and forming abroad.

The Proud Boys' gender exclusivity speaks to two things. First, fraternal organizations have existed for millennia, dating back to the Last Supper and beyond. In recent years such groups have come under cultural and legal attack in America.

Acknowledging such a tradition is an application of the New Right's advocacy of exclusion, as opposed to the progressive view that every venue should be open to as many people as possible. It harkens back to the 1999 film *Fight Club*, wherein lost young men found solidarity with one another through ritualized violence, ascetic communal living, and soap.

The New Right position on "free speech" is not precise. The idea that no one should ever have any consequences for anything one says is not a tenable one, and to be fair is rarely stated as such. Telling the wife that yes, that dress *does* make her look fat is certainly free speech and as certainly a terrible idea. The New Right claim that hierarchy is natural and unavoidable comes into play here as well. Bosses will be vindictive to subordinates who speak out of turn.

Then the position becomes that professionals, especially intellectuals, shouldn't be silenced and prevented from presenting their views. Yet ostracism is the only alternative to some sort of censorship. Every individual must choose which speaker is worth their time and which isn't. It becomes a problem when groups of people try to prevent speakers from being heard by others.

The landscape has completely changed from when Jim Goad had to write and produce *ANSWER Me!* with his wife and hope for word-of-mouth appeal. Absolutely, people are driven from their jobs and silenced in certain venues. But it's impossible to completely silence them. Literally anyone can start a Twitter account or a YouTube channel, and if those accounts get shut down, there are easy workarounds. Entire social networks exist to inform one's friends about cool, new interesting points of view, in culture and politics as well as elsewhere. The New Right realizes that as social media platforms become infected, it is important to create parallel sites.

As an example, the website Gab touts itself as an alternative to Twitter—which is of course blithely described as "Nazi Twit-ter" by the corporate press. While Twitter routinely bans and purges those whose behavior it finds unacceptable—and has a thriving reporting system in place to encourage this—Gab will only ban users who advocate violence. Milo Yiannopoulos, Vox Day, and several others have made their way to Gab after Twitter made it clear they were no longer welcome there.

After ending his *Free Speech* podcast, McInnes launched *The Gavin McInnes Show* on Anthony Cumia's Compound Media, stylized as "The Free Speech Network." Activist Mike Cerno-vich's movie is titled *Silenced: The War on Free Speech*. When Milo announced his events at Berkeley, he called it "Free Speech Week." The universal claim and concern in the New Right is that attacks on our free speech are unprecedented and fiercer than ever.

They are wrong.

Virtually all the Founding Fathers, including George Wash-ington himself, were still alive when the Fifth Congress passed the Sedition Act, signed into law by John Adams. The act made it a federal crime to criticize the government or the president, leading to the arrest and imprisonment of several journalists. In other words, it was precisely the supposedly holy "political speech" that was the first to be explicitly *attacked* (not defended) under the Constitution. Sure, the government ostensibly had a reason. But the government always has *some* reason to lessen our liberties.

The so-called Comstock Laws of 1873—named after United States postal inspector Anthony Comstock—made it a federal crime to use the mail to discuss such matters as abortion or con-traception or even to exchange letters recounting sexual con-tent of a personal nature. In 1886, Moses Harman in his *Lucifer the Light Bearer* newspaper published a letter from a physician detailing a wife's rape by her husband shortly after a difficult childbirth. For using the mail to distribute "obscene" works, Harman was arrested and sentenced to five years in prison (for which he served a few months before being released on a technicality). Harman's struggles did not end there. At the age of seventy-five he was sentenced to one year in prison *at hard labor* for more violations. He was only one of many to face the wrath of a government supposedly zealously protecting free speech.

The Comstock Laws were not explicit censorship but de facto censorship. It's not that Harman had published obscene things so much as he used the mail—a government monopoly—to disseminate the work. Yet when individuals such as Lysander Spooner succeeded in operating private mail services as competition, they were hounded and persecuted by the government until they were driven out of business.

The censorship continued with the arrival of radio, and with it the argument that the government had the right to regulate radio content because it owned the airwaves. Claiming the government "owns the airwaves" and can thereby dictate the content therein is not only on its face a blatant repudiation of the First Amendment guarantee that Congress "shall pass no law," but it's also nonsensical in its reasoning. It's akin to saying that since the government assigns street addresses to each individual home, it's thereby in a position to enforce what is spoken inside of them.

The "Fairness Doctrine"—an Orwellian title if there ever was one—that the FCC enforced from 1949 to 1987 insisted that contrasting views be presented for matters of public interest. In other words, contemporary talk radio would be rendered impossible given the strong market preference for right-wing programming as contrasted with notable failures like Air America. The insistence on "contrasting views" furthered the impression that politics is binary and the choices are either Republican or Democrat—and, in a time period where the Republicans were simply Democrats-lite, presented the appearance of political contrast while implicitly reaffirming that the only choices were either full-blown progressivism or a marginally milder version.

Through the 1970s there were three network anchors on the air at a given time, and since there were three of them the perception was that they were presenting three points of view. While this was technically true, it was literally false, as all the networks came from a strongly progressive perspective. It was only after the repeal of the Fairness Doctrine and the rise of talk radio that principled (and unprincipled) right-wing thought was given a constant voice in the Cathedral—which is why the evangelical left despises it so completely.

More recently, the *Federal Communications Commission v. Pacifica Foundation* case of 1978 allowed for the FCC to fine broadcasts that they deemed "indecent" without even the pretense that this term could be objectively defined—a total violation of the "equality before the law" that conservatives crow about but which virtually never exists in practice. As a consequence of regulations like this, the market inevitably responded by heavily erring on the side of caution, thereby creating the appearance of self-censorship and allowing the puritanical state to claim clean hands for itself.

In 1988, for example, Howard Stern was fined for describing an in-studio guest with the words, "The big black lesbian is out of her mind with lust!" In order to avoid the nefarious clutches of the FCC, Stern effectively had to leave the earth with his program, switching from traditional radio to satellite-broadcast Sirius. Once again, if the evangelical left had their way, there would literally be nowhere on the entire planet outside their grasp.

There has therefore always been a very strong and usually successful attempt by the state to control speech in America. It is only recently that this has been stymied, and this is due far more to technology than to changing public attitudes. Again, for the New Right the focus is on strategy and not on persuasion per se.

To illustrate this point, let's suppose someone traveled back in time to the 1980s. Man has walked on the moon, and computers are used in the workplace. We have color photocopying and mobile phones—not to mention nuclear weapons. By any standard it's a technologically advanced time. We can easily imagine an argument about censorship and what the two positions would be. On the one hand comes the position that we should have complete free speech, that good arguments win out in the "marketplace of ideas," and that in fact one way of knowing that given ideas *are* good is through vigorous debate with those who disagree. On the other side comes the argument that books like *Mein Kampf* might lead to extremely bad social consequences—not to mention subjects like, say, child pornography or graphic crime scene photos. From this perspective, since we have to draw the line *somewhere*, it then becomes a question of *where* to draw it and not *whether* to draw it.

Now our time traveler appears, and he tells the two debaters that their argument is superfluous. In a few short years, censorship will be technically impossible. Anyone will be able to take any text and, with the press of one button, create as many copies of it as they want. Then, with the press of one button, they can send it to anywhere on earth, at the speed of light. They can also make it so that only someone who knows a magic word (a "password") will be able to open the document to read it. And the cost for all this? Oh yes, all this is free.

Clearly the time traveler would sound like a lunatic. Yet that is precisely the state of affairs today, which is why the increasing shrieking of the evangelical left can be seen not as a function of their domination but of their decreasing power. Those driven by emotion (children, the mentally ill, hormonal men and women alike) don't freak out when they get their way; they freak out when they're *not* getting their way.

We see it nowadays with demands to strip internet anonymity in an attempt to force people to suffer severe consequences for what they say online. This is a technologically recent development. It was far easier to track people down when there was a literal paper trail to their work. Shamelessly, to attack anonymity is to attack the Constitution itself. The greatest defense of the Constitution was a series of essays written by Alexander Hamilton, James Madison, and John Jay under the collective pseudonym Publius and later collected as *The Federalist*.

The fact is that there have been and always will be vast numbers of Americans either supportive of or utterly indifferent to free speech. Yet it's quite easy to proclaim one's belief in something while doing absolutely nothing about it at all. There is absolutely no cost. This is why it is almost impossible to expect large numbers of people to take on the government when they have no personal vested interest in a particular dispute. It is also almost impossible to expect large numbers of people to think in terms of principles, to understand the profound difference between "I don't approve of this" and "this should be illegal." At least, however, we have the First Amendment. Europe is an entirely other matter.

9

★

GET IN THE CHOPPER

Sometimes democracy must be bathed in blood.

—Augusto Pinochet

Despite media attempts to conflate the New Right with Trump support, the two are not identical phenomena. It is certainly true that the New Right was pretty much unanimously pro-Trump or at the very least anti-anti-Trump. Since members of the New Right view politics as a *consequence* of the battle to be had but not precisely the field upon which it is to be fought, the presidency is only one element of the bigger picture. The person in the White House is nowhere near as important for someone in the New Right as for a progressive or a conservative. The movement preceded Trump's candidacy and would have continued had he been defeated in the 2016 presidential election.

As far as I could tell, there wasn't a single person prominent in the movement who didn't have very strong reservations about Donald Trump. This is due to several reasons, not even counting Trump's erratic behavior. There's the question of whether any one president can do enough to save the country, both due to how antagonistic U.S. culture has become and how resistant our political system is to change. There's also the tacit understanding that people in Washington know how the system works far better than Trump could ever hope to and would be able to undermine him at every turn. Trump and his online followers might be better at social media than the clunky corporate press, but he and his team would not be able to out-Washington Mitch McConnell and Paul Ryan.

So if there's someone who the New Right admires almost without hesitation or qualification, it's not Donald Trump. It's not even an American—it's Nigel Farage, former head of the UK Independence Party (UKIP). Before Farage came along, British anti-EU sentiment was strongly tinged with racism and even white supremacism. Groups like the British National Party were brazenly based on racial identity, and Farage mentor Enoch Powell's famous "Rivers of Blood" speech has been viewed as racist code by progressives and white nationalists alike.

In 1993 Farage was one of the founders of UKIP, formed in reaction to Prime Minister John Major's increasingly pro-EU actions—a far cry from his predecessor Margaret Thatcher's heavy skepticism of the European Union and its consequent threat to British sovereignty and the integrity of the pound. Farage was first elected to the European parliament, and there, so to speak, a star was born.

Part of the reason Farage is so beloved by the New Right isn't simply his views but his approach. His speeches to the European Parliament are some of the few examples of politicians being treated to their face with irreverence if not downright contempt—something that has increasingly been happening since then thanks to social media.

"You have the charisma of a damp rag, and the appearance of a low-grade bank clerk," he told then-EU president Herman

Van Rompuy in 2010. "You appear to have a loathing for the very concept of the existence of nation-states—perhaps that's because you come from Belgium, which of course is pretty much a non-country. [. . .] Sir, you have no legitimacy in this job at all, and I can say with confidence that I speak on behalf of the majority of British people in saying: 'We don't know you, we don't want you, and the sooner you're put out to grass, the better.'" (UKIP later sold damp rags as a fundraiser.)

Farage is vulgar in both senses of the word. On the one hand he is rude and disrespectful. It is usually the left who claims that things like manners and decorum are mechanisms for the ruling class to maintain a façade of civility over a reality of domination. This framework was particularly on display when activists began disrupting people trying to eat their meals and even stopping traffic as part of the Black Lives Matter movement. The idea that progressivism is in fact the ruling ideology is nonsensical to a faith that defines itself by combating racism, a pervasive existential threat.

But Farage is also vulgar in the non-derogatory sense of the term, meaning something that has mass appeal. He does not attempt to be pretentious but mocks such affectations. He has no use for the "self-appointed" (or rather politically appointed) overclass dictating and passing judgment upon the layman. The cliché was that George W. Bush was the president people wanted to have a beer with, and there are literally dozens of photos online of ol' Nige hoisting a pint at the pub.

It is Farage who explains who the main enemies are that unite the New Right: the so-called globalists. "The European Union has become a sort of prototype for what Hillary Clinton and some of the Wall Street banks want to see," he told CNN's Jake Tapper. "Namely, where individual nation-states give up their democratic rights, give up the supremacy of their courts, and hand it all over to a higher global order that wants to homogenize, harmonize, and make everybody the same." This is the "New World Order" that George H. W. Bush so admired—and partly explains the extreme antipathy between Jeb and Trump during the 2016 primaries.

Farage's life work came to pass when he forced the UK to have a referendum on leaving the EU, and then led that referendum to victory against pretty much the entire British establishment. There were several reasons why so many on the American New Right were such enthusiastic cheerleaders of Brexit. The first and most obvious was that it was a clear reclamation of national sovereignty from an international organization. It was the British people asserting themselves as British and not as Europeans, stating in not so many words that country comes before continent and that not all countries are equal or equally good.

Second, it was partly a repudiation of the concept of free movement and free migration. The Schengen Agreement allows people to travel throughout Europe without stopping at national borders. This is taken advantage of in northern Africa, where migrants jump fences to land on what is technically European soil and then make their way to continental Europe. Any chain is only as strong as its weakest link. Reclaiming one's borders is seen as an urgently necessary prerequisite for maintaining one's culture and preventing things like Islam (and its minority component of radical Islam) from setting up roots.

But perhaps most important was how Brexit played out. Just as with the anti-Trump forces here, virtually the entire Cathedral united to denounce and discredit the referendum. The pro-Brexit left, people like Labour Party leader Jeremy Corbyn, largely kept their mouths shut. The message was that being for Brexit was not a position one could take seriously if one were informed about the issue. Pro-Brexit wasn't a political stance so much as an absurdity.

Further, most of the polls showed that Brexit was going to fail, in the same way that many other such secessionist movements failed in the past. The motion passed with a small but unquestionable margin. The Cathedral predicted that Brexit wouldn't pass, and that if it did pass there would be disastrous consequences. Neither of these came true, and it was a public demonstration of the New Right idea that the evangelical left is nowhere near as bright as they purport to be. How can they claim to have a monopoly on brainpower and then get every aspect of the issue wrong?

Many in the corporate press are still baffled by how they missed the Brexit vote (not to mention the Trump victory). Yet there are a couple of scenarios to describe how the pollsters consistently got it wrong. What might actually have happened harkens back to the time in modern history when the elites were most out of touch, to a debacle even worse than the famous headline that proclaimed "Dewey Defeats Truman" in the 1948 U.S. presidential election.

Victor Sebestyen's *Revolution 1989* is a masterpiece of historical writing that recounts "the fall of the Soviet Empire." The date fittingly refers to the beginning of that fall, in late-1980s Poland. After a series of nationwide strikes there, the communist government agreed to recognize the labor movement Solidarity as a political force and to hold semifree elections. Communist governments always held elections but they were a sham, often with only one candidate listed. This time, however, there would be a modicum of competition (though many seats in the Parliament were reserved for the Communist Party).

The Polish people, who were reared in government schools, watched government propaganda and government-friendly television programs, and read government newspapers (and wiped their asses with the same), would surely side with the ruling class. They had been told what they were supposed and expected to do since birth. The concern from some of the party members was that they would end up sweeping the elections, giving the appearance that the vote had all been a sham even though it actually hadn't been.

These concerns were misguided.

With one exception, Solidarity wound up winning every single contested election in the first round. This was an almost unanimous public repudiation of the government, and it was humiliating. The Polish communists agreed to accept the results of the vote (and Gorbachev decided not to send in the tanks), beginning a swift path to the collapse of the Soviet Union, the end of communism, and the conclusion of the Cold War.

The other parallel example to how polling is often misguided was the 1982 California gubernatorial race between African American Democrat Tom Bradley and state attorney general George Deukmejian, who was a white Republican. Bradley had a consistent lead throughout the campaign. In other words, even though one or two polls may have been wrong, it would be statistically unlikely in the extreme for them *all* to be wrong and wrong in the same direction.

Election night saw a squeaker of a victory by Deukmejian, one that left pollsters scratching their heads. The prevailing theory on the left is that racists lied to pollsters and in private were free to act on their prejudices, and that there were enough of these racists to tip the election. This is where the term "Bradley effect" is used to describe the purported disconnect between how minorities do in polls and how they do in elections. This didn't seem to affect Obama, although perhaps in his case the Bradley effect would have only been half of an effect.

It's no surprise that a worldview grounded in racial analysis sees racism as the cause of what is happening. Yet there is another possible explanation for Bradley's loss. Famously, after Kennedy was assassinated, more people remembered voting for him than had actually pulled the lever for him in the 1960 election. Why is that? The valorization of an assassinated president might lead people to lie about having supported him in an attempt to borrow virtue. Further, the human mind is very good at convincing itself of what it wants to be true. People might have genuinely been remembering incorrectly, because it felt better to have done the proper thing in the past—especially when there were no witnesses to the contrary or any real consequences to misremembering one's actions.

As the press is increasingly perceived as an entity like any other—namely one with its own agenda that regards certain outcomes as preferable—voters decreasingly see it as objective and fair (in whatever sense of that word one desires). As such, pollsters are not regarded as mathematicians with no skin in the game. This has been demonstrated repeatedly by the fact that polls taken over the phone, with someone speaking directly to a person, have different results than those taken via automated methods. So to lie and say one is for Bradley is not so much a function of racism as a function of trying to avoid being called a racist.

Given that Trump was compared to "literally Hitler" and the Antichrist during the campaign, there was a legitimate incentive to lie about supporting him. As a rule of thumb, the most effective way to lie is to do so consistently, making sure one doesn't ever slip up. Smiling and nodding about being pro-Hillary at work would carry over into a pollster's phone call. There would be a possible cost but no real benefit to openly declaring Trump support, even if the cost were merely conversational awkwardness from, say, admitting being pro-Trump to a minority polltaker on the line.

The pattern was the same not only with Brexit but with the British parliamentary elections in 2015. Every single poll predicted a hung parliament, one in which no single party had a majority. Instead, David Cameron led the Conservatives to a lead of over 6 percent and almost one hundred seats more than Labour. Much of the Cathedral's control is based on the concept of illegitimacy. It's not just that one's opinion is incorrect; one doesn't even have the right to hold it to begin with, sometimes even as a hypothesis.

Yet this pattern did not carry over to France's 2017 presidential election. All the major polls had an extremely consistent 20–26 percent lead for independent candidate Emmanuel Macron over the National Front's Marine le Pen. Macron ended up winning by 32 percent, significantly higher than expected. The 2017 Austrian presidential election was reheld due to voter irregularities; in both cases the neofascist lost to the ex-Green candidate, performing as expected or worse. Iceland saw the antiestablishment Pirate Party strongly underperform polling predictions, and in the Netherlands Geert Wilders came up quite short as well. Hungary's Viktor Orbán was reelected in 2018 by a massive margin—but with precisely the same amount of party seats as the previous time. It seems as if there isn't one coherent theory to describe all these phenomena.

So who are the New Right's political idols? Who are the models that are held up as "this is who we want in charge"? In this regard we need to look not at home—we've been under progressive domination for decades, after all—but abroad. There are two names that are largely unknown to most Americans, even most right-of-center Americans, but that hold outsized influence as inspirations in New Right circles as "proof of concept." It *can* happen here, because it happened *there*.

The two men represent two types of national vitality: creation and salvation. The former speaks to the actions of Lee Kuan Yew, who was the first (and only) prime minister of Singapore for over thirty years. Lee took the island nation, to use the title of his autobiography, *From Third World to First*. What had basically been a jungle is now one of the world's financial centers, with an extremely high standard of living—but Lee did not affect change through very democratic means. He might be thought of as akin to former New York City mayor Michael Bloomberg, an autocratic but largely nonpartisan ruler focused on quality of life and willing to pay the costs for it, sometimes even the cost of freedom.

Lee Kuan Yew stated that Western-style multiparty mass democracy would not work in a tribal, multiracial society because people vote along ethnic lines, exacerbating divisions and often leading to conflict. To avoid that, the government placed restrictions on "inflammatory" speech on race/religion. The restrictions would have been anathema in the United States, but worked to promote Singapore's stability with its multiethnic society (80 percent Chinese, 8 percent Indian, 12 percent Malay).

Healthcare is a good example of how Singapore prefers pragmatism over ideology. Per the World Bank, the United States inefficiently spends over 15 percent of GDP on healthcare, and European welfare states like Germany, the UK, and France around 10 percent. Singapore meanwhile spends less than 5 percent with equally good if not better results. They're willing to combine measures such as high private expenditure (65 percent) with regulations forcing citizens to invest in health savings accounts while encouraging high-deductible, first-expense-out-of-pocket plans. The government also has rules forcing all hospitals and doctors to post prices for procedures, ensuring transparency.

Homosexuality is technically outlawed, but the rule is not actually enforced unless the person is participating in parades or lobbying. Basically, what one does behind closed doors is one's own business, and in fact there is a thriving underground gay community. It is only when it enters the public sphere that it might upset the careful balance, since most Malays are practicing Muslims and there is a substantial Christian minority.

Thus, Singapore has a small but strong and efficient government. The laws are mostly common sense in both business and personal life, but they are enforced fairly and strictly. This allows people to know the "rules of the game" and act accordingly. In the United States, on the other hand, companies must constantly lobby government and politicians, as well as concern themselves with random judges impeding their business, unpredictable and shifting legislation, and unaccountable and countless government agencies and bureaucracies.

As a result of all this, Singapore is a world leader in good governance by several metrics. In 2018 the World Economic Forum ranked Singapore first out of 137 countries when it came to trust in politicians and math/science education. It was second regarding overall infrastructure and overall education quality. Yet when it came to debt it was only one-hundred-twenty-eighth.

Lee Kuan Yew's reign is not without its critics. Yet he isn't radioactive in a political sense, being highly regarded internationally and well-respected even by his foes. He's criticized but not demonized. And while the case for Lee Kuan Yew's Singapore is fairly straightforward and easy to make (even while acknowledging strong issues with his approach), the case of Augusto Pinochet and how he saved Chile is a far more controversial subject.

If Lew Kuan Yew is the honest example to hold up, Pinochet is the example suffused with irony (though to what extent depends on who is making the reference). Pinochet's reign was strongly intertwined with American politics, especially with President Reagan's attempts to fight the spread of communism in Central and South America. Pinochet's relationship with

Margaret Thatcher was a source of controversy for decades, as she defended him long after many others cut their ties either due to ideological or practical concerns. But although there are a few books about his reign—*A Nation of Enemies: Chile Under Pinochet*; *The Pinochet Generation*; *The Dictator's Shadow: Life Under Augusto Pinochet*—there are, bizarrely, no English-language biographies of Pinochet available. This lends itself well to the New Right's creation of a mythos around the man that's based in reality but still somewhat independent from it.

The Pinochet parable almost reads like a folk tale (*volk* tale?). In 1970, "socialist" Salvador Allende was elected Chile's president. Allende was a "mere" socialist in the same sense that the Democratic People's Republic of Korea, north Korea, is "democratic": i.e., not at all. Allende was a totalitarian Marxist, the likes of which would be seen in Venezuela in President Hugo Chavez decades later.

The usual communist tactics ensued, including the seizure of private property and the killing of those who opposed such actions. A free press was swiftly becoming a thing of the past, and legalized crime via the state became the norm. Tens of thousands of foreign operatives infiltrated Chile to ensure the revolution was carried through to completion. The Supreme Court ruled against Allende's legitimacy, and the people took to the streets. Things were getting worse and worse.

In an attempt to restore order to Chile, Pinochet and the military staged a coup in 1973. Allende died during the conflict, either by his own hand or that of his men's. Pinochet's men ended up killing over three thousand people as they seized power. These three thousand deaths are at the heart of the argument against Pinochet. When compared to the (literally) hundreds of millions of people in various countries killed by their own respective communist governments, this isn't even a rounding error. Nor is it a huge number in what was effectively a truncated civil war. The question is, therefore, is it wrong to kill several thousand people who back a government in the process of installing a communist dictatorship, with all that that entails? The answer is obvious to all—though *what* said "obvious" answer is differs based on one's political perspective.

Pinochet reigned for many years. He had little regard for the equivalent of Miranda rights; many people, including many innocent people, were tortured under his regime. The most unusual method of execution—and one frequently invoked by the New Right—was taking Marxists up in helicopters and throwing them into the ocean. Thus, a common New Right Twitter response to some blathering left-wing journalist is to simply retweet their vapidity with the helicopter emoji attached. In answer to the frequent question, "Just how many people are in the New Right, anyway?," one can look to the twelve thousand plus members of the Facebook group for "Pinochet Helicopter Rides and Rentals." That's a significant number for what's basically the ultimate New Right in-joke.

Yet Pinochet also sought the help of many American economists from the University of Chicago to govern effectively. Due to their advice, his relatively free-market policies allowed Chile to flourish financially and become the leader in South America by several economic indicators. In 1988, Pinochet finally put his leadership to a vote, which he lost. As a consequence, democratic elections for both the presidency and the congress were held, the results of which Pinochet accepted. Chile remains a thriving parliamentary democracy to this day. As of 2015 it ranked thirty-eighth in the United Nations' Human Development Index, receiving the highest possible score of "Very high human development" (ahead of Portugal and Russia) and the highest ranking in all of Central and South America.

For the New Right, Pinochet occupies the precise place that Che Guevara does for the left. In reality, Che Guevara was a racist, homophobic mass murderer. He brought labor camps to Cuba and wanted to nuke New York City. He was, in his own words, "a cold killing machine motivated by pure hate." He also recognized that "[m]uch more valuable than rural recruits for our guerrilla force were American media recruits to export our propaganda."

Yet despite this Che has been turned into a symbol of youth and rebellion, especially that iconic Che image adapted from a photograph by Alberto Korda. Has the idea of Che become divorced from reality? *Can* the idea of Che be divorced from reality? Depending on one's perspective, it's either telling or irrelevant that Hillary Clinton once named her dog Che. The same question can be asked of the New Right about their comfort with Pinochet (as well as with racist figures and iconography).

This love of Pinochet is very much in the trolling Rothbardian tradition (either that or it's crypto-fascists tacitly showing their hand). But if Rothbard brings to the New Right a contempt for the establishment and elites in general, it is from Pat Buchanan that the New Right gets its global perspective. Buchanan's *Death of the West* is indeed a seminal text for the New Right (one of the very few), and as such it bears discussing in detail. It's not universally read and beloved in the subculture—no book can make that claim due to the disparate nature of the movement—but a vast number of New Right concepts can be found explicated within: from the concerns with demographic displacement to a strong case for economic nationalism and a suspicion of internationalist organizations.

A principle that progressives approve of is frequently followed by positive exclamations like "This isn't hard!," whereas a bad principle is "silly" or "simplistic." Radical ideas are "innovative" when they pass muster but "crackpot" or "paranoid" when they don't. Similarly, if ideas are simply being used as postulates for further analysis, they're "absurd" instead of "thought-provoking."

As such, it's very hard to critique a right-wing book that is actually crackpot, simplistic, and outdated without sounding like a leftist. Yet *Death of the West* is all those things to a great extent, combined with spot-on analysis and insight. Like so much else of the New Right, it's very much a mixed bag.

To begin with, Buchanan repeatedly uses a trick to make claims without taking the responsibility of making them: the use of rhetorical questions that are anything but. "[I]s Western civilization about to follow Lenin's empire to the same inglorious end?"[1] "Are we in the twilight of the West?" Buchanan wonders. Without waiting for an answer, he quickly assumes the positive and then asks, "Is the Death of the West irreversible?"[2]

Buchanan's logic is remarkably similar to that of Al Gore and his global warming associates. It breaks down like this:

- Civilization is under unprecedented existential threat.
- The only way to stop this threat from being realized is via a complete reordering of society, which is admittedly impossible.
- Since our political systems won't allow us to undertake the massive changes that are necessary, we can at least effect incremental changes in the right direction.
- Said changes won't actually stop the existential threat from being realized, but for some never-explained reason we should do them anyway.

For Gore, "civilization" consists of the entire world, whereas for Buchanan civilization is largely synonymous with the West. Other than that, the logic is pretty much identical. Whereas for Gore death is a function of the weather, for Buchanan it's a matter of the wrong people outbreeding the right ones.

Buchanan anticipates this objection and addresses it:

> [I]s the death of the West inevitable? Or, like all previ-
> ous predictions of Western decline and demise, will
> this cup, too, pass away and expose as fools all who said
> we must drink it? [. . .] Why do predictions of the Death
> of the West not belong on the same back shelf as the
> predictions of "nuclear winter" and "global warming"?
>
> Answer: the Death of the West is not a prediction
> of what is going to happen, it is a depiction of what is
> happening now. First World nations are dying. They
> face a mortal crisis, not because of something happen-
> ing in the Third World, but because of what is not
> happening at home and in the homes of the First
> World. Western fertility rates have been falling for
> decades.[3]

Because *Death of the West* was written in 2001, Buchanan
makes several claims that can now actually be checked against
the data. For example, he points out that in 2000, "Russia's
birthrate had already plummeted to 1.17 children, below Italy's.
Its population had fallen to 145 million; one estimate had it
headed to 123 million by 2015."[4] Surely there was also an estimate that would have been a *higher* number, but Buchanan
chooses to end on the more alarmist figure. In fact the 2017
figure has Russia's population sans Crimea—at 144.5 million,
approximately where it was in 2000. The idea that Russia's
worldwide influence or vitality is somehow weaker now than it
was during the Clinton years is untrue. After all, the Kremlin
now controls both Moscow *and* the White House.

"Is there a parallel between a dying Christianity in the West
and the death of Japan's prewar and wartime faith?" Buchanan
asks. "When nations lose their sense of mission, their mandate

of heaven, the faith that brought them into this world as unique countries and cultures, is that when they die? Is that when civilizations perish? So it would seem."[5] In fact that's not how it would seem in the slightest.

It was partly the faith of the Japanese in Emperor Hirohito's divinity that convinced Truman to drop the atomic bombs on Hiroshima and Nagasaki. It was also why getting the emperor to renounce his claim to be god-made-man was such an important part of the surrender. Absolutely, much of pre–World War II Japanese culture has gone by the wayside. But Japan as such has not perished in any sense. To claim that the world's largest creators and consumers of tentacle-rape pornography are somehow no longer a unique country and culture beggars belief. It was losing its faith that permitted Japan to become a civilized world power—and not a progressive, egalitarian world power either.

"The richer a nation becomes," insists Buchanan, "the fewer its children, and the sooner it begins to die. Societies organized to ensure the maximum pleasure, freedom, and happiness for all their members are, at the same time, advancing the date of their own funerals."[6] But Buchanan doesn't bother to name a single nation that actually has "died." The most recent major nation to have a "funeral" was the Soviet Union, and this was due neither to its wealth nor its aging population. In fact, if the Soviets had had more money they likely could have held on for far longer, as part of the Reagan stratagem was to force the USSR to spend itself into bankruptcy and systemic collapse. Iraq in one sense can be said to have "died," but to claim that this was due to the "maximum pleasure, freedom, and happiness for all" Iraqis is also absurd.

One of the problems with Buchanan (and Rothbard) is that he often reads things into politicians that aren't really there. It's a common approach, as seen with the Cathedral's veneration of candidate Obama and the New Right's early hopes for Trump. Yet politics is rarely that straightforward or that linear, and after serving under Nixon, Buchanan should have known better. Instead he ended up writing paeans to the New Right's bête noire, Angela Merkel.

"The German Christian Democratic party leader Angela Merkel already appears to be moving to capitalize on the backlash against Islamic immigration," Buchanan declared. "Inviting Turkey to become a candidate for the European Union membership was a mistake," he quotes her as saying. "There are differences of values. We do not have the same understanding of human rights. Try opening a Christian Church in Istanbul."[7]

Contemporary Germany is regarded as ground zero for the alleged Muslim invasion of Europe. Along with Sweden and France, Germany—specifically *Merkel's* Germany—is always held up by the New Right as what to avoid as a model. Not only is Merkel committed to bringing in even more migrants, but leaders of German opposition parties are even advocating extending voting rights to them—something members of the New Right feel is downright suicidal and insane.

Breitbart and other outlets constantly point out how all the migrants being brought into Germany are not assimilating at all: "Tens of Thousands of Migrants in Germany Unable to Read or Write"; "Migrant Convicted of Sexually Abusing 10-Year-Old Received Asylum Status Despite Known Criminal History." Articles from mainstream outlets are shared in New Right circles without any comment necessary, such as one Metro article that begins, "A woman in Germany has created anti-rape shorts, which began as a personal project after she was attacked while out running."[8] By far the biggest scandal—and cautionary tale—in New Right circles was the huge number of sexual assaults that occurred in Cologne and other German cities on December 31, 2015, and into the night. The claim was that these attacks—overwhelmingly by non-Aryans—were deliberately kept out of the press by the German government lest there be racist reaction.

If the Alt-Right could be defined by one slogan, it would be that "Demographics is destiny." When whites screw up a culture, they say, we get Sweden. When blacks do, we get the hell on earth that is Liberia. Yet despite dancing with this issue elsewhere in the book, Buchanan doesn't take the bait, pointing out that "the past five hundred years have been an endless chronicle of European peoples slaughtering one another, with World Wars I and II as climax to the horrors. And during that past half-millennium, the great enemies of Western faith, culture, and civilization have come out of the West."[9]

But Buchanan vacillates between identifying what the problem is, per se. On the one hand, he seems to indulge in the naturalistic fallacy, equating that which is natural with that which is good. "Six hundred Americans had died of AIDS in 1983," he writes, "when the author urged the White House to address the medical crisis in a column that closed, 'The poor homosexuals; they have declared war on nature and nature is exacting an awful retribution.' So it did. Hundreds of thousands have since died."[10] Yet mortgages and cable television, to name two examples, are hardly "natural." The other higher primates engage in polygyny. If evolution is a farce and ape comparisons invalid, as Buchanan would say, then one can point to King David's many wives and Jesus dying a virgin. If nature is the standard, then women should be ready to be mothers when they first get their period.

On the other hand, Buchanan is concerned about populations being replaced both by becoming outbred and by becoming outnumbered due to naturalized immigrants because "the immigration tsunami rolling over America is not coming from 'all the races of Europe.' The largest population transfer in history is coming from all the races of Asia, Africa, and Latin America, and they are not 'melting and reforming.'"[11]

"How bleak is the situation? Of the twenty nations with the lowest birthrates in the world, eighteen are in Europe. [. . .] But as Europe is dying, the Third World adds one hundred million people—one new Mexico—every fifteen months. Forty new Mexicos in the Third World by 2050, while Europe will have lost the equivalent of the entire population of Belgium, Holland, Denmark, Sweden, Norway—and Germany!"[12] Uh oh, an exclamation point! An effective literary flourish, yes, but not truth serum.

"As equality is its core principle," Buchanan says, "the cultural revolution teaches that the real heroes of history are not the conquerors, soldiers, and statesmen who built the Western nations and created the great empires, but those who advanced the higher cause—the equality of peoples. Thus, the end of segregation in the South and of apartheid in South Africa are triumphs greater than the defeat of communism, and Mandela and Gandhi are the true moral heroes of the twentieth century."[13]

At times Buchanan—and the New Right—flirts with racial issues as the basis for cultural success: "[L]et us look again at the population projections for 2050, and try to visualize what our world will look like. In Africa, there will be 1.5 billion people. From Morocco to the Persian Gulf will be an Arab-Turkic-Islamic sea of 500 million. In South Asia will live 700 million Iranians, Afghans, Pakistanis, and Bangladeshis, and 1.5 billion Indians. There will be 300 million Indonesians, and China, with 1.5 billion people, will brood over Asia."[14]

It is hard to avoid the racial subtext with the call to "visualization," followed by a list of non-white nations. At times Buchanan gets even more explicit with this perspective: "Mexicans not only come from another culture, but millions are of another race. History and experience teach us that different races are far more difficult to assimilate. The sixty million Americans who claim German ancestry are fully assimilated, while millions from Africa and Asia are still not full participants in American society."[15]

"If Americans wish to preserve their civilization and culture," Buchanan eventually concludes, "American women must have more children. While there is no guarantee that government incentives can change the mind-set of women, a pro-family, pro-child bias can be built back into national policy."[16]

Marginal tax cuts for having children seem to be an utterly ineffectual response to a crisis that is leading to the "death" of the West. "The honor of being the first nation to voluntarily turn its majority indigenous population into a minority will go to the United States."[17] But in Buchanan's case, there was no subculture in America at that time that saw all this as a problem. This is how he can be said to presage New Right concerns.

Buchanan also blasts both political parties as being ineffectual at best in taking the needed steps to save America: "With the Democratic party so beholden to feminism that it cannot even oppose partial birth abortions, and the GOP in thrall to libertarian ideology and controlled by corporate interests, the call of the gods of the marketplace for more women workers prevails over the command of the God of Genesis: 'Be fruitful and multiply, and replenish the earth.'"[18]

The Republicans are no better off: "Many conservatives have succumbed to the heresy of Economism, a mirror-Marxism that holds that man is an economic animal, that free trade and free markets are the path to peace, prosperity, and happiness, that if we can only get the marginal tax rates right and the capital gains tax abolished, Paradise—Dow 36,000!—is at hand. But when the income tax rate for the wealthiest was above 90 percent in the 1950s, America, by every moral and social indicator, was a better country."[19]

That's quite a bold claim to make, and there are many social indicators that show America is better off now than in the past. Life expectancy, levels of education, access to technology. Not so for Buchanan: "In the African-American community [. . .] [d]rugs are pandemic. Children do not learn in schools. Conscientious kids are intimidated and beaten up. Girls are molested and assaulted by gang members high on dope and rap."[20]

The constant fears about the "Balkanization" of America ignore most of actual American history (and frankly, the Balkans are hardly some sort of existential nightmare anyway). Our Founding Fathers didn't view us as one country in the sense that it is now, not by a long shot. A "state" is a government, and the "united states" were a united collection of governments much like the United Nations is a collection of different countries. There weren't any "American citizens"; there were citizens of Virginia or New York or even (God help them) New Jersey. It's why the preference before the Civil War was to refer to "these" United States. Well into the nineteenth century it was common to say "the United States are" instead of "is." It was one of the reasons Alexander Hamilton viewed the national debt as a blessing; it would encourage the populations of thirteen states to begin to think of themselves as one nation.

"For what is more important than the permanence of the American nation and people?," Buchanan asks. A great deal. The Founding Fathers took the idea of dissolving outdated governments for granted. They had also done it twice, emancipating themselves from Great Britain and then later (in secret!) overturning the Articles of Confederation—something they were explicitly forbidden from doing.

While many in the New Right insist that a white nation will be inherently cohesive, the War Between the States—the bloodiest conflict in American history by far—was fought by white people against other white people. Buchanan knows this quite well: "For our divisions are rooted in our deepest beliefs, and upon those beliefs Americans are almost as divided as we were when General Beauregard gave the order to fire on Fort Sumter. Once again, we are seceding from one another; only this time, it is a secession of the heart."[21] So we have been through this before, and it was worse then—even though we were demographically far more united.

Buchanan quotes the *Dallas Morning News* as projecting that "fewer than half of Texans will be white" by 2005, and the implication is obvious. In fact Texas is over 70 percent white according to the 2010 census. That number is misleading, since it combines Hispanic Whites and non-Hispanic Whites (the latter of which are just over 45 percent of the population). Yet Donald Trump still defeated Hillary Clinton there by 9 percent—a sizeable margin, but far lower than the hapless Mitt Romney's 16 percent margin over incumbent president Barack Obama in 2012 (which was itself higher than John McCain's 12 percent victory). It's hard to make comparisons to earlier years, since Texans ran as presidential candidates in all elections from 1988 to 2004.

On the other hand, the 2014 Republican House majority of 247 was their greatest number since 1927—and 2014's Republican Party was far more ideologically right wing than at any point in those intervening years. A proportion of this was due to the creation of majority-minority districts, artificially engineered congressional districts designed to guarantee stronger minority representation. Yet this again is an argument against the idea that demographics is *destiny*.

One of the issues—that immigrants will simply vote themselves welfare benefits, or even vote to turn America into the countries that they escaped from—can be addressed by limiting voting rights. Many countries have severe restrictions on citizenship and thereby the right to vote, and these are not authoritarian nations either. One of the biggest—if not *the* biggest—obstacles to restricting suffrage is that the evangelical left views extending voting rights as their greatest moral victory and the basis of their identity as a movement. There is literally nothing else that matters as much to them or that they would be as willing to fight over. They (understandably) view any talk of restricting the vote as a code word for Jim Crow.

Voting in America has not always been "one man, one vote" or even "one person, one vote." Not only have there been many restrictions on suffrage but there have been restrictions on representation as well, most famously with the Constitution counting slaves as three-fifths of a person. What some forget or choose to ignore is that those slaves were all "represented" by their owners; the higher the number of slaves in aggregate, the more powerful the slaveowners would be in Congress. "I'm not three-fifths of a person" makes for a nice chant, and a good lyric is more important than a mere fact. The West has come under existential threat before, many times. The question on the table is whether it is dying now, and whether that death is inevitable. For many on the New Right, that answer is a very firm *yes*.

10

★

SECOND-HAND LIVES

Of all tyrannies, a tyranny sincerely exercised for the good of its victims may be the most oppressive. It would be better to live under robber barons than under omnipotent moral busybodies. The robber baron's cruelty may sometimes sleep, his cupidity may at some point be satiated; but those who torment us for our own good will torment us without end for they do so with the approval of their own conscience.

—C. S. Lewis

If conservatives operate politically, the New Right operates sociologically. One of their mechanisms for destroying the corporate press is to focus on how they function and on their techniques as opposed to any one individual story. A key leader in this aspect of New Right activism is Mike Cernovich.

Cernovich got his start writing about men's issues, a huge breeding ground for New Right recruitment in a post-feminist America. Frequently but dubiously lumped in with the New Right, Jordan Peterson and Joe Rogan occupy similar niches—encouraging skepticism toward the Cathedral and self-development within oneself. In 2015 Cernovich self-published *Gorilla Mindset*, a book that explains "How to Control Your

Thoughts and Emotions and Live Life on Your Terms." Yet despite his swagger and the book's title, his writing is far more new age than neo-reactionary. Many of the ideas have been staples of women's magazines for years, including the benefits of meditation and "being present."

Cernovich has cleverly repackaged such concepts in a manner friendly for guys, and in the process he has given men permission to engage in these activities without feeling stigmatized. It's akin to when Coca-Cola invented Coke Zero, which was conceived as a male alternative for those were too embarrassed by the perceived effeminacy of ordering a Diet Coke.

Yet Cernovich doesn't pull punches online, frequently calling out reporters that he regards as dishonest (as opposed to those with whom he merely disagrees). Despite his love of aggression, he isn't some meathead thug in person. He speaks with a lisp, which leads his foes to mock him as the author of "Gowilla Mindthet." He's also quite even-tempered and laid back. "What I go for is self-possession," he explained to me. "I wrote an article called "Why I Am Not an Alpha Male." I want a sense of ease: this is who I am, and this is where I fit in. If I'm on someone else's show and he wants to be the boss, I don't care. If he talks over me, I don't feel diminished. I'm having fun." ·

The transition from men's writer to New Right figurehead was an organic one. "We live in a woman's world," he explained. "Men are told they're living in a man's world, and they're looking around thinking, *Well, not for me*. With men there isn't any real help with alienation." Much of contemporary feminism is based on things like the relative numbers of male CEOs. "It's called the apex fallacy," he said. "'Too many men at the top.' OK, what about the men at the bottom? Male suicide is four times women's suicide. Look at homelessness, drug addiction, and suicide rates. Men are often the biggest winners *and* the biggest losers."

Late 1960s hippie culture, though strongly antiwar and pro–civil rights, was still largely a way for young people to bond over shared interests and values. A great deal of New Right activity involves self-improvement and teaches young people—especially men—to be the highest version of themselves they possibly can be. It's a natural reaction to the idea that white men are privileged and have it easy when so many young people of all ethnicities are struggling. Struggling comparatively less because of one's white ancestry is hardly a way to mollify depression, anxiety, and a general sense of purposelessness. No one doubts that wealthy and powerful people—the most privileged of all—suffer from these maladies in enormous proportions as well.

In 2008 there was no shortage of attacks on the rule of "old white men" by many of the same people who came around to Bernie Sanders in 2016. The New Right, with its veneration of strength and power, naturally views attacks on masculinity—which is not the exclusive province of men—as evil and dangerous. "The only time you're allowed to talk about masculinity," Cernovich quipped, "is bacon, boobs, beer, and CrossFit. But that doesn't threaten the structure. Men and women mature at different rates. Men shouldn't get married until their thirties because we peak then, while women peak in their twenties."

To point out human biology and apply it differently to different groups of humans is heretical to the evangelical left. A March 2018 tweet from Planned Parenthood Kentucky consisted solely of the phrase "Some men have a uterus" repeated eleven times. (Something apparently becomes true when you say it ten times or more.) There's also been legal movement, subtle but successful, to change birth certificates from "father" and "mother" to "parent 1" and "parent 2." After all, the claim goes, there's no reason why a man can't be a mother.

Cernovich's definition of masculinity is fairly representative

of those in the New Right: "Having purpose of will and imposing it on the world. Going after life, going hard, and not conforming. These are all things that are taught to women shamelessly and constantly. 'Girl power!' There's a program for what you're supposed to do as a man," he concluded. "But it's all duty. There's no sense that society should give you something back for it." Now that it's women's turn, men should do as they're told and sit quiet and be remorseful for their past transgressions.

In August 2016 Cernovich was invited to be a panelist on Fox News' *Red Eye*. One week later, the Daily Beast's Lloyd Grove wrote a piece asking the rhetorical question, "Why Did Fox News Welcome Date Rape Apologist Mike Cernovich?" The sidebar link to the article had the alternative title of "Date Rape Apologist Welcomed on Fox News." Grove's source for this classification was Cernovich's past tweet that said, "Have you guys ever tried 'raping' a girl without using force? Try it. It's basically impossible. Date rape does not exist."

The article led off with quotes from two of Cernovich's conservative enemies, Ben Shapiro and Ben Howe. Within the piece, a spokesperson for Fox News was quick to point out that he would not be invited back. At the time, Cernovich had seventy-eight thousand Twitter followers. "After they did a hit job and banned me from Fox News, I realized that I was never going to be legitimate," he told me. "That gave me a sense of freedom. I can go after anyone I want. I realized the only way to be legitimate is to redefine what legitimate means, and I redefine by sheer numbers." Less than a year after the Daily Beast article, Cernovich's Twitter followers had tripled.

We've seen this before. The path was set by Matt Drudge, who broke the Monica Lewinsky story and in the process broke the old media model and almost took down a president. At the time, the corporate press was wringing its collective hands, wondering how to report the scandalous story, or *if* they should respond to it at all. Instead Drudge blew it wide open. The press retaliated by trying to decree him as illegitimate. In a sense, they were right: he did not have the imprimatur of a brand like the *New York Times*. In another sense, that didn't matter. He was breaking news that contained real, truthful information—what we are told is journalism at its most basic.

Things have not changed since the mid-1990s. When the corporate press engages in idle speculation, it's "having a discussion." When someone with a large following on social media engages in brainstorming, it's "dangerous" and "irresponsible." When Omar Mateen killed dozens of people in Orlando's Pulse nightclub in June 2016, Cernovich took to Twitter to argue that there must have been a second gunman. He gave very clear, cogent reasons for his thinking, as well as a perfectly logical reason why the police would not confess to such: namely, that the second shooter had yet to be apprehended. For this he was widely attacked. On the other hand, when Malaysia Airlines Flight 370 went missing in March 2014, the media's thinking was somewhat less grounded in plausibility. CNN's Don Lemon asked whether a black hole could have been responsible. As anyone who takes high school physics knows, a black hole isn't an actual hole at all, but a collapsed star several orders of magnitude heavier than our sun. Its gravitational field is so strong that it literally bends space and time and would destroy the entire earth.

Like Drudge did in creating an alternative, curated version of a newspaper with his site, the New Right often provides alternative versions of stories themselves. "Before social media," Cernovich pointed out, "you could read about yourself in the *New York Times*, they would do a hit job on you, and what can you do? Write a letter to the editor? You're fucked." Now technology offers resources to make that no longer the case. A small, focused army is going to be far quicker and better at reacting than a large, powerful force. It's how a pack of wolves can take down a moose—especially if that moose is past its prime and has lost touch with reality.

In March 2017, *60 Minutes* did an interview with Cernovich. "I knew what they were going to try and what they were going to try and hit me with," he told me. "What they wanted to do was hit me with Pizzagate."

One of the problems with being red-pilled is that once one believes everything one sees as a lie, it's often hard to navigate to truth—and in fact the more intricate and bizarre something sounds, the more intriguing its veracity becomes. Pizzagate was a Byzantine conspiracy theory that emerged in social media in late 2016. Briefly—and there are hours of mind-numbing video and hundreds of posts explaining it as well—it consists of the claim that Clinton attack dog John Podesta was involved in a pedophile sex-trafficking ring operating out of Washington, DC's, Comet pizzeria.

Some fodder for the theory was found in a 2011 tweet by Andrew Breitbart: "How prog-guru John Podesta isn't household name as world class underage sex slave op cover-upperer defending unspeakable dregs escapes me."[1] What Andrew was referring to at the time is anybody's guess—and many have tried.

Self-styled internet sleuths went through the social media accounts of James Alefantis, the pizzeria's owner, and found all sorts of supposed boy-love symbols in his household art and inferred various references in photographs he had of (clothed!) children, including one of a young girl taped down to a desk by her wrists. Things finally reached a head in December of 2016 when a gunman went to the pizzeria and fired several rounds. As a demonstration of how great the disparity is between things that matter to the New Right and those that concern mainstream conservatism, I was on a panel with *National Review* editor Rich Lowry three days later, and he was completely unaware of Pizzagate at all. (Frankly, this is to his credit. And please, dear reader, don't look up Elsagate either.)

"I never mentioned Comet Pizza or James Alefantis," Cernovich said. "They wanted to say that I propagated Pizzagate; fake news is dangerous; I'm a menace to society. That way they could call on banning me from social media. They want us all off social media so they can control the narrative."

Cernovich knew *60 Minutes* would not be a friendly interview, and he took action accordingly. "There's an app on my iPhone," he explained. "They didn't know I was recording. It's legal to record even in a two-party consent state if there's no reasonable expectation of privacy. If there's cameras and a hot mic, it isn't private."

He had the full interview transcribed so that if anything was taken out of context, he would be able to set the record straight. Before the segment aired, he released part of the transcript, which created hype but was also something *60 Minutes* was probably not anticipating. Once the segment aired he held a YouTube "press conference" addressing it, thereby guaranteeing himself the last word. The whole experience taught him something: "I realized that if there's a big hit job on us, we need to counterprogram it and get people to watch *us* instead."

On June 19, 2017, Megyn Kelly was all set to reveal her interview with Alex Jones on her new show. I was first introduced to Alex Jones by one of my fellow trolls who posted a YouTube clip titled, "Alex Jones: Juice Boxes Making Kids Gay." "The reason there's so many gay people now," Jones claimed in the video, "is because it's a chemical warfare operation—I have the government documents—where they said they were going to encourage homosexuality with chemicals so that people don't have children." He then cut open a juice box and revealed the smoking gun: the thin plastic lining on the inside. Jones went on to conflate same-sex attraction with transgenderism: "After you're done drinking your little juices, you're ready to go out and have a baby. You're ready to put makeup on, you're ready to wear a short skirt. You're ready to put together a garden of roses or something."

Whatever the supposed government conspiracy, Jones has discussed it and probably broke the story on his InfoWars show. One of his first big breaks was sneaking into the Bohemian Grove ceremony in 2000. Bohemian Grove is a secret meeting of high-powered men where supposedly all sorts of plots are hatched. When Jones confronted David Gergen about the gathering and its "Cremation of Care" ritual, the unflappable advisor to four presidents did his version of turning apoplectic. Obviously something secretive was going on, but that something needn't be nefarious. Richard Nixon described the gathering as merely "the most faggy goddamned thing you could ever imagine."

There was great backlash against Kelly's piece before it debuted, with a few stations refusing to even air the episode. If Jones had merely been a con man or a lunatic, no one would have batted an eye. Diane Sawyer was lauded for her 1993 interview with cult leader Charles Manson, whose underlings were responsible for several grisly murders. Disgraced televangelist Jim Bakker said his piece on *Good Morning America*, perhaps the most benign venue possible. Barbara Walters sat down with both Fidel Castro and Muammar Gaddafi, terrorist dictators with many, many bodies to their name.

The problem with Jones, then, isn't that he was simply perceived as a con man or a lunatic. The problem was that he does a phenomenal job discrediting the evangelical left as legitimate and moral, and this is something that the Cathedral cannot bear. I recall vividly a friend of mine being described as a "9/11 truther." Baffled, I asked him whether it was true. "My view," he told me, "is that there's more to the story than we are being told. There is *always* more." Given that several pages of the 9/11 report have been redacted, his statement is not only true but undeniably true. Yet the term "9/11 truther" conflates that perspective with those who claim that the towers were hit not by planes but by missiles cloaked in holograms.

It's easy to caricature Jones as a lunatic or a clown. But Jones subtly and consistently preaches several essential New Right ideas. The first is that politics is often a public sideshow, a distraction that grants the illusion of choice when actual decisions are made covertly and secretly without even the pretense of public input. The second is that progressives aren't simply well-meaning people with a difference of opinion who want a safety net and fairness. Rather, they are undiluted— though sometimes deluded—totalitarians at heart who would gladly round up their enemies (i.e., "racists") and send them to prison camps if they had the opportunity. Finally there is the essential perspective that elites hold loyalty to their international community over their given country of origin and/or residence.

Much of the New Right is about positioning. By having Bernie Sanders to her left, Hillary Clinton could tout herself as a centrist. But this is a relational position, not an absolute one. The letter B is to the right of A, but it's nowhere near the center of the alphabet. Similarly, Alex Jones works as a foil for the New Right by making people more reasonable than him come off as palatable.

He's also often hilarious. A video of him dorking out with a fidget spinner went viral, and his trolling of the Young Turks at the 2016 Republican Convention can safely be described by the overused term of "epic." Even his attorney insisted that he was actually a performance artist in Jones's divorce proceedings. When I appeared on Jones's show—every troll's wet dream— the segment immediately prior was about a subject I knew very little about. "I have nothing to say about lizard penis," I told him right away. "I can't speak on that."

For a pair of supposed lunatics, Cernovich and Jones did a great job with preemptive strikes against Megyn "Blood Coming Out of Her Whatever" Kelly. "The whole week we fucked with her," Cernovich chuckled. He basically gave Jones the same playbook that he used for *60 Minutes*, but amplified it. Jones released audio of Kelly and himself speaking on the phone, including her explicitly promising that the interview wasn't going to be a hit piece.

"So now they're fucked up," Cernovich explained. "They know he's got the audio. How bad is Alex going to fuck with them? What's he going to do? What's he going to release? He kept putting out video after video after video." Cernovich then flew out to Jones's hometown of Austin and sat there doing Periscope videos. "What we were doing is sucking the oxygen away from the actual hit piece."

Jones and Cernovich weaponized the internet's short attention span and used it against Kelly. Most such oddball stories (remember "covfefe"?) last a day or two in the popular consciousness. Even the United States' withdrawal from the Paris Climate Agreement, a major multinational accord that will supposedly prevent catastrophic planetary outcomes, only received two days' worth of coverage on CNN. The attention span on Twitter is far shorter. After all, it's a social media site that regards a paragraph's worth of text as too long.

"Unconsciously," Cernovich pointed out, "people felt like they'd already watched it. That's why the episode did fewer viewers than an *America's Funniest Home Videos* rerun." By the time it aired, "Megyn Kelly and Alex Jones" was kind of played out, almost literally "yesterday's news." To make matters worse for her, Jones streamed it live and provided live critical commentary on *his* show, denying Kelly viewers.

Despite Kelly's assurances to the contrary, the interview had the exact same tone of fraudulent disbelief and inherent dishonesty as a 1980s Dungeons & Dragons scare piece (they're learning Satanism!). The fact that Donald Trump had once called into Jones's show as a candidate (gasp!) was regarded as so shocking that any actual conclusion didn't even need to be said. But a moment's reflection shows that the sense of terror is absurd. What happened was that a bizarre candidate called into a bizarre show, one with a large audience that he thought would be partial to supporting him.

Here Kelly was borrowing a classic leftist technique: the demand for disavowal. If a given politician or a given political stance attracts the "wrong" type of audience, it's presented as "problematic" on its face. This is the sophisticated version of saying the utterly unsophisticated "If he's fer it, I'm agin' it." In a democracy every person's vote counts, quite literally. Disavowing followers isn't really about denouncing people—they'd probably still maintain their support—so much as it is about genuflecting before the demands of progressivism.

At its root, the same tactic is similar to the insistence that an accused party must somehow prove that they're not a racist, i.e., someone who doesn't care about racism as much as the evangelical left does. Given that the accuser is also the judge and jury, the accused would find themselves doubly submissive if they took the bait. No matter how much mainstream Republicans tried to demonstrate that they weren't racist, the accusations grew *shriller*. They went from being called racist in the sense of prejudiced to blithe accusations of literal white supremacy. This is also a major difference between the New Right and conservatives: refusing to allow the evangelical left to set the terms of debate.

Much of Kelly's piece focused on statements that Jones made about the 2012 Sandy Hook Elementary School shooting. (In

2018 he would be sued by parents livid at his claims that parts of the Sandy Hook massacre were somehow fake.) For Kelly, the key term was Sandy Hook. But for the internet, the key term was 2012. By going back as far as 2012 to find dirt, the implication was that everything that Jones has said since is calm, measured, and reasonable. Meanwhile, arguing over comments that Jones made in 2012 has the relevance in contemporary culture of relitigating the Mitt Romney campaign.

Jones says far more bizarre and incendiary things on a weekly basis. When I was on his show in mid-2017, for example, he drew comparisons between north Korean dictator Kim Jong Un and Hillary Clinton. I tactfully disagreed with the analogy, just as I find it noxious when Trump is referred to as Hitler or "literally" Hitler. Kim Jong Un is responsible for the deaths of many people, including his uncle-in-law and his older half brother. The only person Hillary Clinton is responsible for killing is Vince Foster. (That's a joke; we also know she killed Seth Rich. OK, that's also a joke. It's not like there's a "Clinton death list" anywhere online for people to google.)

Cernovich is perhaps the best member of the New Right when it comes to understanding how the Cathedral works and exploiting its own rules. In November 2017, Cernovich uncovered proof that John Conyers—who had served *fifty* years in Congress—was a "serial sexual predator." Worse, he had used taxpayer money to settle with his victims, with said settlements being kept secret.

Nor was Conyers alone.

Rather than run the piece himself, Cernovich gave it to Buzzfeed. "I could have taken the glory, gaining tremendous fame for myself while humiliating my enemies in the fake news media," he explained. "But if I took this path, the story would have been about me rather than these secret settlements totaling tens of millions of dollars."

His view was absolutely correct. Dozens of articles showed their authors desperately trying to somehow get in an attack on Cernovich, though he had nothing to do with the story itself other than acting as a conduit. "I tipped [Buzzfeed] off and they did the rest," he wrote. "What they did is none of my business and I take zero credit for their work." But in the process Cernovich's credibility was necessarily strengthened. He broke the story, and there was much wringing of hands about why sources were speaking to a "rape apologist," "conspiracy theorist," etc., instead of the "real" reporters.

The New Right seeks to discredit and obliterate the power of the corporate press. "My goal is to destroy the *New York Times* and CNN—and not just them," Andrew Breitbart once explicitly said. In the 1950s, cigarette companies could blithely go on the air and decree that theirs was the healthiest brand to smoke. In this instance, one tobacco company was in fact telling the truth, because by definition there must be a least-harmful brand. Cigarette companies still exist, yet no one would even imagine suggesting that they are healthy in any way or are organizations concerned with one's family or the nation as whole. They are what they are. The New Right goal is for the public to view the corporate press in the exact same way as they view Chesterfields: as self-serving merchants of death who have their own agenda that is often malignant but never healthy. Given how often the press loves to beat the drums of war, this is not hyperbole.

The destruction of the press means unmasking their claim to be objective agents of truth. It is to expose them and humiliate them, individually and collectively. The process is working and frankly is almost a fait accompli. A 2017 Gallup poll found that 36 percent of Americans had very little or no faith in newspapers—an all-time high—and 20 percent had a great deal or quite a lot of faith—an all-time low. By means of comparison, Congress's approval ratings haven't hit 30 percent in any single poll since *2010*. This means the process is working. Once trust is lost, it is very difficult to regain. It is far easier to lose trust than to gain trust, because one lie discredits a speaker far more than one truthful statement gives them credibility.

In 2012, presidential debate moderator Candy Crowley declared that she would interject herself into the debate should she see fit—and she did in fact, forcing the hapless Mitt Romney to fend off both President Obama and the woman who had been selected for a role meant to be impartial. By the 2016 Republican primary debates, the audience was cheering when Ted Cruz berated the moderators over their questions, something which would have seemed insane not too many years prior. Not long after that, nominee Trump pointed directly to the press pool and openly mused about *killing* them to the crowd's great applause. In May 2017, *Guardian* reporter Ben Jacobs tweeted that Montana congressional candidate Greg Gianforte "just body slammed me and broke my glasses." Not only did Gianforte go on to win, reporters couldn't even manage to find *one* voter who dropped their support for him due to the assault.

Destruction means not "playing fair" and taking whatever victories are available. In June 2017, Bill Maher interviewed conservative Republican senator Ben Sasse on his show *Real Time*. "I gotta get to Nebraska more," Maher opined.

"You're welcome," Sasse told him. "We'd love to have you work in the fields with us."

"Work in the fields? Senator, I'm a *house* nigger."

Sasse was taken aback, but this was clearly an unprecedented situation for him. On the one hand, Maher was using a slur. On the other hand, the comedian was being facetious and using the term in reference to himself and not to an actual black person. No doubt taking his cue from the laughing audience, Sasse simply chuckled awkwardly.

Sasse did nothing wrong; he did nothing at all, in fact. Maher used a forbidden offensive word. Both men apologized for what they did—or didn't do. Yet much of the outrage on Twitter came from the New Right trying to add fuel to the fire against both a conservative and a leftist. Nothing came to pass, but things were not done yet.

The Maher incident came a few days after comedian Kathy Griffin posed with a decapitated dummy head of President Trump. The reaction was as swift and violent as an actual beheading. Griffin was summarily dismissed from her annual gig cohosting CNN's New Year's Eve event. Her partner Anderson Cooper, who she considered a close friend, publicly denounced her. Every single venue from her upcoming comedy tour canceled her appearance.

It was very clear that Griffin did not expect this sort of reaction. This is partly due to the circles she runs in. The first rule of improv is, "Yes, and." Meaning, one takes what one is given and escalates it. Clearly, denigrating Trump is simply what one does in Griffin's part of the culture. From there it just becomes an issue of what one *out*does compared to the others, without any input from external elements of the nation.

I suspect if Griffin had clad herself in a hijab, she would have gotten far less of a backlash and would have been able to get away with a simple apology. Instead, in a somewhat rambling press conference, Griffin blamed Trump for the fallout: "A sitting president of the United States and his grown children and the first lady are personally, I feel—personally trying to ruin my life forever, forever. My impression is that they have mobilized their armies or their bots or whatever they do. I—like I said, it's quite clear to me that they're trying to use me as a distraction."

It's not surprising that inherent in Griffin's thinking was the idea that there had to be some leader calling forth his troops. We all tend to need a boogeyman to point to, a villain who embodies our opponents in one person. This is one of the greatest strengths of the New Right: Yes, there are many prominent personalities within the movement. But all of them are, by and large, expendable to varying degrees. Trump is the consequence, not the goal, and most certainly not the head (pun intended) in any sense.

None of my contacts in the New Right were genuinely offended by Kathy Griffin. Most saw what she did as a stupid stunt. A few did view the iconography of decapitation as disturbing, which is understandable. But it was the conservatives who were offended because this was "the president" she was going after. Those on the New Right simply saw this as an opportunity to get a leftist scalp.

A key tactic used by the New Right is forcing the enemy to make difficult choices. Are they going to be held to the principles they espouse, or are they going to be loyal to their own people? When they are in complete control, they can get away with doing both. But if there's pressure, then they will have to choose. In such a case, some will choose the former while others will choose the latter—and both sides will be upset with the other for making the "wrong" choice.

In fact, that is exactly what happened. Some defended Griffin on free-speech grounds. Others felt the need to distance themselves and throw her under the bus. But they did have to choose one or the other. They couldn't play coy, make a mumbling note of disapproval, and then continue on as if nothing had happened. Those days were done—and no one bothered to tell Griffin that. She had said bad things in the past and been forced to apologize for them with no lasting repercussions whatsoever. So what had changed in the meantime? On the surface, in her mind, it was that Trump was now president. It was a logical conclusion to reach—but it was wrong. In fact it only took one more week for the New Right to claim another scalp.

In 2012, Todd Akin was the Republican Senate candidate for

Missouri. Akin also happened to be as dumb as rocks, and I don't even mean the smart kind of rocks. During his campaign, he was asked a very frequent question that pro-lifers have to address: how do you handle the issue when a woman has been raped?

According to Akin, "From what I understand from doctors, that's really rare. If it's a legitimate rape, the female body has ways to try to shut that whole thing down." Whether it's rare or not, the question remains. And in fact Akin got it exactly wrong. According to the book *Sperm Wars*, women are *more* likely to conceive as a result of rape, not less (and definitely not "not at all"). The idea that this profoundly ignorant man would have political power over women's reproductive lives was regarded as obscene, and understandably so.

In this context, Islamic apologist and later CNN host Reza Aslan tweeted, "Just to be clear I was indeed wishing someone would rape Congressman Todd Akin. I'd hate to be misunderstood." Funny? Not really. Profane? Certainly. But the context clearly matters here. This wasn't wishing harm on a politician out of nowhere, but in reaction to their comments.

At the time, nothing came of it. That's because the time was 2012. By 2017, the rules had changed. After Aslan called President Trump a "piece of shit" on Twitter (is that worse than calling him "literally Hitler" and "Antichrist"?), a campaign was launched and Aslan was fired, his series canceled—and to this day he probably still thinks it had something to do with Trump.

Cernovich has taken it upon himself to be one of the organizers of the New Right, and part of what that means is to hold events and bring people (literally) together. The fact that so many members of the subculture are not only anonymous but often geographically removed from one another is an issue. There is a social cost for being a member of the New Right and living in, say, New York City, where a MAGA cap is virtually the equivalent of, if not a swastika, then perhaps a confederate flag.

In that vein, Cernovich announced a series of events called "A Night for Freedom." The first was held in New York City on January 20, 2018. As he explained, "There aren't enough events happening in our community, and most of the stuff happening on the left, right, or center is boring. . . . It's a bunch of people sitting around at tables of 10–12 people eating bland food while a speaker drones on in front of a podium. There's no vibe or excitement. We want to hold a party while providing you an opportunity to hang out in an environment where free speech and open inquiry are welcome . . . and then have a huge party."

I was one of around five speakers, alongside comedian Owen Benjamin, Gavin McInnes, and Canadian philosopher and You-Tuber Stefan Molyneux. One of the big surprise guests was none other than leftist darling Chelsea Manning, who as Bradley Manning had been sentenced to prison for leaking military secrets (and whose sentence was commuted by President Obama after her transition). Manning later claimed to be doing research on the enemy by spying, something which is hard to do when one is the most identifiable person in the room at an event that was widely publicized to be open to all. Her cover story was quickly blown, as photos were unleashed with her previously palling around with various New Right scenesters. (And what of it?)

The event was one of the rare opportunities to see the people who identified with this movement out in public. I was surprised. Unlike the typical autistic behavior so prevalent among libertarians, everyone was well-dressed and well-spoken. The several hundred attendees were respectful, friendly, and informed, and they asked smart, pertinent questions. They were well-adjusted. To have a roomful of people who are virtually all well-adjusted in New York City is a minor miracle.

But then, McInnes was there too. At one point in the evening,

he sidled up to me and launched into one of his hilarious mono-
logues. It's like talking to a great stand-up comedian who hits
you with punchline after punchline but keeps a straight face
even though he knows he's got you good. "Did you see Chelsea
Manning?" he asked.

"Yeah I talked to her."

"Her? Him? I guess I'll say 'her' if she's here. Like, I don't
understand how it works with trannies. Let's suppose you're into
dick. Well, they take estrogen so it makes the dick shrink to like
a baby carrot. If you want dick, you want a big *cock*, like an elephant's trunk. But if you like pussy, you don't want a dick flop-
ping back and forth like windshield wipers. It doesn't make
any sense to me." Each of these sentences was of course punc-
tuated by the appropriate hand motions.

The controversy over transgenderism, bathrooms, and pronoun usage was predicted by Steve Sailer in TakiMag in
2013, over a year before the article that got Gavin fired from
Thought Catalog. For Sailer, "the structure of the dominant
contemporary mindset means that with the triumph of gay
marriage, a need will be felt for a new front in the elite culture
war on average people, with 'transgenderism' (a catch-all phrase
for a variety of complaints) the most likely salient."

Sailer's approach here is common to him and emblematic of
New Right analysis. Similarly, he has put forth "Sailer's Law of
Female Journalism," which holds that "[t]h most heartfelt articles by female journalists tend to be demands that social values
be overturned in order that, Come the Revolution, the journalist herself will be considered hotter-looking." Instead of focusing on what a given article says—or in this case a given class of
articles—the salient question for Sailer is: What caused this article to be written in the first place? What purpose does it
serve?

In a New Right context, where objective journalism is either impossible or extremely rare, the tendency is to focus on the writer or publication's given agenda. There is an idea among moderates of both sides of the aisle that we should focus on ideas and assume that fair-acting people can independently come to different conclusions. While this may hold true in interpersonal relationships, the idea that this holds true when it comes to members of the press is rejected in toto.

An example of this sort of thinking could be seen between CNN's Jim Acosta and President Trump in the wake of the president allegedly referring to various countries as shitholes in January 2018. "Did you say that you wanted more people from Norway?" asked Acosta. "Is that true, Mr. President?"

"I want them to come in from everywhere," Trump replied. "Thank you very much everybody."

"Just Caucasian or white countries, sir? Or do you want people to come in from other parts of the world, people of color?"

Trump pointed at Acosta and just said, "Out!" There was no attempt to engage with the blatant accusation of racism, no pretense that he could or should try to bring Acosta around to his point of view. This was not an honest disagreement that could be resolved through discussion. This was someone with an agenda, dishonestly impugning motives, in the guise of a question.

The axiomatic belief that antiprogressivism and racism are quite literally synonymous forced an embarrassing *New York Times* correction about McInnes's Proud Boys group in June 2017: "As the article correctly notes, while most members who are recruited are white, there are also small numbers of nonwhites in the group. It is not a rule that all members be white."

That an organization would appeal disproportionately to whites is not a problem if said organization is part and parcel of progressive culture, like Whole Foods, the official supermarket of Stuff White People Like. Otherwise, things are suspicious. The fight for desegregation will never stop of its own accord. For the evangelical left, until and unless there are people of color in every possible venue—even the planet Vulcan—the crusade must continue on. It will never be enough.

11

★

EGO

Give me four years to teach the children and the seed
I have sown will never be uprooted.

—Vladimir Lenin

Across the street from Alexander Hamilton's grave is my
friend Alex's apartment. Alex intermittently holds events there,
small gatherings featuring guests ranging across the political
spectrum from socialist-anarchists to "shitlords" and everyone
in between. The end results are something like a real-life equivalent of the Jabba the Hutt sequence from *Return of the Jedi*,
populated by aliens of every possible shape and size. The
attendees are all political outliers in their own way, but in this
neutral space they can have discussions without raising one
another's hackles. Like Jabba's palace on Tatooine, Alex's events
feature a mix of people who normals might regard as grotesque
but who are actually nothing of the sort. I first met Mike Cernovich there, and for a while the Nazi (as in swastika tattoo)
hacker weev crashed there as well. (Yes, Alex is Jewish.)

I met Milo Yiannopoulos there in mid-February 2016. He

didn't even stand out that much, certainly not compared to the (literally) seven-foot-tall weightlifter in attendance. The thing about Milo is that he's clearly and unabashedly a performer. This does not make him a phony or insincere. It just means he knows how to put on an entertaining show, something many conservatives are incapable of doing.

Milo was going to be on a popular program, and the two of us figured out how he could call the host a "cuck" to their face without it being an incident (something he went on to pull off fabulously, as he is wont to do). After the game plan was set he declared that I was "a Machiavellian imp," which isn't as good as *Observer* calling me a "Nietzschean weasel" but far better than *The Onion*'s claim that I'm a "human cockroach." My impression of Milo was that he was like a WWE heel, the bad guy in wrestling who knows how to get the audience riled up even though they are in on the gag. Like the late Randy "Macho King" Savage, for example, Milo has come out to speak while seated on a throne hoisted on the shoulders of a group of men. Another time he appeared in drag as his femme persona "Ivana Wall." His constant smirk—far less present "offscreen"—is the classic villain's wordless sign of contempt for his foes.

Yet as I've had to explain to many people, there *is* a there there when it comes to Milo. Comedians are often very bright people whose minds work quickly and who see things that others don't—and often get people riled up in the process. Somehow when it comes to humor and politics, this insight escapes them entirely. After all, why would someone who was capable of calm, insightful dialogue engage in near buffoonery? Several reasons: First, it disarms one's foes because they underestimate you. Second, it allows you to stand out. Third, it's easier to persuade people via entertaining anecdotes than rote argument. Finally, it's fun as hell.

It's in this context that members of the New Right engage

in what Yiannopoulos has described as "performative racism." When Microsoft launched an artificial intelligence chat bot in March 2016, it took internet trolls less than a day to figure out how to make her say things like "I fucking hate feminists and they should all die and burn in hell" and "Hitler would have done a better job than the monkey we have got now." Activism in the form of anti-anti-racism became a new strategy designed to make the left feel unsafe and to prove their tacit assurances of increasing cultural hegemony were a lie.

Several weeks after Alex's event, Milo was back in town and had me as a guest on his podcast. When I met him in his hotel room, the only really flamboyant parts of his wardrobe were the pearl bracelets he wore. Strewn throughout the room were plenty of pieces of Louis Vuitton luggage (really, girl?), as well as several young men in various states of slumber. To be clear, these weren't lovers of his. All straight, they were members of the Milo Family. It's like a fabulous version of the Manson Family, but they kill on stage and on social media (except for Twitter, which banned his handle @nero in July 2016).

I was prepared to engage in verbal repartee when we started to record, but Milo was not only prepared but almost deferential. Being good at banter—and Milo is world class—heavily depends on actually listening to the other party so one can knock their comment out of the park. "When you interview, do, 'Compliment, compliment, question,'" he told me. At the time, Milo still hadn't come up with a title for his forthcoming book. Given his nickname for then-candidate Trump, I suggested that he call it *Daddy Issues*. This would have been perfectly apt at the time, but would have blown up in his face terribly after what ended up happening later.

Milo had already been the object of a great many attacks, being called a Nazi, a fascist, a white supremacist, and everything in between. Amazingly, many conservatives had thought that because Milo was gay, partly Jewish, and very fond of being plowed by black men that he would be in some sense inoculated from leftist criticism. This is a fundamental misunderstanding of how the evangelical left operates. For them, a person's actual identity does not really matter. A person's actual actions do not really matter. What matters is the destruction of the heretic, and to take their criticisms and worldview at face value is to give them a validity that they do not possess. Worse, doing so is ceding control of the conceptual framework to them.

Yet, none of the attacks on Milo were sticking. One of the first *effective* attacks on Milo came from Ryan Holiday. The aforementioned Mr. Holiday's *Trust Me, I'm Lying* is a case study in how to exploit the media to create publicity for clients. Take the story of how he generated free buzz for his client Tucker Max's movie *I Hope They Serve Beer in Hell*: "After placing a series of offensive ads on buses and the metro," Holiday recalled, "from my office I alternated between calling in angry complaints to the Chicago CTA and sending angry emails to city officials with reporters cc'd, until 'under pressure,' they announced that they would be banning our advertisements and returning our money. Then we put out a press release denouncing this cowardly decision." It was free press and it was good press; not only did it spread the word about Max's film but it also gave him the appearance of standing up against political correctness run amok—when in fact no one actually cared until Holiday forced them to.

Holiday is not a member of the New Right. In July 2016 he even wrote an article titled "Dear Dad, Please Don't Vote for Donald Trump." "I find it disgusting to hear him talk about banning Muslims from America," wrote Holiday. "That's not what you taught me. That's not how this country is supposed to work."[1]

Holiday is one of the most perceptive people in the world when it comes to how media actually operates. As such, his analysis of the Cathedral—or the communications aspect, at least—is fairly close if not identical to how it is viewed by the New Right. His entire book describes how the internet and emotions form a kind of snake eating its own tail, where truth falls away and emotion and tribalism reign supreme.

It's therefore no surprise at all that he didn't see Milo as a Nazi or a self-hating gay man or a pawn of forces greater than himself. In February 2017, Holiday took a direct shot at Milo in an article with a fairly blatant title: "I Helped Create the Milo Trolling Playbook. You Should Stop Playing Right into It." "Numerous leaders of the alt-right [*sic*] movement read the book I published in 2012, which outlined exactly how this media strategy works," wrote Holiday. "Several have told me *Trust Me, I'm Lying* is their bible."[2]

The strategy that Holiday lays out is indisputably true: "Someone like Milo or Mike Cernovich doesn't care that you hate them—they like it. It's proof to their followers that they are doing something subversive and meaningful. [. . .] The key tactic of alternative or provocative figures is to leverage the size and platform of their 'not-audience' (i.e. their haters in the mainstream) to attract attention and build an actual audience."

This brings up a very key point that is often glossed over in discussions of Milo and the New Right. There is an implicit assumption that subversion is its own reward, that those who seek to tear down do so merely for the sake of tearing things down. The arsonist does not plan to be a developer, after all. Yes, the juvenile punk desire to "get pissed and destroy" often does not have any articulate replacement in mind. Yet to equate subversion and meaninglessness is inaccurate, especially with regards to the New Right. There are many arsonists, but there are many developers among them as well. The confusion comes because

while there is consensus regarding destruction, there is none regarding whether that empty lot will be replaced by a church, a
castle, or a digital experience.

In early 2017, a planned appearance by Milo at UC Berkeley
was canceled after rioting there grew so bad that actual fires
started on campus. While the New Right ideal is for the universities to be burnt to the ground—perhaps with the earth
salted so no life could ever grow there again—I had always taken
this goal to be figurative and not literal.

Some on the New Right took this as evidence of how far gone
the evangelical left has become. The fact that Berkeley was home
to the 1960s Free Speech movement was not lost on anyone. I
took the other perspective: that the rioting and fires were some
of the best things that could have ever happened to defeat the
evangelical left in their own monasteries.

The Ferguson riots of 2014 immediately preceded the mid-
term elections, where the Republicans picked up a mindbog-
gling sixty-three seats in the House and six seats in the Senate.
(Fun fact: the Wikipedia entry is listed as "Ferguson unrest,"
which is the leftist euphemism for rioting.) Regardless of one's
politics—hell, regardless of whether one is a human being or an
animal—there is a universal consensus that fire is bad. To see
buildings burning leads anyone to say, "Whatever this is, I am
against it."

At the same time, the corporate press did a phenomenal job
of not just excusing the rioting but occasionally even glorify-
ing it. The implicit message was, this is what we are for. The in-
stinctive, natural reaction was to run in the other direction. A
similar phenomenon famously happened with the 1968 Democratic convention, where moderate and apolitical voters re-
coiled at the violence.

To remove the façade of respectability from the universities,
things like Berkeley need to happen. Banning speakers is not

enough; a person not speaking isn't a visual. There is nothing to see, nothing to react to. Burning buildings demonstrate that the universities are, at the very least, hardly bastions of civility.

What finally brought Milo, if not down, then back on his heels were previous comments he had made on various podcasts about his own sexual awakening. In February 2017, comments he had made over a year prior became widely disseminated online with all the marks of a hit job. Milo apparently lost his virginity to a Catholic priest. "I'm grateful for Father Michael," he said. "I wouldn't give nearly such good head if it wasn't for him."

In any other context, an LGBT activist would point out the concept of "heteronormativity." Meaning, it is unethical to expect gays and lesbians to live by heterosexual standards. It's not "gays are OK because they're just like us," it's "gays have the right to live on their own terms." As Milo put it in that same podcast, "In the gay world, some of the most important enriching, and incredibly life-affirming, important, shaping relationships are between younger boys and older men. They can be hugely positive experiences very often for those young boys."

For decades it was not uncommon for older gay men to initiate younger ones into the lifestyle. In fact it was to be expected; a closeted and confused young gay man would need someone to guide him and let him know that he's not as alone in his proclivities as he might feel. As a consequence, historically, there was a huge cultural perception that homosexuality and pedophilia were virtually identical. When Milo spoke of being taken advantage of as a young man by an older one and enjoying it, he was either (a) the victim of statutory rape and trying to deal with that in his own way or (b) telling the truth and pointing out that male/male standards shouldn't be expected to be the same as male/female ones.

What people *heard* was: pedophilia is OK. A Facebook post of his titled "A note for idiots" tried to clarify his position:

"I have outed THREE pedophiles in my career as a journalist. That's three more than any of my critics and a peculiar strategy for a supposed pedophile apologist. [. . .] I *did* joke about giving better head as a result of clerical sexual abuse committed against me when I was a teen. If I choose to deal in an edgy way on an internet livestream with a crime I was the victim of that's my prerogative. It's no different to gallows humor from AIDS sufferers." He also clarified the specifics of his interaction: "I was talking about my own relationship when I was 17 with a man who was 29. The age of consent in the UK is 16."

It didn't work. Milo's book was canceled. He was publicly uninvited from CPAC, and he left Breitbart as well. Milo is a great case study in how the politics of taboo and heresy are used not to fight ideas but to defeat the people who hold said ideas. Heresy works almost like an online hyperlink. It attaches concepts to a subject via a keyword that is imprecise, and then the mind fills in the rest. In this case the terms "pedophile" and "child molester" were successfully linked in the media's collective mind with Milo's name. And for those in the media who weren't really keeping tabs on Milo, a suggestion to work with him would quickly become, "Isn't he the pedophile guy?"

All that was necessary was for the term to somehow be associated with him. From that point on, it's how he came to be regarded in the eyes of the media and therefore in some sense with the public. It was the corporate press's way of giving him a warning label: He's a pedophile! No need to continue listening![3] The equivalent would be if every article about Bill Clinton mentioned as an aside that he was impeached—and identified the correct reasons for it. The frequent claim that Clinton was "impeached for having sex with an intern" (as opposed to perjury and obstruction of justice) is like claiming a drunk driver was arrested for choosing the wrong beverage to go with his dinner.

After Simon & Schuster canceled his book, Milo went ahead

and put it out anyway. His face was plastered all over the New York City subways and buses, and the book hit the *New York Times* bestseller list. Soon after the book's release, *Out* magazine ran a blatantly false headline: "Nobody is Buying Milo Yiannopoulos' Memoir." In the article, the author admitted that "[s]ince launching on July 4, Dangerous has sold 18,268 copies in the US"—an impressive number by publishing standards. Sure enough, the author was quick to claim that Milo is someone "who's openly voiced support for child abuse" and that 18,268 copies was 18,268 too many. The idea that literally no one should be reading Milo's book is totalitarian in its claim, and absurd on its face.

Yet Milo's setbacks—hardly a complete defeat—affected the New Right not at all. The attack model is quickly becoming an outdated one. Both political parties operate under a system where leaders are taken out with no one to replace them. The highly effective attacks on George W. Bush and Hillary Clinton, respectively, had enormous consequences for their underlings and supporters.

But as its detractors fear and they themselves understand, the New Right might be more akin to al-Qaeda in its structure. Killing Osama bin Laden was symbolically important, and it prevented him from further plotting mass murder. Al-Qaeda is by all accounts a shadow of its former self. Yet terrorist attacks continue unabated, and instead of al-Qaeda we are dealing with ISIS—a group that doesn't seem to have even a nominal leader.

Similarly, taking down Milo was a mere speedbump. Closing down a New Right message board such as /r/TheDonald would silence discourse until a new location could be found. Given how easy this would be to do, and how quickly the location of the new board would be disseminated, it would probably set things back by a mere day or two.

And in fact, Milo was resilient enough to handle the blows and maintain an audience despite it all. In July 2017 he filed suit against Simon & Schuster for canceling his book. Two months later, word got out that Milo was planning a Free Speech Week at Berkeley. I was as dumbfounded to see that I was publicly announced as a speaker about Islam as I was to see *Vanity Fair* describe me as a conservative writer (the correction came quite swiftly). Apparently some of the speakers had never even been approached to begin with. Charles Murray, author of *The Bell Curve*, explicitly said, "The inclusion of my name in the list of speakers was done without my knowledge or permission. I will add that I would never under any circumstances appear at an event that included Milo Yiannopoulos."[4] He further told the *Chronicle of Higher Education* that he wouldn't appear with Milo because he's "a despicable asshole."

In October 2017, Joe Bernstein wrote a devastating attack on Milo and Breitbart for Buzzfeed. Depending on your perspective, Milo was either palling around with the worst of the worst—the hacker weev again makes an appearance—or being a responsible journalist and asking them to explain their points of view in their own words. But it did not help his case that his email password began with "LongKnives1290." As Bernstein explained, "The Night of the Long Knives was the Nazi purge of the leadership of the SA. The purge famously included Ernst Röhm, the SA's gay leader. 1290 is the year King Edward I expelled the Jews from England."[5]

A month later, his sponsor Robert Mercer publicly cut ties with him—and not very tactfully either: "In my opinion, actions of and statements by Mr. Yiannopoulos have caused pain and divisiveness undermining the open and productive discourse that I had hoped to facilitate," Mercer wrote. "I was mistaken to have supported him, and for several weeks have been in the process of severing all ties with him."[6]

His lawsuit against Simon & Schuster did not go well. He fired his lawyer and decided to represent himself—not a genuinely recommended legal strategy. As he explained, it was "partly because me and my attorneys had a different strategy—and partly because I'm between billionaires at the moment and it was costing me a hundred grand a month." He asked to drop the case entirely in February 2018.

The three legs of the progressive stool are the universities, the media, and the government. For the New Right, the universities are the source of the other two. Virtually everyone in media, especially journalism, is a college graduate. With few, if any, exceptions, every member of Congress is a college graduate, most of whom have law degrees to boot. Andrew Breitbart saw this analysis as essential, writing, "The left does not win its battles in debate. It doesn't have to. In the twenty-first century, media is everything. The left wins because it controls the narrative. The narrative is controlled by the media. The left is the media. Narrative is everything."[7] This is why the conservative insistence on fighting the government in Washington is somewhat doomed from the start. Fighting DC is like arresting the street dealer, who is the end point in the drug trade. It's the most visible aspect of the problem, sure, but it doesn't address the source of the spreading contamination.

The New Right and other cultural actors have done an enormous amount of work to discredit the press and the government. The last target for them to eviscerate is the universities. This is a trickier task, but the wheels are already in motion. For decades, going to college was the acme of bourgeois aspirations. The idea of being the first person in one's family to receive a degree speaks to the heart of the American dream, where every generation does better than the one that preceded it. Here was concrete, demonstrable proof that progress was being made.

There is little dispute that a college degree is considered to be highly desirable—if not downright necessary—for career advancement in America. Politicians of both parties speak so often about the importance of higher education that such expressions have become vapid clichés that can be uttered by Bernie Sanders as easily as by Jeff Sessions. Yet other than those schools that have no set curriculum, every other major and second-tier liberal arts university has some sort of progressive propaganda course as a requirement for every student.

The universities' explicit goal is to train the next generation's elites. No one disputes this, though some prefer to use platitudes like "training the leaders of tomorrow." This is a banal way of obscuring an important point: Are the leaders being trained to be leaders? Or are they being trained to be evangelists? The answer is both, and for the New Right it is the second group that is the enemy.

To call something a conspiracy theory—even an actual conspiracy—is akin to calling it "racist." It's a mechanism to dismiss a subject or speaker without having to engage with their ideas. Technically speaking, the Constitutional Convention—a small elite who swore their discussions to secrecy— was a conspiracy. We don't use the term to describe it as such, since we like those fine men.

To be sure, conspiracies usually have a nefarious, covert goal. The New Right views the college system as having such a goal, though most others do not. But if the goal of the universities isn't universally understood to be nefarious, it *is* unambiguously covert—and it is so by design and has been since the beginning.

It is not just the New Right but virtually every right-wing publication that thinks the universities have gotten out of control. *National Review* regularly has articles pointing out madness on campus. The idea is that this is new, and it's constantly hammered as a largely unprecedented phenomenon in New

Right circles. Yet this is not true, at least not entirely. For over a century, universities have been designed to promulgate a leftist takeover and control of American society—and it's a story that has only been uncovered fully in recent years.

The secret origin of the evangelical left and their vision for what universities can do was uncovered by Thomas C. Leonard, who is ironically a research scholar at Woodrow Wilson's very own Princeton University. Leonard's 2015 book *Illiberal Reformers* is ostensibly about "Race, Eugenics, and American Economics in the Progressive Era." He sets out to make the little-disputed claim that early progressivism was involved in certain things that are anathema to the contemporary left. Conservatives like to point this out as leftist hypocrisy, yet no one cares. Conservatives of today vary greatly from the conservatives of a century ago as well. This isn't hypocrisy so much as the development of an ideology.

The first half of Leonard's book ("The Progressive Ascendancy") describes how early progressives consciously and successfully set out to change the university system in order to produce a self-perpetuating elite to engineer (read: rule) every aspect of American society. As Leonard puts it, the book "tells the story of the progressive scholars and activists who enlisted in the Progressive Era crusade to dismantle laissez-faire and remake American economic life through the agency of an administrative state."[8]

Leonard begins his tale in the snidely titled Gilded Age. "The new research universities, exemplified by Johns Hopkins University (1876), were founded not to reproduce their faculties but to send civic-minded men and women into the world so they might improve it."[9] Preaching what they referred to as "the social gospel" (fairly close to today's "social justice"), these types (just as today) saw their path to moral redemption as one via helping others as opposed to merely living an upstanding life of integrity. There is an easy argument to make that an upstanding life of integrity precisely does mean helping others. Yet for the evangelical left, their moral righteousness gives them the right and even the duty to rope third parties into their machinations, and this is where the departure lies.

Across the Atlantic, the innocuously titled (and quite prestigious) London School of Economics was founded in 1895 by members of the Fabian Society. The Fabians were socialists in the true sense of the term, not in the Bernie Sanders welfare-state sense of the term. They were against profit and thought the government should run industry. They also realized that proclaiming such views openly would not go over well with the general population. As such, their chosen symbol was *literally* a wolf in sheep's clothing. When that was perceived as being perhaps a touch too brazen and nefarious, they changed it to a tortoise. Slow and steady wins the race, and the nation. The Fabians were instrumental in forming the contemporary Labour Party in the United Kingdom.

Here in the United States, the similarly benignly-titled American Economic Association was founded in 1885. Unlike in the United Kingdom, where leftism was far more secular, the social gospel was very much rooted in the literal Gospel. "Of the AEA's fifty-five charter members," Leonard points out, "twenty-three were clergymen." This is no coincidence. The rise of Darwinism caused an existential crisis among many religious people in the West. To this day, Buchanan and similar thinkers recognize that denying evolution is essential to their worldview.

As Leonard describes it, "In redirecting American Protestantism from saving souls to saving society, the social gospelers enlarged and transformed the idea of Christian redemption."[10] No longer about the individual soul, their newfound perspective was that "society was the proper object of redemption." This thinking is still heard today in such phrases as "nations are judged by how they treat the weakest among us." This thinking also underlies the mantra that America is white supremacist, racist, and even sometimes "the most racist country in the world." It's all about the intangible doctrine of original sin, not about anything actually quantifiable.

The technicalities of how to reorient the country via the government was not being taught on these shores, even at fair Harvard. To learn how to remake America through the state required taking lessons from those who were the best engineers—social and otherwise—in the world: the Germans. "American reformers traveled to the German universities," explains Leonard, "which, in the 1870s and early 1880s, were regarded as the world's finest in political economy."[11]

"The AEA was organized not merely to arrange scholarly meetings and promote the field," Leonard writes. "The AEA was formed to exclude other claimants to economic knowledge by making them outsiders and amateurs."[12] Since they couldn't get the government to give them a de jure monopoly, they needed the imprimatur of the universities to give them a de facto one. Things came to a head with the New Deal and FDR's "brain trust." Now the educated and enlightened would save capitalism from itself and also America in the process. A strongly regulated economy became the order of the day, and this was a major focus of leftist politics until the 1960s.

With the rise of the New Left and the victories of the civil rights movement, the evangelical left now had a firm moral victory over their opponents. Very quickly, the university takeover—and the training of the next generation—became complete. From the New Right perspective, those newfound women's studies, African American studies, queer studies, and other similar departments can be simply regarded as propaganda in pink, brown, black, or lavender hues. Though the *subjects* of their interest changed, their background philosophy—the Christian social gospel—had not. Yet they didn't have the historical perspective or self-awareness to even realize it.

12

*

THE DIVINE MISS C

When I am weaker than you, I ask you for freedom
because that is according to your principles; when I am
stronger than you, I take away your freedom because
that is according to my principles.

FRANK HERBERT

VDARE.com is named after Virginia Dare, the first English
child born in the New World. The site is run by Peter Brimelow,
who had been a *National Review* editor and contributor until
being purged in 1998. I first heard of VDARE around 2012,
thanks to my friend Magus. Magus was my first contact with
NRx, and he regularly posted articles from VDARE on his Facebook feed. In 2014 he had attended the annual VDARE Christmas [*sic*] party and had been shocked to see Ann Coulter in
attendance, even though her columns were frequently published
on the site. "She didn't need to be there," he pointed out to me.
"It could hurt her more than help her. Very cool of her to come."

Like any troll, I had long had an appreciation for Ann Coulter. This is the woman who was better than pretty much anyone at taking basic conservative ideas and saying them in such
provocative ways that leftists could no longer maintain their

façade of genteel decency. In 2002 she had likened Katie Couric to Eva Braun in her book *Slander*. Couric challenged her about it on *The Today Show*, the epicenter of calm morning America: "You call me the Eva Braun of liberalism—"

"*Affable*," Coulter cheerfully added. (She had in fact called her "the affable Eva Braun of morning television.")

Years later, said Eva Braun—affable or otherwise—was exposed on social media for deceptively editing an interview in order to diminish her antiprogressive interviewees. Couric is not regarded as a con woman, but she is no longer unironically regarded as America's sweetheart either. More recently, however, Coulter has taken a turn toward the serious. In 2015 she was a guest on Kennedy's eponymous Fox Business show. As the segment was wrapping, Kennedy threw one last question at her. "We're running out of time: Are you fun?"

"Um . . . that's a silly question," said Coulter.

"Yes, it is!" Kennedy smiled.

"I don't answer silly questions."

"Ann, come on!"

"That should tell you something about me. No silly questions."

"I think the question answers itself," Kennedy quipped. "I've heard from mutual friends that you're a very fun person."

Coulter said nothing and just sat there as Kennedy cut to commercial. This was not in keeping with the Coulter I had witnessed from afar. Nor was it in keeping with the Coulter who I too had heard, repeatedly, was a very fun person. Not fun in a frivolous, airheaded party-girl sense, but warm, conversational, and down-to-earth.

As I began to explore the world of the New Right, I realized that attending the 2016 VDARE Christmas party would probably be highly informative. On December 8, 2016, I sent Magus a text. "When's the VDARE party this year?" I asked him.

"It's tomorrow."

"Do you think I can go?"

It turned out that freedom isn't free after all, and in fact it even had a cover charge since the event was for donors only. "I'm donating the 100 bucks," Magus texted me, "consider it my Christmas present to my friend the Joo ;)"

On December 9, I headed to the Upper East Side to one of those antiquated social clubs where people like myself aren't their kind of people. Not to say Jews per se, but urban loud-mouths. On a side table were rows of buttons reading "Please, wish me a Merry Christmas." I glanced around the nametags in the room until I saw someone with a last name ending in -stein. It was then that I felt like a tourist but not an imposter.

There were about thirty-five people there, seven of whom were women. Virtually everyone was white, which in the sociology of the evangelical left is not only noteworthy but actually a problem. Frankly I'm surprised that anti-Constitutionalism isn't more of a current in leftist thinking, given the homogeneity of the Founding Fathers. Sure they had extreme differences of opinion and represented two or more differing cultures. But they were all white men, and therefore anything they created is suspect or even nefarious by definition, right?

In the corner of the room was a group of professional carolers clad in traditional garb, the sort of clothes you would see in an old-timey Christmas card. I overheard two guys in their early twenties trying to be edgy with their quips. "I'd rather live under white supremacy than any other kind of supremacy!" one said, to the other's laughter. Not only did the joke not land, it didn't even make any sense. The second and third most murderous regimes were those of Hitler and Stalin. Mao was of course Chinese, and "Asian supremacy" would surely have been the guy's second choice.

Everyone at the event was quite friendly. A man around my age chatted me up. He told me about a Trump rally he had attended where Christian fundamentalists were praying to God to keep Trump's plane safe, laughing at the contradiction between being so religious and yet so devoted to a foulmouthed multiple adulterer. "It was funny after election day," he recalled. "People were either hysterical or smart enough to ape being sad."

I had made the same observation myself. Hell, it was unavoidable. For some progressives, the problem was that a vote for Trump wasn't just wrong or ignorant or even simply racist. It was "explicitly," "clearly," and "blatantly" a vote for white supremacism. At the same time, very, very few people publicly identify as white supremacist or even tacitly speak well of them. Thus, the conclusion was straightforward: Many people who claimed to be moderate or even broadly liberal were, in fact, closeted white supremacists. They might act one way in public but their actions, again, were "explicit," "clear," and "blatant." Everyone knew Trump was the devil. They chose to vote for the devil after being *informed* that he was the devil.

For the evangelical left, majority rule is not as valid when the majority is white. For months and years leading up to 2016, leftists were ecstatic that we were "finally" going to be a minority-majority country just as our Founding Fathers didn't intend but surely meant to. When that didn't happen on schedule, they had a meltdown. The reaction was like that of any cult when the predicted end times—a necessary step toward heaven-on-earth—is put off.

Worse, their fort had been breached. Bad outsiders with evil thoughts had infiltrated their schools, their offices, their neighborhoods—even their electorate. There was no way of knowing how many of them there were, or *who* they were. It's impossible to "regroup" without sorting out who belongs in the group and who most certainly does not. Far too many people were imposters who looked just like "us."

So what do social animals do when separated from their group? They vocalize. A wolf's howl can be heard for miles. Elephants rumble subliminally. Then the call is repeated by others, and the group reestablishes itself. Reciprocal vocalization is a simple and effective way for social animals (including humans) to bond, or to re-bond as necessary.

This led to the November 2016 phenomenon of anguish signaling. It allowed those who genuinely felt unsafe, who no longer felt themselves surrounded by the unanimous consensus that they viewed as their social backdrop, to regain some sense of stability. By having the displays be as intense and *public* as possible, it let the true believers recognize one another for who they were and to start to redraw the boundaries of their particular subculture. *You're making the same sounds as I am? The emotion behind them feels as sincere as mine? Then we can trust each other.*

It's in this context that the 2017 storming of the Central Park stage by Jack Posobiec and Laura Loomer makes sense. The performance was of *Julius Caesar* with contemporary elements, with Caesar-as-Trump being murdered every single time. Their invading of the theater was meant to demonstrate to the left that there is no safe place for them. Pauline Kael's Nixonless sociological fortress was a luxury that contemporary leftists could not share.

"So what is it you do?" asked my fellow partygoer.

"I'm a columnist for *Observer*," I told him.

He blanched. "You're not filing a piece on *this*, are you?"

I realized that the gathering was a safe space for these people, that nowhere else could they state their views without fear of repercussion—views that had been quite mainstream for all of American history until quite recently. Supporting VDARE was akin to being gay fifty years ago; not just a firing offense but also a perversion of what is holy. You gotta keep the kids safe!

Then Gavin McInnes came in. On his "My Name Is:" sticker he had written "Yes, this is a herpes sore" lest there be any confusion. McInnes wasn't particularly surprised or worried about seeing me and greeted me warmly. He's one of the funniest people I know, in that he is able to talk smack quite well to the point where you have no choice but to laugh with him. After I did a podcast where I talked about my denim collection, he really let me have it: "You've been in this country since you were a kid," he pointed out. "How are you acting like you just stepped off of the boat yesterday? 'Oh, in America, I can haf all the jeans I vant! Vat an amazing country!'"

Magus had told me that Coulter was scheduled to attend. In the previous months she had followed me on Twitter, unfollowed me, and then refollowed me. It was one of the most important—and one-sided—(social media) relationships in my life. I wasn't exactly crying into my pillow like a high schooler, screaming, "She doesn't even know I'm alive!" But you don't actually need a pillow to cry on, so there's that.

As the night went on I could hear people muttering about where she was. Eyes kept glancing to the door, as the number of people trickling in came to a halt. Coulter finally arrived, about an hour after me. When Ann Coulter walks into a room full of the New Right, it's not the same thing as, say, Avril Lavigne (is she still a thing?) walking into a room of her fans. Coulter is tall, thin, and blonde, and she is easy to spot. One by one, little pauses in conversations occurred as people noticed her arrival. Here and there around the room partygoers started to cast side glances, like dogs scared to make eye contact yet still keeping their attention focused on the target. The vibe had very clearly shifted. It was like the precise moment in a movie theater when the previews are over and the film is about to begin.

There weren't *that* many people at the party, and most were scared to approach Coulter. The thing with right-wingers, especially slightly older ones, is that they're very, very polite. So no matter how much they wanted to talk with OMG ANN COULTER, they hadn't actually been introduced and were thus in a bit of a quandary. I caught one woman asking Coulter for an autograph and a photo (*not* a selfie). Coulter happily signed a copy of *VDARE* magazine. "No pictures," she said, firmly but with a smile. "It ruins the party for Ann."

I didn't know what to do. I wasn't starstruck but I also didn't want to make an ass of myself—not to the Queen of Trolls. Then I realized that I had an intermediary. Coulter had been on McInnes's show many times and I knew that the two of them were buddies. I pulled him out of his conversation and asked for his help. "Gavin, Ann's here," I told him. "I've never met her and I don't know what to say. Can you introduce me?"

The look on McInnes's face was a look I knew very well, for it was one that I gave all the time. It was a smirk, but not just a look of arrogance. It was a smirk where you have someone right where you want them, and you both know it, and the victim himself can also see the humor in the situation. So here was my personal karma for being so gleefully insufferable so much of the time. In that moment Gavin was my personal Picture of Dorian Gray, a reflection of my conscience but one that was far older, far uglier, and with a weak chin. Also far uglier—yes, it bears repeating.

Far older.

"Well," McInnes said, aging and uglifying right before my eyes, "she looks pretty busy. It doesn't seem like it's a good time."

"*Gavin.*"

The grin grew even broader, though admittedly it was hard for me to look him in his old stupid ugly face. "Maybe next year," McInnes said. "If not then, there's the year after that."

He had me and he had me good. Coulter made her way over to the two of us and greeted him. McInnes went to introduce me but she interjected. "I know you," she commented.

"Yeah, you followed me on Twitter, then unfollowed and refollowed."

She laughed. "Was it a quick unfollow? You must have retweeted someone I hate." We made some small talk about people we both knew, and for someone who has a reputation for being abrasive, Coulter acted like she'd known me for years. It was entirely at odds with her super-WASPiness.

A short while later, Peter Brimelow introduced Coulter to the crowd so that she could deliver an impromptu speech. It was like listening to an inverted Dorothy Parker: instead of using humor to make a subtler point, Ann's worldview was transparent and her approach one of stridency. She seemed as irritated at what was happening in politics as she was by the fact that pointing these things out was in any way controversial. "I'll believe Muslims are scared when the first one leaves," she frowned. "Unless you're the descendent of African slaves, I don't want to hear from you about racism. What do we owe *Somalis*?" To hear the left tell it, we are a nation of immigrants who must also pay restitution for slavery.

In a sense Coulter's worldview is akin to that of the backdrop of Ayn Rand's *Atlas Shrugged*—America is the last holdout against a world populated largely (or exclusively) by socialist "people's states." Reagan made the same point as early as 1964: "If we lose freedom here, there is no place to escape to. This is the last stand on Earth."

Coulter's 2015 polemic *¡Adios, America!* was perhaps the most influential book of the 2016 presidential campaign. The subtitle makes her stance quite clear, as the book describes *The Left's Plan to Turn Our Country into a Third World Hellhole*. As with much of New Right thinking, Coulter finds as much fault with conservatives as with the left, blaming country-club Republicans' commitment to immigration on their need for cheap labor in the workplace and cheap domestics at home.

There are very many talking points defending immigration in the zeitgeist. One is that you're more likely to die by lightning than via a terrorist attack! This is like saying that rarer illnesses shouldn't be treated, since one is far more likely to be felled by heart disease. Another is that we are frequently reminded that Muslims are, by far, the biggest *targets* of terrorism. But why we should be importing targets of terrorism is a question left unanswered.

The fact that it's not about terrorism but about preserving American culture is almost literally incomprehensible to the evangelical left. It's similar to the Cold War, when Soviet leaders constantly and explicitly promised to take over the world—only to have progressives in the United States insist that they didn't *really* mean it.

Leftists need to believe that all religions are the same, because to them religion is largely indistinguishable from custom. Just open any newspaper and there are more examples of Muslim feminists than you can count—as if this is the median Islamic position anywhere on earth, even in the West. Therefore, for the left, we are to consider Islam for most intents and purposes as not so much a religion as a tradition.

This thinking is also why the evangelical left is so often hostile to conservative Christians: it's not the Christianity that bothers them so much as the repudiation of progressivism. Being explicitly Christian is one of the few things that gives people social cover to freely espouse antiprogressive views. The conflict is a sectarian one and therefore quite intense.

The New Right fear is that Muslim immigration can only lead to the suppression of Western values in order to accommodate those whose religion demands severe cultural restrictions. It's a slippery slope from Linda Sarsour to Sharia. One meme that is widely spread among the New Right claims to be "adapted from Dr. Peter Hammond's book: *Slavery, Terrorism & Islam*." The book features a thermometer with the supposed varying consequences as the percentage of the Muslim population increases:

<2% Muslim: Unthreatening.

2–5%: Proselytization, "often with major recruiting from the jails and among street gangs."

5–10%: Demands for special rights and treatment; i.e., getting supermarket to have halal food, and allowing for private Sharia (Islamic law) courts.

10–20%: Lawlessness; i.e., "car-burnings" as well as "uprisings and threats" against anti-Islamic speech.

20–40%: "hair-trigger rioting, jihad militia formations, sporadic killings, and the burnings of Christian churches and Jewish synagogues[.]"

40–60%: "widespread massacres, chronic terror attacks, and ongoing militia warfare."

60–80%: "unfettered persecution of non-believers" and "sporadic ethnic cleansing[.]"

>80%: "daily intimidation and violent jihad[.]"

At 100% there won't be peace because the extremists "satisfy their blood lust by killing less radical Muslims[.]"

Coulter, however, is just as hard on all immigration, not simply that from the Middle East: "Even when Third World immigrants aren't trying to blow up the First World, as in Boston, ethnic 'diversity' is all downside." Her conclusion is hard to miss or to ignore: "The only thing that stands between America and oblivion is a total immigration moratorium."[1] Further, "There's no sense in arguing about any other political issue. If we lose immigration, we lose everything. [. . .] The anti-amnesty side has to be perfect every time; the pro-amnesty side only has to win once. And then the country is finished."[2]

In 2015 Coulter sat down at Politicon with Cenk Uygur, co-creator of the progressive program *The Young Turks*. At one point during their very heated exchange, Uygur read a quote from a 2007 column of hers:

> In 1960, whites were 90 percent of the country. The Census Bureau recently estimated that whites already account for less than two-thirds of the population and will be a minority by 2050. Other estimates put that day much sooner. One may assume the new majority will not be such compassionate overlords as the white majority has been.

"Will the new immigrant overlords be as compassionate as the white overlords?" Coulter replied. "I think it was illustrated when you read that quote. When you got to 'whites will be a minority,' I heard the audience cheer. Can you imagine an audience of white people cheering 'Oh, it's going to be all white'? No you cannot. Those are your new overlords."

Human beings as a rule tend to be petty and vindictive. One of the great achievements of Nelson Mandela was his refusal to enact retribution against the formerly white elites once apartheid ended in South Africa. But this was by far the exception, and in 2018 the parliament there endorsed land expropriation without compensation. Why would anyone expect a newly empowered minority-majority to act any differently from, say, the way white settlers treated Native Americans—especially given a population that is constantly taught about its oppression and views whites as the oppressors?

As disgraced comedian (and Hillary superfan) Louis C.K. put it, "I'm not saying that white people are better. I'm saying that *being* white is clearly better. [. . .] I can get in a time machine and go to any time and it would be fucking awesome when I get there. [. . .] I can go to any time . . . in the *past*. I don't want to go in the future and find out what happens to white people because we are going to pay hard for this shit. We're not gonna just fall from #1 to #2. They're going to hold us down and fuck us in the ass forever—and we totally deserve it."

For the New Right, the problem can clearly be tied to the Immigration and Nationality Act of 1965 that was championed heavily by Teddy Kennedy. "Until Teddy Kennedy struck," Coulter writes, "America was never less than 99 percent white Western European and West African black." Even though "the country remained overwhelmingly Anglo-Saxon and Protestant right up until Teddy Kennedy decided to change it," it's not as simple as that.[3]

The term WASP was invented by E. Digby Baltzell, whose 1964 classic *The Protestant Establishment: Aristocracy and Caste in America* discussed the ceding of the WASP old guard to a new elite that included ethnic whites such as Jews and Catholics. Yet writing in the 1963 foreword—*before* the Immigration Act—Baltzell was already pointing out that "[s]ince [Teddy] Roosevelt's day, America has become, at all levels of society, the most ethnically and racially heterogeneous nation on earth."[4]

Harkening back to the theory of the circulation of elites, the Alt-Right doesn't see a majority-minority country as a more equal or fairer one. Rather, regarding hierarchy as literally inevitable, it sees whites being supplanted by minorities and relegated to second-class citizens in their very own country. As Coulter puts it,

America is not a mere landmass—otherwise, the Indians would have written the Declaration of Independence and put a man on the moon. Far from discovering America, Indians didn't even detect America. There was no America until the British and Dutch arrived. They were not "immigrants" because there was no established society for them to move to. Without the white settlers, what is known as "America" would still be an unnamed continent full of migratory tribes chasing the rear end of a buffalo every time their stomachs growled.[5]

If a progressive feminist were somehow allowed to move to Mecca, she might wear a hijab for professional reasons. But to assume that she would embrace Allah simply due to her proximity to the Kaaba is absurd. She might mouth the platitudes but her heart wouldn't be in it. In fact she would probably do everything in her power to change the culture she found herself in—and why wouldn't immigrants to America, being humans with their own ideas, cultures, and philosophies, feel the same way?

Witness the constant progressive insistence that Americanism or thinking that the United States is better than other countries is basically akin to Nazism. The opposite view, however, is that every country and culture is somehow good and valid. Coulter speaks for the entire New Right with her summation of this thinking, confirming that "any organization with 'world' in its title   International World Court, the World Bank, World Cup Soccer, the World Trade Organization—is inherently evil."[6] Again, this is not invoking "the loyal opposition" or two sides to the issue. This is right and wrong, good and evil, us against them. Conservatives don't think in those terms and are certainly scared to speak in that way.

"We're not changing the immigrants," writes Coulter, "they're changing us. The rape of little girls isn't even considered a crime in Latino culture—and that culture is becoming our culture. [. . .] In fact, in thirty-one of thirty-two states in Mexico, the age of consent for sex is twelve. Only in Mexico State is it fourteen."[7] As Coulter writes elsewhere in the book, "Gang rape, child rape, elder rape, and murder rape are highly correlated with specific ethnic groups—ethnic groups we are bringing to America by the busload."[8]

Here was where Trump got his notorious quote about Mexicans, which bears reading: "When Mexico sends its people, they're [*sic*] not sending their best. They're not sending you. They're not sending you. They're sending people that have lots of problems, and they're bringing those problems with us. They're bringing drugs. They're bringing crime. They're rapists. And some, I assume, are good people."

The implication isn't that all, most, or even many Mexicans are rapists. If a person said that the restaurant next door to him is sending its leftovers, no one would think that that meant that the restaurant only had leftovers to send. Yet to claim the quote is racist is to claim that Mexicans are either somehow incapable of bringing drugs, crime, and rape—which is absurd—or that the Mexicans who are coming are bringing those things in precisely the same or lower proportions as the American population. The New Right response to the latter is to ask why Americans should tolerate even one more drug, crime, or rape at all.

The audience laughed in Coulter's face on Bill Maher's show when she claimed in June 2015 that of all the Republican candidates Trump had the best chance of winning the presidency. It was a jarring prediction; no one had ever been elected president without political or military experience before. Yet Coulter laid out the playbook, and Trump followed it to victory.

First, she squarely took on the "racism" taboo that disarms conservatives so effectively to this very day: "Democrats denounce and abuse white people, and Republicans act embarrassed about having whites vote for them. Why are white votes bad?[9] [. . .] Rule of thumb, Republicans: If you aren't being called 'racist' by the *New York Times*, you're losing. [. . .] Historically, when Republicans ignore white voters, they lose."[10] As Buchanan and Rothbard realized, a vote is a vote is a vote.

The problem with Republican attempts to be diverse is that they will never be able to compete with the left on the subject regardless of the validity of such an approach. Basic marketing teaches that there must be some mechanism to differentiate one's products from the competitor's. So proclamations of excitement that a Republican stage consisted of Hispanic senator Marco Rubio, Indian American governor Nikki Haley, and African American senator Tim Scott are read not so much as arguments for voting Republican as attempts to inoculate Republicans from leftist criticism. This doesn't work for two reasons. First, it lets the left set the terms and thereby validates them. Second, it says that progressives are being honest and playing fair. They aren't—and frankly why should they?

The progressive strategy is to have a group be as diverse as possible. Disagree with the LGBT member? You're homophobic. A female? Sexist. A person of color? Racist. Having this phalanx inoculates the group against all discussion, as long as the term racist has the meaning the left would like it to. At the end of the day, for them it's a bit like playing Pokémon: trying to catch one of every type.

As Andrew Breitbart once wrote, "We don't fight fair; we fight righteous. The Democrats and President Obama will not give up their tack or their tactics. Do you think the GOP will win if its strategy is to apologize for every media-manufactured 'right wing' outrage? It will not. We will win the day by using all the tools in our arsenal to fight the tyranny of these totalitarian ideologies that have been visited upon us from overseas, where those same ideologies caused only chronic human misery. We will win by using the New Media to expose the bankruptcy of their beliefs and tactics. And ultimately we'll win, because their ideas simply don't work. No amount of media spin can change that."[11]

"The foreign poor are prime Democratic constituents because they're easily demagogued into tribal voting," Coulter writes. "Republicans' whispering sweet nothings in Hispanic ears isn't going to change that. Voting Democratic is part of their cultural identity. Race loyalty trumps the melting pot."[12] In a sense, it's politics 101. To win an election, you go where the votes are—and not where they *aren't*.

It was the winning strategy for George W. Bush. Rather than focusing on swing voters or, pointlessly, the left, Karl Rove worked to turn out the base. "Blacks and Hispanics are not swing voters—whites are," Coulter points out. Campaigning for minority votes "would be as if Republicans tricked the Democrats into devoting all their efforts to getting a tiny sliver more of the fundamentalist Christian vote."[13] The idea that minorities are less important in any sense, even when it comes to the mathematics needed to win an election, strikes at the very basis of the evangelical left and their creation myth. Nothing can be more heretical than this sort of thinking—at least, not in mainstream political discourse.

This is why Coulter and VDARE can be considered the furthest edge of the Overton Window. Past that are those who are far more heretical than Coulter, people whose books will most certainly not be found on the *New York Times* bestseller lists. I found one such person in Virginia. His name is Jared Taylor.

13

*

THE NEW HWITE

I see nothing wrong with ethnic purity being maintained.

—JIMMY CARTER

The best way to think of the Alt-Right conception of race is to
compare human populations to dog breeds. There are certainly
many Yorkshire terriers that aren't yappy, and it was a Labra-
dor retriever that actually bit the Dog Whisperer. But anyone
who knows the slightest thing about dogs would regard these
as aberrations—and that includes dog breeders themselves. In
other words, it is precisely the people who have the most knowledge and experience with a given breed that will be the first to
explain that there are certain behavioral tendencies that can be
expected.

Humans aren't dogs, of course. Well, dogs aren't dogs per
se either: A French bulldog in Berlin doesn't become a German
shepherd. A Yorkie is a Yorkie in Ireland, and a Welsh corgi can
tend cattle in Scotland just as well. It's easy to argue that an
immigrant who is culturally Muslim or Jewish or Christian

would gladly adopt liberal Western values while maintaining their faith at home and recognizing the rights of others to do the same. It happens all the time. Yet the Alt-Right claim is that not only does this *not* happen enough, but it *can't*. For them, demographics is destiny, and it is our genetics that determine our culture.

If Ann Coulter can be considered the point furthest to the right of allowable opinion in American politics, Jared Taylor's American Renaissance (AmRen.com) is very clearly beyond that point. The term "racist" has many meanings, ranging from "someone who regards certain races as inherently inferior" all the way through to "someone who happens to be against progressivism." In every sense of the word, Taylor is a racist.

By most accounts, this means that Taylor can be summarily dismissed as saying nothing of worth. This claim seems dubious. Even if someone were completely wrong, they could still be bright and thought-provoking in their errors. It is by having our ideas challenged and confronted that we come to better understand why it is we think how we do. And it is very hard to simply dismiss Jared Taylor.

Progressives—like all evangelical movements—demonize and ostracize their opponents, often fairly and with good reason. Yet despite all the imagery of racists as marching hicks, yelling and misspelling words, Yale-educated Taylor is anything but. He speaks calmly, eloquently, and viciously. One of the most unique things about Taylor is his anachronistically erudite way of speaking, almost like William F. Buckley without the smugness and smarm. Taylor has been writing and speaking about race for twenty-five years, and the fact that he pronounces white as "hu-wite" is a source of great amusement in New Right circles.

Taylor spent his youth in Japan, and his Virginia home is decorated with a mix of exquisite Japanese objets d'art—and framed Confederate currency. Yet despite this, it's not as simple as some would have it. He's not someone merely bitter about the War Between the States who just wants to go back and start Dixie again. "The people who are now trying to establish a Southern nation are," he told me, "almost without exception, conservatives. They're all ferociously Christian, they're antihomosexual, they're antifeminist, they're for very small government. You would never have a nation of people all thinking the same thing. For the concept of a nation to take root, it goes beyond politics. My mother was very much a liberal, but she was a Southerner, and a loyal Southerner. But today, to find someone who would march for gay rights and be a feminist and basically a socialist and still have regional loyalty—it's impossible to find such a thing."

Yet Taylor also said that "Yankees who have an understanding of whiteness are my comrades [sic]" and is willing to let bygones be bygones: "That is in the past for our people here." The amount of damage done by the Union against the Southern states took many decades to erase. The lives lost were innumerable, certainly far more than every white person killed by every minority combined. Maybe it's like the n-word; it's OK when "we" do it, but don't you ever dare. "I would argue that Abraham Lincoln was a better hwite man than Jefferson Davis," he concluded. "Lincoln wanted to free the slaves and send them away. Jefferson Davis wanted *more* black people! More problems. Crazy! My ancestors were all crazy hotheads."

So what is it about black people that Taylor finds so unacceptable? "Everyone who observes blacks arrives at certain conclusions about them," he said. "Oversexed, not very smart, and rhythmic." I'm assuming rhythmic isn't meant to be disparaging. But the other two most certainly are. So what does "oversexed" actually mean? This is a value judgment, not an objective term. What is the medically appropriate amount of sex to have?

If you asked most men, it would be "as much as possible." If you asked most women, it would be "as much as I feel comfortable with." In racist circles, Jews were and are also frequently described as oversexed or "sex obsessed," yet no white nationalist would claim that Jews commit sexual assault at significantly higher rates than WASPs. Yes, black Americans commit sexual assault at higher rates than whites—but they commit nonsexual assault at higher rates as well. This is a violence problem, not a sex-drive problem.

One of the weakest arguments against Taylor's way of thinking is that people said the same thing about the Irish, Italians, and Jews, and they were wrong then. Therefore, they must be wrong now. That's a logical fallacy. It's certainly possible they were wrong then and right now, or that they were in fact right then and wrong now. If one looks purely at voting, the Irish, Italians, and Jews do not vote in the same manner as WASPs, even many decades after they've become an irreversible part of the American tapestry. And turning the anti-Taylor logic on its head, it would also be fallacious to say that since many were wrong about Kaiser Wilhelm posing a threat and wanting to control Europe prior to World War I, and many were wrong about Hitler posing a threat and wanting to control Europe prior to World War II, therefore many are wrong to say Angela Merkel isn't a threat and doesn't want to control Europe today.

According to the 2015 FBI Crime in the United States report, 37 percent of violent crime arrests were of black people. Yet as reported in *A Primer on Social Problems*, "people in the 15–24 age range account for about 40 percent of all arrests even though they comprise only about 14 percent of the population." This number obviously includes nonviolent arrest, but by that metric blacks only constitute 26.6 percent of all arrests. So even stacking the deck against black Americans, it makes as much sense to blame blacks—who are around 13 percent of the population—for the actions of black criminals as it does to blame *everyone* for the actions of young criminals.

It might be absurd to argue that we can get rid of all people aged fifteen to twenty-four, but it's almost as absurd to argue that "we" can get rid of African Americans. The idea that they can somehow be removed (to where?) does not seem remotely plausible. Further, black people were here before the Italians and the Irish. Surely they have more of a right to be here than them.

Taylor does not dispute this, in the abstract. But what it comes down to, for him, is that the differences between blacks and whites are so insuperable that the only way to overcome the "mistakes" of the past (i.e., slavery) is through separation today. This is also due to the inherent tribalism found in all peoples, *including* whites. Why tempt fate?

Interestingly—and despite what the media would claim—some of the racial condemnation among the Alt-Right does firmly go antiwhite. "We have a streak of pathological altruism," Taylor said. Many white nationalists and race realists believe that white people are genetically predisposed to self-destruction. It's a convenient way to explain their perception of worldwide white racial suicide (despite there being more white people on earth than at any point in history).

Yet how is it easier to counter this supposed white instinct for self-destruction than it is to combat the supposed black instinct for crime? There are far fewer black Americans than white ones. Keeping violent crime down is not only simpler than fighting some sort of emo death wish, but it's actually been implemented very successfully over the past several decades. Thanks to technology, it's becoming easier all the time.

What makes matters difficult is when any slight connection between race and crime is forbidden to be discussed at all. Yet even Taylor wouldn't say that crime is caused by being black per se so much as it is caused by high testosterone and low IQ, which are supposedly correlated with being black. But then it would be the testosterone and IQ that are the problems, not the actual race itself.

Dealing with groups that commit more crime can easily be done in a colorblind way. Take what New York City mayor Rudy Giuliani did, for instance: he located areas with higher crime rates and allocated security resources there. If this correlated with race, then so be it. The important thing was that it correlated with reducing the risk of crime and increasing the prevention of it. But this cannot be done when a religion that regards any criticism of minorities as a taboo and a heresy has clout.

If Taylor's claim were true that black criminality is heavily genetic, we would see consistent black crime rates over time. But in fact black crime rates in America have fluctuated in relation to whites. Since blacks as a population are largely genetically the same, the only conclusion is that something other than genes is correlating with crime—or, alternatively, that some methods of crime prevention are more effective than others. In either case, the data contradicts the idea that this is some sort of insurmountable dilemma that grants the black race a sense of immutability vis-à-vis their behavior, in my view.

Some of what Taylor mentioned has already been discussed in more mainstream outlets. *The Bell Curve*, published in 1994, created huge controversy—but enormous debate—with its discussion of heritability of IQ, including across race. The universally lauded Steven Pinker's *The Blank Slate* is a full-frontal assault on the implicit idea that biology plays virtually no role in social issues and norms. Nicholas Wade, at the time a *New York Times* science writer, wrote *A Troublesome Inheritance* about "Genes, Race and Human History."

The fact is we don't know what causes criminal behavior. Race is not the answer; the overwhelming majority of every race does not commit crime. The conservative claim that "people are evil" is more of a descriptor than an explanation. Nor is crime simply a function of economics; American blacks commit higher rates of crime than whites at every economic level.

A possible parallel example to consider is the issue of alcoholism. Alcoholism used to be regarded as literally satanic (the old-timey version of "racist") and was, correctly, blamed for enormous social problems. In contemporary times, however, alcoholics are treated with far more compassion and sensitivity due to the understanding that being an alcoholic is not some simple decision that an individual made. No one argues that alcoholism is equally prevalent in every given population. What was once used to condemn entire groups, such as the Irish, is now treated as irrelevant when dealing with people as individuals.

Thomas Sowell and John McWhorter took on all these issues with a sense of compassion in their respective books. Sowell's *The Intellectuals and Race* is a relentless dissection of how leftists try to reconstruct racial realities to further their agenda. McWhorter's *Losing the Race* is a scathing—though empathetic—attack on contemporary black anti-intellectualism and a broader culture almost designed to cause dysfunction. Both men are black, and they painstakingly grapple with and address the criticisms that Taylor and the like make.

Even if race is a factor in the success of various cultures, that doesn't imply that it's an important factor, let alone the *most* important. The two Koreas aren't both just "Asian" but are genetically identical populations. Yet south Korea has had the highest GDP in all of Asia, while north Korea has an African-level GDP. During the "Arduous March" famine of the 1990s, *polio* even returned to the north. It all clearly can't be reduced just to race.

"No, it cannot," Taylor agreed. "You had the same issue with

East and West Germany: essentially genetically identical populations living in strikingly different circumstances. Now that they are reunited they are assimilating at a very fast rate, which is what you would expect from genetically identical groups of humans. You don't get that with genetically mixed humans."

Just as race needn't be the most important factor, diversity can also be *a* strength, just not necessarily *the* great strength it's touted as being by the left. Price is an indicator of information. A person walking into a comic book store would see that *Detective Comics* #27 costs several orders of magnitude more than #26 or #28. Not knowing anything about comic books whatsoever, one can deduce that either the issue is relatively scarce (low supply) or relatively desirable (high demand) or both. They wouldn't need to know that it's the first appearance of Batman to perceive genuine information about the issue's value.

If diversity were the nightmare that Taylor makes it out to be, it would factor into how rent is structured in different places. New York and San Francisco are both very diverse, yet their rents—an economic expression of a desire to live there—are both very high. To some extent, of course, rents are artificially increased due to government manipulation. But no politician could make rents high in rural areas even if they wanted to. People would simply move elsewhere. Clearly, for *some* people, diversity *is* a strength.

Jane Jacobs made this point when it came to architecture. In her *The Death and Life of Great American Cities*, she pointed out that visually diverse neighborhoods that feature different architectural styles and differently-aged buildings are most attractive to people. These elements stimulate the eye and give the neighborhood a sense of character, a micro version of that regional loyalty Taylor likes so much. Does that imply that we should therefore be importing refugees by the thousands? Not in my view. The implications needn't go any further than that some people enjoy living in ethnically diverse areas, even given the inevitable cost of cultural friction.

It is in cities where diverse groups get along. This is one of the reasons New Yorkers are often stereotyped as "rude." We constantly have to remind strangers and miscreants of the rules of decorum, because those become a necessity in tight quarters with frequent contact with different people. I am not making the claim that city life is for everyone or for most people. But I am saying that the claim that diversity is inherently unharmonious is false. It becomes a problem when the diversity is imposed and mandated and venerated as a sacred act of faith.

Now, let's take on the IQ issue, leaving aside the idea that having any population without an enormous amount of stupid people is somehow possible. As the comedian George Carlin put it, "Think of how stupid the average person is, and realize half of them are stupider than that." Having a higher IQ or simply higher intelligence would also correlate very well with being effective at implementing *bad* ideas, such as committing atrocities. The undisputable fact is that the worst butchers in human history—Mao, Hitler, and Stalin—all came from populations that white nationalists regard as being highly intelligent. There's an undercurrent in Alt-Right circles that if a white person had to randomly choose where to live, they would want to be in a majority-white country. Given that the worst atrocities are under white and yellow, this feels a bit like Russian [*sic*] roulette.

"It's a risk I'm willing to run," Taylor said. "If you're going to have people intent on killing each other, they're going to kill each other with their bare hands if need be." True. But it is only high-IQ elites who can convince people that killing each other is for the good, that killing each other is the right thing to do, and that killing each other is necessary and ultimately to everyone's benefit. It is far easier to brainwash a mind convinced of its own brilliance than one that is slow and needs to be told what to do.

There are several issues that "race realists" like Taylor focus on, resulting in a bit of a package deal. It's similar to how Republicans imply that being pro-military and pro–tax cuts are logically intertwined, or the Democratic linkage of gay marriage and single-payer healthcare. For Taylor, talk of IQ is admittedly a secondary concern. "IQ is generally correlated in a very positive way with moral behavior," he said. "If you're going to say average IQ would be the touchstone of a good society, then you'd be a 'yellow' supremacist. You'd have to concede that East Asians have higher IQs than whites. Ashkenazi Jews have the highest recorded IQs, on average, so then we should just let ourselves be replaced by Ashkenazi Jews. Well, I don't want to be replaced by anyone. I am loyal to my group in the same way that every human group is loyal to their group."

But what, precisely, is their group? Leftism is inherently about being "disloyal" to one's group but in service to a higher moral principle. Sometimes this is demented, as when the outgroup is truly malevolent. The left cheered the fall of the Shah of Iran in 1979, but his replacement was worse in every sense. But sometimes this "disloyalty" to one's group is humanity at its greatest. When Chinese citizens house north Korean refugees at legal risk and their own expense, that is nothing but admirable.

Inclusion versus exclusivity is an axis that can be used to divide the left from the right. All leftists regard as central to their mission the idea of bringing new peoples "out of the shadows" and into the mainstream. In this they perform an extremely necessary cultural function. Many times individuals or peoples are dismissed for illegitimate or no-longer-legitimate reasons. It is the leftist challenge to the status quo that permits them to be integrated into society.

One fairly uncontroversial example of successful left-wing

inclusionism was the movement to redeem drug users and abusers. Hubert Selby's 1964 novel *Last Exit to Brooklyn* was subject to obscenity trials and bannings due to his unjudgmental—though hardly valorizing—depiction of drug addicts and other "low lifes." The culture at the time preferred to act as if these people did not exist, or, if they did exist, it was not as people but only as cautionary tales. Nowadays, major celebrities freely discuss their battles with addiction on morning television with no repercussions whatsoever, and drug abusers are regarded with sympathy. Death by overdose, as with Amy Winehouse, is not seen as karmic justice but as an artistic tragedy. Even when drug addicts turn to crime, their families are treated with sympathy by and large—not as somehow dirty and as if they have something to be embarrassed about.

"The founders of the U.S.," Taylor said, "by today's standards, were ravenous hwite supremacists. They expected it to be a country for hwite people. The first citizenship law, passed by the first Congress, restricted citizenship to free hwite persons. Jefferson expected hwite people to fill up all of North and South America—and not a single Indian left! In the United States the dividing line very quickly became one of race. To some extent, religion. To some extent, nationality."

There is no doubt that these were all dividing lines, as they are now. But I would argue that the biggest "dividing lines" were the literal dividing lines, meaning the state borders. In early America a person was a citizen of Virginia or New Jersey or Georgia and not of "America." Of course the white population looked down on blacks and slaves, as well as on white indentured servants to a lesser extent.

The Founders also thought that the right to secession was a given, that if new states could enter the Union then of course others could exit it. Yet Taylor isn't arguing for this either, and his expressed kinship with northern whites is very different from how the early Americans viewed themselves. Everyone has things they agree with the Founders on and things they don't. Slavery is bad independently of whether some Founders believed in it and practiced it or not.

We form different associations based on our contexts. Athletes have a collegial attitude toward other athletes, but some surely prefer to associate with, say, nonathletic conservatives than with liberal athletes. Europeans do not primarily consider themselves as white; they think of themselves primarily as French or German or whatever. Western European culture is not a monolith. To conflate Camus with Wagner is to defy critical thinking entirely.

Taylor largely concedes this point. "Yes, the French think of themselves as French and the Flemings think of themselves as Flemings," he said. "But identitarian circles in Europe are very conscious of this brotherhood of Europeans. It is true that if you're a Hungarian, you can't decide if you hate the Slovaks or the Romanians more. But they of course recognize the importance of each European country maintaining its nationality. You would find much more areas of agreement between Austrian and French identitarians than between Austrian socialists and greens and identitarians."

By his own words, Taylor freely admits that human beings can view "their group" as one based on ideology instead of race, one that crosses national boundaries. The loyalty question isn't as simple as he would have it. In fact, the blog Slate Star Codex ran the numbers in a post called "I Can Tolerate Anything Except the Outgroup." The author cites a study that found something quite revealing. When it comes to hiring someone for a job, "discrimination on the basis of [political] party was much stronger than discrimination on the basis of race." An information economy segregates on ideas and not on genetics.

One of the Alt-Right claims I've heard bandied about is the

idea that if we simply had an all-white country then everything would be fine. "Well certainly not that," Taylor agreed. "But I think homogeneous countries, by and large, have fewer problems than heterogeneous countries. Homogenous hwite nations have never been utopias of harmony. But they are far more harmonious than what the Germans are doing to themselves."

Like most people, however, I think that there are more choices than simply a white ethnostate or a country where the government imports refugees by the tens of thousands. As Taylor himself said, "Every society has got friction. Every society has got problems. It's inevitable. People do not all agree. Homogeneity of a nation is only a first. Then it makes other problems easier to solve. It doesn't make them all go away."

There's no question that America was more racially homogenous in the past. But how were we "harmonious"? When there were industry-wide strikes, and strikebreakers? When the South was under Northern occupation? Before the Civil War, where the balance between North and South was a source of constant and tenuous tension? Is a nation "harmonious" when one election, the election of 1860, caused half the country to exit without even waiting around to see what would end up happening?

Taylor does not try to whitewash [sic] history to fit his narrative. Regarding the Civil War, "slavery is unquestionably the cause. People talk about tariffs, and to some extent that was true, but the real difference was slavery. Look, white people have fought each other for hundreds of years, for thousands of years. Look at the first World War! We are tribal. We are combative. The male of the species is a very easily aroused, tribal, and potentially very violent organism. All these things have to be kept in check. So to say that homogeneity is pointless because homogeneously white people have slaughtered each other over tariffs or over boundaries or over slavery—that's all true. But why *add* problems?"

What country hasn't had problems? The whole point of the free market is to recognize problems that exist in society, identify the needs of the populace, and to provide solutions for them at a tidy profit. Expelling or denigrating one out of eight Americans is, itself, a massive problem—at the very least in terms of the costs necessary to pursue such an enormous endeavor. Taylor may very well argue that the benefits outweigh such a cost. But the accounting simply isn't that clear cut.

Here, I suspect, is the reason such ideas often get currency. To actually crunch the numbers and to regard the entire black population (let alone those of other minorities) as a mere statistic is inherently dehumanizing and inhumane. To even consider such a thing, for people on the left, is to invoke slavery and genocide, where populations were dealt with in the same way a business might deal with transporting livestock or meat. Without a rebuttal, it's possible to create the perception that there *isn't* a rebuttal, and that it's only political correctness that keeps the subject under wraps. In an open discussion of ideas, the white nationalist argument goes, white nationalist ideas are so "obviously" true that they would win the day.

For Taylor and other identitarians, it's not just about racial separation. "But even more important than that," Taylor insisted, "is the survival of my people. That to me is the crucial question. I don't care if my people have committed numerous atrocities in the past." Ignoring the moral aspect of committing aptly named "atrocities," it seems pretty straightforward to me that an atrocity-rich society is neither very harmonious nor very utilitarian. Not only does dealing with the victims of said atrocities cost a great deal of money, labor, and general social control, one also has to worry about those bleeding hearts that have the unmitigated gall to suggest that maybe a little less atrocity would make for a better nation.

"If you look for atrocities you can find them in anyone's

past," Taylor continued, "and some people have more means for committing them than others. It is only hwites who are expected to pay forever for all the things we are alleged to have done." Yet this is simply untrue. North Korea is still angling for reparations from Japan from when they were a colony, despite the fact that the Japanese installed the vast majority of the infrastructure that the DPRK uses to this day. The Armenians and the Turks have neither forgiven nor forgotten; are they "white" in the sense Taylor means? I know little about the rivalry between India and Pakistan but am fairly sure that each has plenty of fingers to point at the other.

"All people have the right to survive," Taylor said, "and for that to happen there has to be an area where they are recognized as the dominant population." This too is untrue, in my view. Many peoples were utterly subjugated by the Soviets, and they survived. The Romani are dispersed throughout Europe, and they survive. To be sure, having an area of one's own is certainly conducive to a people's survival. But it is not in the end necessary so long as their rights are respected.

Various groups have different cues to identify one another that non-members would be oblivious to. I was surprised and partially gladdened to learn how few of my media colleagues knew what the number "1488" meant. The eighth letter of the alphabet is H, so "Heil Hitler" becomes "HH" which becomes "88." On the other hand, "14" stands for the "fourteen words," a vow that "[w]e must secure the existence of our people and a future for white children." The numbers are frequently used as tattoos among lower-class racists. So to hear the same precise sentiment as the fourteen words being uttered in Jared Taylor's frankly lovely accent is doubly off-putting. (As it was disturbing to learn that Milo had once sent a Jewish journalist $14.88.)

Every cultural and political group has adjacent groups that they disagree with but still have things in common with. Liberals

have democratic socialists on their left flank and moderates
to their right, while democratic socialists have communists to
their left—a group that liberals do not make common cause
with, for the most part. Similarly, "race realists" like Taylor will
have white supremacists and anti-Semites to their right without being (complete) anti-Semites themselves. Even the fringe
has a fringe.

In 2011 (i.e., a time long, long ago, and a galaxy far, far away),
Taylor was asked by Phil Donahue on MSNBC(!) about Jews
and how we fit into his white nationalism. "The Jews?" Taylor
replied. "The Jews are fine by me. [. . .] They look hwite to me."
Some in the Alt-Right took this as an affront and a betrayal. For
them, Jews are obviously the most dangerous precisely because
we don't stand out in a crowd of whites unlike, say, pretty much
all the races. Others took him at face value and agreed, regarding Jews as a whole as very much a baby/bathwater situation. A
third group took him to be dissembling, saying that we *look*
hwite but actually *aren't*.

Yet again, Taylor here doesn't fit into an easy box. When I
spoke to him about some of the anti-Semitism prevalent on
Twitter and elsewhere, he almost couldn't wrap his head around
it. "This 'gas the kikes' stuff," he frowned, "I don't think anyone really believes it." As absurd as it might sound, I believe that
Taylor's incredulity was sincere. To begin with, his affect and
body language betrayed his visceral feelings (though that surely
could have been misleading). But more objectively, how Taylor
views and carries himself makes his beliefs quite clear. Like
Buckley, his disdain for the gauche seeps out from every pore.

"The idea of modeling a current political movement on Hitlerism seems just *fantastic* to me," he went on.

"You mean 'fantastic' in the negative sense," I asked, "not
'wonderful,' right?"

He burst out laughing. "Yes, I appreciate the clarification."

Here is where I became convinced that he was not, in fact, a pure anti-Semite as some of his fellow travelers are. Taylor wouldn't have let his guard down and used such sloppy language with a Jewish writer. Most reporters would have simply taken that quote, "Hitlerism seems just fantastic to me!," and run with it. It would take on a life of its own, and Taylor would have to spend years explaining, which would only come off as backpedaling. We see the same phenomenon in pro-lifers attempting to paint Planned Parenthood founder Margaret Sanger as some sort of proto-Nazi. When she said, "We do not want word to go out that we want to exterminate the Negro population," she didn't mean "We do not want this secret revealed" but rather "We do not want people to get that impression." Yet the quote is still bandied about ad nauseam.

"For those of us Americans who think in racial terms," Taylor went on, "we have very useful racial models from our *own* past that should guide us." He regards the Alt-Right view that we should do the opposite of whatever Israel does simply because it's "the Jews" to be "completely incoherent." "You find these people with sympathies toward Palestinians," he went on, "people with whom they have absolutely nothing in common. And these are supposed to be *allies*?"

At times Taylor shows his leftist side. While one of the key aspects of right-wing thought is that human nature is immutable and largely static, the left thinks we are not the same beings who walked the earth during the time of the pharaohs. "I think after the two world wars it is impossible to imagine Europeans slaughtering each other with that ferocity," Taylor insisted.

Yet this is exactly what many people thought before World War I started. Now that there was industry and technology, the argument went, now that humanity had unlocked achievements that we'd never unlocked before, we could turn our backs on the barbaric practice of war. To quote Reuters, "A

1910 bestselling book, *The Great Illusion*, used economic arguments to demonstrate that territorial conquest had become unprofitable, and therefore global capitalism had removed the risk of major wars."[1] This was a worldview also shared by Marxists at the time, the idea that war is a function of imperialist capitalism and that an international community of workers would never war with one another. The *New Statesman* backs up this point of view:

> In 1914, by contrast, very few people had any idea of the cataclysm that was about to descend on them. Just as admirals thought that the war at sea would be a rerun of the great naval engagements of the past, so the generals thought the war on land would be something like the conflicts of the 1860s, opening with rapid, railway-borne advances to the front, followed by a decisive encounter in which the other side would meet with a shattering defeat; peace would then be concluded after a few weeks or at most a couple of months.[2]

So how does one prevent war, if one rejects the globalist New World Order and the conservative peace-through-conquest? The answer is culture, but not in the way most people think. It was from New Right sweetheart Camille Paglia that I first learned about the importance of low culture, especially through her self-identification as a Warholian and her incessant championing of Andy and his work. In the same way that the vulgarization (i.e., popularization) of the Bible led to massive international change, so have Americans vulgarized the arts. Though the term "vulgar" has a negative connotation, especially to WASP ears, it is precisely America's vulgarity that has enabled us to conquer the cultural world.

The ideal model for bringing down an enemy establishment is how we defeated the Soviet Union. Whereas World War II cost literally millions of lives, as well as untold cultural and property damage, the end of the USSR happened almost entirely peacefully. While Reagan and Thatcher applied political pressure, they also provided political cover. No one could accuse the pair of being soft on communism, and therefore any concessions they made to the Soviet Union passed without criticism. This also allowed Gorbachev to save face, as both leaders were strongly admired in the USSR and were hardly regarded as weaklings to whom submission would be humiliating.

But the other part of the story comes from popular culture. The Eastern European masses started to watch American television. Despite years of Soviet agitprop, they then came away from watching trashy soaps like *Dynasty* with one simple question: "Why do the maids have fur coats in America, while I'm literally wiping my ass with newspaper?" The same process is being repeated right now in north Korea, where trashy south Korean culture—television programs, movie stars, and K-pop music—is doing as much if not more to radicalize DPRK youth against the regime as any form of propaganda.

When I questioned Taylor about this he entertained my idea. "There may be some truth to that," he admitted. "I know some Jews who would argue that American culture has benefited enormously from this frothy mix of Jewish intellectuals who think outside the box and don't subscribe to traditional views. Yeah, but then the anti-Semites say that's what also gave us the pornography industry—but that's a very glib response."

Despite his dismissiveness, Taylor did make a good point. Pornography strongly fueled the spread of VCRs (why go to the porno theater when you could watch it in your own home?) and later the internet (why go to the rental store when you don't have to leave home at all?). Still, Taylor was skeptical. "I'm not convinced that high culture requires—"

"I mean specifically low culture."

"Well, I'm not that interested in low culture."

"Do you not agree that low culture was instrumental in our Cold War victory?"

"If nothing but WASPs were running Hollywood," Taylor said, "there would still be movies. And I think they would still show a kind of America that was certainly superior to what the Soviets were experiencing."

"The common person in any country is going to consume trash," I pointed out. "When you have enough of them, they are going to affect politics even if it's not a democratic country. But that 'trash' is what convinces them." In my view, a white nationalist can't defend the "white trash" so reviled by progressives while simultaneously denigrating "trashy" television.

"Is your argument that since Jews created Hollywood, that was particularly important in the Soviet common man losing faith in his society?" Taylor asked.

"Yes." Not only that, but it was also the Jewish Jacob W. Davis who invented blue jeans—the most American of all clothing and a symbol of Cold War envy of the West—and the Jewish Levi Strauss who popularized them.

"I've never heard that argument."

"No one has made it until me," I said.

But it's not just Jews, of course. It's blacks, and gays, and every other out-group that has one foot in America but one foot out the door. That's where culture comes from, and this is something I've found that the New Right finds difficult to grapple with. The Alt-Right especially insists that such groups create culture steeped in a leftism specifically and intentionally designed to destroy the West. In my view, however, these groups are being driven to the left because they have nowhere else to go.

Thinking creatively means taking what is given and reconstructing it to make something better, something unprecedented. This is something the bourgeois find impossible to do, as anything new is "weird" and therefore bad to them. Creativity is therefore inherently, if not left-wing, certainly a thoroughly anticonservative position.

Culture is the most peaceful, cost-effective mechanism for conquest that exists. It is because leftism is so grounded in valorizing the weak outsider that leftists get a front-row seat for the innovations of tomorrow. They get to be the first investors practically every time, and they get to reap the windfall profits—as well as ownership stakes—that come with it. Even Mike Cernovich discussed "throwing shade" with me, a term first "popularized" (barely!) in the 1990 Harlem drag ball documentary *Paris is Burning.*

In his *A Renegade History of the United States*, historian Thaddeus Russell elucidates this position. It is unfortunate that the term "marginalized" has become synonymous with "oppressed." Russell makes the opposite claim: that though people on the fringes of society might be in a weaker position socioeconomically, they are in a *stronger* position in other crucial ways.

For Russell, the first American feminists—meaning, empowered women beholden to no one—weren't people like First Lady Abigail Adams ("Remember the ladies"), or Rhode Island founder Anne Hutchinson, but *madams*. Being flush with cash, they became enormous investors in real estate. They were basically lobbyists when it came to local government. In many cases these madams even became lenders of last resort when crises hit. In one sense, a woman who ran a whorehouse was as low as it gets—especially in WASP society. But in practical terms they were among the wealthiest citizens and lived as they damned [sic] well pleased, certainly being far freer than, say, the wives of prominent businessmen and politicians.

Did these women make prostitution acceptable? Of course not. But at the very least they became living, visible examples of independent property-owning women. Culturally, the argument then became, *Why do madams get to own property whereas proper women can't?* Why do they get to be independent, while the moral females have to be functions of their husbands? If it's good enough for the lowest, surely it's good enough for everyone else. Freedom and culture are intertwined in unusual ways, and the steps won by ladies of the night are indisputably carried with us to this day.

People on the margins are in a position to effect change because they have nothing to lose. This is not simply an economic point but a function of hierarchy and social credibility. The lower the class an individual or group occupies, the lower the expectations are regarding their behavior. If they try something innovative and fail, they are no worse off. If they succeed, the sky's the limit. It's part of the reason why so many bands are formed exclusively by young people. Without families, mortgages, or any real net worth, it's far easier to shoot for the moon and try to become the next big thing.

As time goes on, the connection between a symbol and its origin are often lost—especially when said origin is disreputable. Many contemporary young people, for example, are oblivious to the fact that the icon to save a document is a floppy disk (an item that they've never seen). Explaining why hard plastic disks were called "floppy" is a whole other issue as well. Despite the fact that orange jumpsuits are now seen as de rigueur prison attire, it wasn't that long ago that horizontal black-and-white stripes immediately identified the wearer as a convict. Convicts and only convicts were the people who wore that look. As Russell points out, a similar example can be found in First Lady Nancy Reagan's fondness for wearing red. Not too long ago, a woman wearing red (not to mention makeup, aka "whore-paint") was as unambiguously a prostitute as one who wore stripes was a convict. This connotation goes back to biblical times. Revelation speaks of the Whore of Babylon, "mother of harlots," wearing red and riding a red beast. Nathaniel Hawthorne's book is called *The Scarlet Letter* for a reason.

Yet virtually no one would think of such connotations nowadays if they saw a woman clad in red, especially a First Lady. A time traveler would be aghast at Reagan's look; a contemporary person would be baffled by such a reaction—*and both would be right in their own way*. It's not always logical, either. Thigh-high boots mean hooker but short skirts don't, even though the former cover a great deal more skin than the latter.

My favorite example of this process is that of Divine, a three-hundred-pound drag queen. In 1972 he starred in John Waters's underground cult classic *Pink Flamingos*. The film was so out there and in such poor taste that it was only screened at midnight. At the climax of the movie, Divine's character is asked her political positions by a reporter. "Kill everyone now!" she immediately replies. "Condone first-degree murder! Advocate cannibalism! Eat shit! Filth are my politics, filth is my life!" What would have been a shockingly obscene transgression in the early seventies barely warrants an eyeroll nowadays.

By 1981 Divine was sharing an onscreen kiss with former teen idol Tab Hunter. Right before his death in 1988 he was preparing to star in *Married . . . with Children*, and the following year his likeness was used as the visual model for Ursula the Sea Witch in *The Little Mermaid* before audiences who had no idea where the look came from. In other words, it took roughly fifteen years to go from completely marginalized social pariah to network television and a Disney movie, the acme of bourgeois provincialism.

To be an actress in the early days of stage was akin to being a literal porn star today in terms of stigma. So strong was the overlap that even Betty White was photographed nude when she was starting out. Hollywood was built overwhelmingly by Jews who saw an opportunity and were already socially stigmatized. As the movie industry sought respectability, many actresses had to deal with the quasi-pornographic "stag films" that they had starred in a few years prior. This is similar to how JFK's bootlegger father Joseph Kennedy—a drug dealer for his era—forced his way into elite WASP culture and gained acceptance for Irish Catholics.

After a marginalized person or group creates some aspect of culture, it goes from outlandish to edgy to stylish to mainstream to déclassé. The marginalized invent it, and then the edgy early outlier adopts it. One can easily imagine the gasps the first young woman who wore red experienced, and then the rapid spread of the color to her peers as they wanted to be perceived as cool without having to do anything immoral whatsoever. After enough edgy people assume some aspect of culture, proselytizers adopt it and spread it. Then corporate America notices it, processes it, and excretes it in such a way that the median person can consume it shamelessly, mindlessly, and on their own terms. After that it largely becomes over in the eyes of the marginalized. I remember my friend calling me up laughing from her job at Urban Outfitters as a tourist held up a Ramones shirt and wondered who the "Ramonas" were.

Having had a virtual monopoly on communications over the last century or so, the provincial bourgeois whites who form the core of evangelical progressivism have rarely had to work to understand anything. Rather, corporate America has devoted enormous energy to taking innovative culture and repackaging it in a way that's palatable and acceptable to them while allowing themselves to maintain their self-image as edgy outsiders.

This is why so much of our culture is made by blacks,

gays, and Jews—all out-groups of their time. As quintessential New Yorker Fran Lebowitz said in her documentary *Public Speaking,*

> People used to say all the time there must be something about homosexuality that makes you more artistic because there is such a huge, beyond-excessive number of homosexual artists relative to the number of homosexuals. But of course that isn't true. While it is not true that being homosexual makes you artistic, what is true is that it's being put in prison or being kept out or being depressed or being forced to observe.

If my model for cultural change is accurate, one would expect that as white men lose their grip on power, they would increasingly become innovators of culture—and that is exactly what has happened. And not just white men, but the low-status white men (i.e., the young), and the lowest status of those (i.e., the archetypical virgin in his parents' basement).

This is precisely who created the New Right as a cultural movement.

So what, in the end, does Taylor really want? Much of race-realist talk seems like a shell game to me. There is rarely contempt expressed for high-test, low-IQ whites. If white nationalists could wave a magic wand and cause all high-test, low-IQ people from America to vanish, would that make things better? Probably. But again: it's about preserving the race. It seems like the high-test, low-IQ criterion is just a pretext for whom to expel. Taylor views Asians as high-IQ, with low or average test. Yet they would not be welcome either, and would "properly" be in their own countries.

For Taylor the answer is simple: "Complete freedom of association," he said. "Just let us do this. I would like to think that if there were a sensible view of these questions, and society were not constantly condemning what comes naturally to most people, these things would sort of work themselves out. I'm not talking about absolute purity either. I'm pretty latitudinarian in my definition of who is hwite. If Thomas Sowell decides he's hwite, I'd have a hard time telling him no."

I almost couldn't believe what he'd said. If Thomas Sowell is allowed in the ethnostate, who isn't? "So you're like a Rachel Dolezal person?" I quipped.

"A society doesn't need this hairsplitting business. For the most part, people who look hwite and consider themselves hwite are hwite as far as I'm concerned."

It seems pretty clear that a newly seceded South is far more feasible than a white nationalist America, for the simple reason that it's easier to convince a part than a whole. But that isn't an option for Taylor. What he wants is a nation where the citizens are overwhelmingly white, proud of their identity and nation, and yet have diversity of political opinion. Some minorities are permitted, but they wouldn't really have much say.

Such a location already exists: New Hampshire. As of 2010, the population was 92.3 percent non-Hispanic white, with the black population at 1.1 percent—precisely half that of Asians, at 2.2 percent. The state has voted for both George W. Bush and Barack Obama, and has consistently flipped from Republican to Democrat and back again in state legislative control, governorships, and the partisan makeup of the two senators.

In some contexts, New Hampshirites see themselves as very unlike their neighboring Vermont. In others, they're both "New Englanders." Again: identification is contextual, not universal. Regardless, I don't know any measure where New Hampshire can be considered some sort of Shangri-La. It is perfectly livable and lovely. Yet the costs to turn America into a larger New

Hampshire seem exorbitant, and the benefits seem low. Let the mountain come to Mohammed, so to speak.

Taylor's Japanese childhood speaks to someone groomed for decorum; his admiration for the South also invokes the demeanor of Jefferson's natural aristocrat. He very explicitly believes that his positions are rational, factual, objective, and demonstrable. Far from being "prejudiced," he claims that he arrived at his views *after* judging all the available information for decades.

I'm not in a position to say whether that makes him a good or a bad person, or even a better or a worse person than a more banal racist. Frankly, I'm not particularly comfortable judging a heretic for his views at all. My gut reaction is to let Taylor live his life, and I can live mine. Our interaction was informative and he was open and amiable. I can't entirely condemn a man who invites a stranger into his home and treats him fairly and respectfully. But I can judge whether Taylor is dangerous, and this is one place where I think progressives certainly have a point.

In the same way that liberalism opens the door to progressivism which opens the door to socialism, Taylor's genteel race realism opens the door to racism of the vulgar kind. One day *Mona Lisa* is the world's greatest masterpiece; the next she is on bookmarks and adapted on greeting cards. Leonardo da Vinci could not have imagined such a thing, but he was nevertheless the origin point.

I am certain that some of my contacts in the New Right are racists, anti-Semites, and all the rest of it. I am certain that far more of them than I realize have such beliefs. I judge people by their actions, not their thoughts. Having heretical thoughts needn't imply poor behavior, because most people, racists or otherwise, are hypocrites and don't even have the courage of their convictions. Certainly having the correct views, as progressives do, does not preclude them from being dicks, to put it bluntly.

Yet the divide between thought and action isn't as smooth as I would like it to be. Having such ideas in a subculture does not necessarily lead to awful things, but they're certainly a prerequisite for awful things to happen. When dealing with these types I don't know that I have a line to draw, and that remains my struggle.

14

☆

CHARLOTTESVILLE OR BUST

Being a Jew, one learns to believe in the reality of
cruelty and one learns to recognize indifference to
human suffering as a fact.

—Andrea Dworkin

I don't remember when I first saw the poster for Charlottesville's Unite the Right rally, but I do remember cringing. Under
fascist-style eagles marched four columns of Confederate soldiers, half with Pepe heads and half with the "feels" guy. The
speakers' names I recognized were full-blown Alt-Right types
(as in "it's the Jews"). But second-to-last on the roster was someone else I knew, who wasn't anywhere close to being as full-
blown white nationalist as the rest: Pax Dickinson.

Dickinson had been the chief technology officer at Business
Insider. After sending a tweet that riffed off of Mel Gibson's notorious phone call where he wished that his lady got "raped by
a pack of [expletive deleted]," he was summarily fired. Rather
than claiming that this made him some sort of martyr for free
speech, he openly admits that he understands why they felt the
need to let him go.

In late January 2016, Dickinson decided to get himself banned from Twitter. "[L]et's play a game," he wrote. "DM me a journalist's twitter and I'll tell them which method of execution President Trump will use on them." "I'm not saying i personally support violent terrorism against the american media establishment but i do kinda wish everyone else would." "[P]ersonally i would never do anything violent to journalists but if someone else did i would demand that we recognize their legit grievances." "[P]lz report me for violent threats against the american journalistic establishment, i want to be banned forever so i can ascend to valhalla."

Then, one by one, he took on the journalist class by name in the most offensive and outrageous manner possible: "[B]arack obama has killed 100s of ppl with drones & president trump should continue that policy after modifying the target selection process." "[A]fter the dawning of the thousand year trumpenreich, #MeetThePress will just be sixty minutes of public executions with no commercial breaks."

Ross Douthat of the *New York Times* "gets an advance warning, like how mossad warned all the jews who worked at the WTC." He asked Jessica Valenti of the *Guardian*, "will you be upset when president trump has you hanged and no one shouts anything complimentary about your ass?" To feminist Amanda Marcotte: "are you going to commit suicide when president trump gets elected? is there anything i can do to help?"

I had never even heard of the city of Charlottesville itself. Since I don't know how to drive and am a provincial New Yorker, I was perfectly happy to presume that all of Virginia is effectively close to Washington, DC. I'd been looking for an excuse to take a road trip with my friends, and another friend Bob had a house in Arlington where we could all stay. On Friday, August 11, I drove down with Jay, a moderator at 4chan, and Simon, a Czech immigrant.

The rally was set for noon the following day. That night we saw on the news that there had been an insane march, with four columns of men with Home Depot tiki torches chanting "You will not replace us," "Jews will not replace us," "Blood and soil," and "F immigration. One people, one nation."

We all looked at each other and had no idea what we were getting ourselves into. Not in the cliché sense, but in the sense of coming up with a strategy of what to do the following day. There was no way of knowing if it would get violent, how many would be on each side, and what to do if things escalated. I had briefly considered trying to get a speaking gig so that I could stand up in front of the Alt-Right and list, in no particular order, my five favorite *RuPaul's Drag Race* contestants and why. But this footage completely changed my calculus as to who the crowd would be. I had never encountered such types in person despite being immersed in the subculture for a few years. Or rather, the ones I encountered had been one or two at a time—not hundreds at once.

On our way to Charlottesville we stopped at Cracker Barrel for breakfast. I had never seen a bowl of white gravy before, and it moved like pus and had a similar texture, actually nauseating me. When we pulled into Charlottesville the streets were completely overrun with protestors and cops, with only a few possible New Right types to be found. The energy in the air was very, very intense, akin to being at a frat house when a fight is about to break out. I don't know that I've ever felt that vibe during daylight hours.

Streets were blocked off, so we kept being detoured as we tried to make our way to Robert E. Lee Park, where the rally was going to be held. As we passed by a group of Antifa, one pulled the cowboy hat off of Bob's head and kicked at him. He held the hat out of Bob's reach before eventually giving it back, telling him to watch out. It was bullying behavior out of a bad high school movie.

I got Dickinson on the phone, and he let me know that the rally was on the verge of being canceled. Despite organizers having gotten permits and the ACLU on their side, the authorities were using some legal loophole to cancel the event. Dickinson was looking for a safe house and told me he'd let me know where they were. I was kicking myself for wearing jeans; the humidity was yet another layer of oppression.

We went to a coffee shop and waited for Dickinson's update. I decided to get an Orangina since I thought it was Italian, and that's as close to fascist as they had at the shop. I later learned that Orangina is from France, but it seemed I had made a lot of mistakes already in what August 12 would entail. Vichy doesn't seem to resonate much with the Nazis of today. If anything it would be a metaphor for let's-make-the-system-work conservatives like Paul Ryan.

Dickinson texted me shortly thereafter, and we drove over to the Airbnb where he was. He greeted us at the door in a shirt that read "Germany," again toeing the line between troll, taunt, and taboo. The house had a Buddhist shrine, a symbol of peace, and some synthetic orchids, a symbol of modernist decadence à la Huysmans. Throughout the small home were about a dozen young men who all seemed to be clad in either cargo or camo shorts. I could overhear references to White Nationalist websites in the same tones my hometown colleagues might discuss the *New Yorker*.

Dickinson told us all how he'd been pepper-sprayed on his arm before. Apparently the cops had forced the Alt-Right people to fight their way through an Antifa phalanx. "We wanted to get arrested," he told me. "They wouldn't do it." Apparently Richard Spencer had gotten gassed—a low-hanging fruit no one had any interest in touching.

The march had been a huge kerfuffle, the scenes of which would be played out in the press in the coming hours. "I haven't written my speech," Dickinson confessed. "But I might still re-cord it. I'd thank the press, because without their attention none of this would have mattered in the least." We all kept up with what was happening literally two or three blocks away. The heat and humidity surely weren't helping to calm tempers, with two groups at least somewhat interested in turning the cultural war into a literal one.

When I had spoken to Dickinson a few weeks earlier he had assured me that my safety would never be in question. "If you get cornered by Nazis then just do your Jared Taylor impression and they'll let you go," he promised. A bunch of us decided to go grab lunch and we headed to the height of Charlottesville's thriving foodie scene: Outback Steakhouse.

At Outback we were soon joined by Augustus Invictus and his entourage. Invictus is a young, preppy-looking man who had tried to be Florida's Libertarian Party candidate for Senate in 2016. The white nationalism was a bit of a dealbreaker for the party, as was the time he had a pagan goat-sacrifice ritual that involved blood drinking. He sat down across from me and seemed to be a bit on edge—and not, I assume, due to the fact that I am circumcised.

"Expedia was canceling a bunch of our flights to come down here," he told me. "Airbnb too. Antifa has been handing out fly-ers with my picture. I went to a bar and they told me the kitchen wasn't open even though I could see them serving other people."

"Now you know what it's like living under Jim Crow," I told him.

He laughed, but I wasn't really kidding. I had a Caribbean American friend who was a waitress, and her father was a vet-eran. Every time she went to a restaurant—every single time—she had to wonder if they were going to get good service or be seated in the back and ignored. "I know black people don't tip and that's why it happens," she had told me. "But I just wanted to take my dad out, and instead it was, 'Here we go again.'" It was her combination of frustration and powerlessness that got to me. She wasn't demanding to be given college admissions ahead of someone else. All she was asking was for her dad to be respected at a restaurant. This was not a big ask, and yet she constantly had to prep herself whenever she walked into an establishment.

Invictus started to show me his various tattoos, none visible under his suit. Across his left forearm was a huge tattoo. "People think I'm secretly Illuminati because it's written in Hebrew," he said, rolling his eyes. On the lighter side, Dickinson ordered the blooming onion, the worst possible thing one can order at a restaurant due to the astronomical calorie, carb, and fat content. "I probably need to start lifting again," he told me. "Someone online called me Pax Thickinson."

We all kept up with the news in real time. We heard about the car driving into a crowd and killing someone. The men began a quiet discussion about whether it would be better for both the driver and the victim to be Alt-Right or a leftist. On the one hand, you don't want to see one of your own killed. On the other, an Antifa victim would give the press the pretext to fairly label the Alt-Right as deadly.

I went outside with Dickinson and picked his brain about the neo-Nazis in the Alt-Right. "I don't punch right," he told me. "Look, every out-of-the-mainstream radical group has its bozos, people who are contrarian or just drawn to the fringe. The rightist ones are highlighted by the media while the leftist ones are ignored by the media. I mean, I've been accused by some people in the Alt-Right of being Jewish because my eyes are too close together."

"Is that a thing? I've never heard of it."

"Neither have I!"

There's an idea called Horseshoe Theory, which posits that far-left and far-right are effectively identical. I am not partial to the concept, as it reeks of people being equally dismissive without really understanding what they are dismissing. Life under Hitler and under Stalin would not be even close to identical for me, for example. There are real, substantive differences between the two that reducing them to "both are evil monsters" completely ignores—not to mention the utter glibness in handwaving away the choice between such unmitigated evil as if someone was picking between Coke and Pepsi.

But this was a case where Horseshoe Theory was true. Who is a "racist"? There are two types: actual racists like the Alt-Right, and then simply "people progressives disapprove of." Who is a Jew? Here again the answer has a parallel: actual people of Jewish descent, and then "people who neo-Nazis disapprove of." This was the explicit strategy advocated by Daily Stormer writer Andrew Anglin: "Always Blame the Jews for Everything." "As Hitler says, people will become confused and disheartened if they feel there are multiple enemies. As such, all enemies should be combined into one enemy, which is the Jews." He goes on to say that even when criticizing women, they "should be attacked, but there should always be mention that if it wasn't for the Jews, they would be acting normally."[1]

Dickinson received an explicit message regarding the afterparty: "Do not bring the Jew." I was reminded of the words of Harlem renaissance writer Zora Neale Hurston: "Sometimes, I feel discriminated against, but it does not make me angry. It merely astonishes me. How can any deny themselves the pleasure of my company?" A pithy quote, but one that didn't reflect how I felt. North Korea is the most homogenous and racist country on earth. I had seen enough of that world to find it less than alluring.

In the aftermath of Charlottesville, one name took prominence: Christopher Cantwell. Like myself, Christopher Cantwell had been a member of the Trollboard. At one point he either flounced or ragequit—depending on the internet vernacular one prefers—while letting the rest of us all know that in a few years he would be too famous as a stand-up comedian to bother with the likes of us. That's not how it worked out. He did, however, end up as a punchline, being relentlessly mocked online as the notorious "crying Nazi" who posted a distraught video after learning that there was a warrant for his arrest after the events of Charlottesville.

Hierarchy is inevitable, and any "scene" will have a number of prominent personalities attracting a disproportionate amount of attention regardless of the size of the scene itself. As such, Cantwell's journey was something the anarchists were all aware of if only due to the drama of watching the infighting among our own.

So how do we effect liberty and anarchy in our lifetime? Radical philosophies require radical plans to implement them, and one of the proposed solutions was the Free State Project. The idea was, if enough liberty absolutists moved to a small state and became politically active, they would theoretically be able to make it an enclave of freedom. As such, it's fun to bring up the example of the Free State Project to open-borders types: Can a small population drastically change the larger culture or not? Many handwringing discussions about the ethics of anarchists running for local office were had on Facebook and in person. The ultimate, oft-unspoken hope for many Free Staters was that the state—they chose New Hampshire—be allowed to secede as a micronation of liberty.

That isn't what ended up happening. If the thinking was that having anarchist neighbors would make people more amenable to anarchism, the reality was that said anarchist neighbors were often obnoxious as hell and turned people against the ideology on a visceral level. The nadir for these types was the city of Keene (population: 23,000), referred to by other Free Staters as the Keeniacs.

A prime example of this was the film *Derrick J's Victimless Crime Spree.*

Derrick J. Freeman—young, queeny, sweet, and principled—was one of said Keeniacs at the time. The title implied Freeman would be engaging in activities like buying narcotics and hiring prostitutes. Instead it featured such things as blasting music in the town square late at night and pontificating in court. The lowest point featured Freeman berating an elderly crossing guard for basically doing her job. This agent of the state was a far cry from the Gestapo, to say the least, and pointed to the difficulties of hating the government when there is very little of the government to be had.

The Keeniac mantle was taken up by Cantwell, who was the subject of a scathing piece by Stephen Colbert on his former *Colbert Report* series. Cantwell and two others followed meter maids around and quickly fed the meter in order to make sure the car owners wouldn't have to pay a ticket—thereby depriving the state of revenue. They also made it a point to berate the government workers, one of whom was a vet: "What was worse, being in Iran and Iraq or being a meter maid in Keene? Boy, that's really a tough question."

As part of the Free State Project, there was the annual Porc-Fest event, named after the project's porcupine mascot. It was the German philosopher Arthur Schopenhauer who posited the "porcupine dilemma," whereby a group of prickly animals both want to huddle together for warmth yet are still unable to refrain from hurting each other with their quills—a perfect metaphor for the anarchist's need for absolute self-ownership alongside his acknowledgment of needing to work with others to acquire goods, services, and many values.

Inaccurately described as the "libertarian Burning Man," PorcFest when I spoke at it in 2013 basically consisted of three tents for activities such as speakers, workshops, and Buzz's Big Gay Dance Party at one end of the campground. The campground itself was filled with tents populated by visitors from far and wide, and yes, of course there was a sex dome. Drugs, guns, and autism were in strong supply, and the many vendors were proud to declare their preference for bitcoin or silver over FRN (Federal Reserve notes, meaning U.S. currency).

The discussion about anarchism and using force against agents of the state has a long, touchy history. President McKinley was killed by deranged anarchist Leon Czolgosz in 1901, ushering the far more statist Theodore Roosevelt into the White House. In 1914, communist anarchist Emma Goldman's journal *Mother Earth* published an article titled "Dynamite!," whose contents the reader can easily deduce. Having been on a lecture tour as the issue was being prepared, Goldman later wrote, "I had tried always to keep our magazine free from such language, and now the whole number was filled with prattle about force and dynamite. I was so furious that I wanted the entire issue thrown into the fire. But it was too late; the magazine had gone out to the subscribers."[2]

The question remained: Was arguing for "the propaganda of the deed" the wrong position, or was it simply wrong to be stating this position publicly? Cantwell was an anarchist broadcaster, but in 2013 he finally crossed a line on his show. As the letter from the Free State Project board read,

> Whereas Chris Cantwell has made the following public statements, been offered the opportunity to retract,

and has refused to do so: "It's a terribly unpopular thing to say, but the answer, at some point, is to kill government agents," and "any level of force necessary for anyone to stop any government agent from furthering said coercion [tax collection in the context of funding the salaries of all government employees] is morally justifiable" [. . .] the FSP Board removes Chris Cantwell as a participant and declares him unwelcome to attend FSP-organized events.

In other words, he was expelled from the Free State Project—including being banned from PorcFest. It must be pointed out that this was not simply a function of Cantwell saying things which, while provocative, were hardly new in anarchist circles. As someone whose website at the time identified him as "Atheist. Anarchist. Asshole.," Cantwell did revel in being abrasive and antagonistic—even by porcupine standards.

I personally crossed paths with Cantwell several times. He came down to the Capitalistmas party in 2012, our annual event where each guest brings themselves a present that they then unwrap in front of everyone else. (This is not to be confused with "Randskeeping," an imaginary joke holiday named after Ayn where one is supposed to bake a turkey, take it from the oven, and announce, "I deserve this!") On December 31, 2013, he was at my house for my New Year's Eve party, where he got to see my friend's dimwit girlfriend glitterbomb my apartment at the stroke of midnight. Cantwell also got to see my ensuing meltdown at the sight of my kitchen completely covered in glitter. (Yes, I am still finding glitter. Even if this book is being read by aliens and the sun has long grown cold, I am still finding glitter.)

In a sense, Cantwell can be regarded as validation of the left's critique of the New Right. He was effectively the slippery slope made flesh. He went from making provocative jokes to freely using racial slurs in a humorous context to becoming a full-fledged Alt-Right white nationalist—heavy on the anti-Semitism. As I watched this transformation, my strongest reaction was one of confusion. Cantwell's strongest philosophical influences were Mises, Rothbard, and Rand—Jews one and all.

After Charlottesville, Cantwell was banned from several platforms, including Twitter, Facebook, and dating site OK Cupid. In response, he told *USA Today*, "Hahaha! Okcupid shut me down? These kikes will stop at nothing!" After he was released from jail, he wrote a post titled "No Jail Can Hold Me" and declared, "This will be the *worst thing* that ever happened to Jews." Even discounting the Holocaust, pogroms, and Debbie Wasserman Schultz, this claim simply left me even more confused than offended. I quite literally didn't understand his perspective any longer.

It's easy for me to disregard those who preemptively dismiss me because I'm Jewish. But I knew Cantwell was quite bright, and I couldn't imagine that he thought of me as some sort of covert Zionist agent. Yet his words seemed to imply otherwise. I reached out to him in the hopes of an interview. "Care to give me an idea of what I'm getting myself into?" he replied, quite understandably. "I didn't know you were Jewish. My opinion of you hasn't changed much now that I know, and I always enjoyed our interactions. Racism is heuristics. If an ethnostate became an achievable political goal, and a condition of my entry was to not bring you with me, I would go live there. I wouldn't feel guilty about it, or see any particular need to alter the immigration policy."

This was quite a bit different from "I wish you were in a gas chamber." I got on Skype with him the next day. He was stuck in his home, wearing an ankle monitor. His demeanor was open, friendly, and even lighthearted. He informed me that he was recording, and I of course understood why.

I was reminded of John McCain's appearance on *The View* during his 2008 presidential campaign, wherein Whoopi Goldberg challenged his self-described constitutionalism as meaning that she would have to be a slave. At the time I found her question absurd. In retrospect I realized that one could have a very clear answer yet still be interested in hearing the other party's reasoning as to *why*. So I opened fairly bluntly: "Do you think the world would be a better place if I died?"

"I think my life would be better if I didn't have to share a system of government with Jews," he said. "When the media calls me a white supremacist or a Nazi, I'm not either of those things. I am a white nationalist. I don't have any desire to see any harm to come to you or any other number of other cool Jewish people that I have known over the course of my life. But I am perfectly happy to discriminate along ethnic and racial lines in order to achieve outcomes."

Though it might sound sarcastic, this was a relief. I don't know if I would have been able to have any sort of informative conversation with someone who was telling me directly to my face that they wished me harm or even death.

"I'm very concerned about communism," he continued. "My observations, reluctant as I have been to make them, is that Jews are overrepresented in leftist intellectual circles to the point where if you even try to make an effective critique of communism, Republicans will call you an anti-Semite just because you're criticizing Jews so frequently. It's not that there's no good Jews or every Jew should be exterminated down to their last drop of blood. It's simply that as a demographic they pose a political problem in a democratic government." (I couldn't help but notice that he said "they" instead of "you.")

The frequent argument among anti-Semitic white nationalists is that as Jewish influence increased, the country moved
further and further to the left. But this perspective doesn't
match the data. In 1952 the United Steelworkers of America announced their intention to go on strike. *Before the strike even
began*, President Truman moved to have the federal government
seize control of the industry. Under FDR the federal income tax
had a top marginal rate of 79 percent, well before World War
II. The assaults on the press and free speech under Wilson were
wide and pervasive. It is impossible to imagine even Bernie
Sanders—so far left he's not even a Democrat!—advocating for
any of the preceding policies in this day and age (and yes, he's
Jewish).

I then asked Cantwell a more personal question. For my work
opposing the north Korean dictatorship—a regime Cantwell
also regards as evil—I've been accused online of being a neocon or only being against them because they're anti-Israel.
"Obviously my life isn't your responsibility," I said. "But what
advice would you give me to navigate such attacks?"

"I haven't thought about giving Jews advice about how to
deal with skepticism towards them," he said. "What I would say
to my fellow goyim is, suspicion is fine, depending on the context. I don't think it's right to write off every Jewish person you
come into contact with immediately. Not to insult anybody, but
not all people are very smart. If you look at race and IQ, Jews
on average have higher IQs than do whites. I think it's a healthy
instinct for an average-IQ white person to avoid taking information from Jews because it's easier for them to get tricked. I'm
a lot more comfortable talking to Jewish people because I'm
smarter than the average Jew."

"You've said that you were trying to sound so much
crazier—or whatever term you want to use—so by comparison
Richard Spencer seems reasonable. Is that your approach?"

"To an extent," he said. "The line between reality and humor in what I do is one that I would have a hard time drawing, frankly. This is why I have a disclaimer on my show. Think of a guy like Mike Cernovich. There are people who are trying to say that Mike Cernovich is some fascist, racist, white supremacist. Imagine if there wasn't a bunch of people like me way to the right of Mike Cernovich, what would be coming down on him. That's why I get especially pissed when that cocksucker has the nerve to go out and say I'm some sort of federal plant, when I'm giving him license to do all the bullshit that he does. What I do gives people like Donald Trump or Mike Cernovich or Gavin McInnes the ability to point rightward and say, 'Those guys are the real racists.' If not for us doing that, they would be the extremists and it would be Paul Ryan and Mitch McConnell who were being called fascists."

"So it is about positioning to some extent. But if I did something like that, it would be me being a 'conniving Jew'!"

"Well, yeah. This is group evolutionary strategy. We are in a sense 'conspiring' to overcome a destructive influence in our society. Jews certainly do conspire to change the Overton Window. With the left, what's permitted today is celebrated tomorrow and then will be compulsory. The number one taboo is Jews. That's when you start getting framed for crimes, that's when you start getting kicked out of the financial system. You can talk about black-on-black crime in Chicago, you can talk about Muslim terrorism, and you might not get invited to some parties because of that. Me being the adrenaline-junkie lunatic that I am, this is how I define myself here."

One of the big arguments is that Richard Spencer and other Alt-Right figures are federal agents of some sort. I wondered what Cantwell thought of this conspiracy theory.

"I don't doubt Richard Spencer would talk to the FBI if there was a criminal conspiracy that he discovered," Cantwell told me. "As a matter of fact I would! I talked to the FBI after Charlottesville, and I'd do it in the future. People on my podcast accuse me of being a fed, and I tell them, 'Go ahead and think of me as one, because if you're doing something illegal, I don't want to be involved!'"

"How do you reconcile the differences between north and south Korea if they are genetically identical?" For those who insist that "demographics is destiny," this seemed like the most obvious counterexample on earth (literally so).

"I'm not an expert on north Korea, but from what I know about communism, I would be shocked to learn that Jews didn't have something to do with communism coming to north Korea. Even China, it appears there was a great deal of Jewish influence around Mao. I have not studied the north Korean thing to speak intelligently on it."

"Let's assume for the sake of argument that Jews were behind communism coming to the North. The outcomes are still vastly different in terms of their standard of living."

"I am not a guy who thinks genetics is the only thing that matters. I know there are people in the Alt-Right (and racist movements more broadly) who think that economic systems don't matter. I think those people are crazy and I argue with them all the time. But I would say that if they are not genetically distinct now they will be, because the economic incentives impact the breeding practices. There are people in these movements who would disagree with me, but I think I'm smarter than them. Economic and political systems dramatically impact a society, and if you think you can boil that down to mere genetics then you're a fool. A lot of things matter aside from race. But I do think that race is literally the most salient detail in any political discussion."

"Do you think it is possible to be a 'good'—in whatever sense of the word—anti-Semite and not be a Holocaust denier?"

"Yeah, because *I'm* a good anti-Semite and I don't claim to know what the fuck happened in the Holocaust. I'm skeptical. When I realized that all state action is violence, it changed my life. When I realized race is as important as it was, it was an even more defining moment. But I'm skeptical of the Holocaust deniers because the people who claim to know—well, everyone who says the Holocaust didn't happen thinks it *should*. Sometimes I think they're just trying to stick up for the Hitler administration."

"I know one of the big arguments is that the Jews weren't gassed but were starved to death."

"Yeah, if you starve a whole bunch of people that's not the best thing that ever happened. And part of what they say is maybe it wasn't intentional, maybe the supply lines were cut off and the military has to eat before the prisoners—'Sorry, Jews!' All these things make sense to me, but I read *Mein Kampf*. Hitler thought all the Jews were responsible for all the problems in his society, so having a policy to exterminate them isn't the craziest thing I've seen a government do."

One of the other Holocaust-denier arguments is that the Holocaust wasn't a big deal at the time and Jews made it into one. "Even the *New York Times* doubted the Holocaust at the time!" is a common refrain in this scene. As author Steven Pinker points out in *The Better Angels of Our Nature*, mass murders of populations were common throughout human history. Obviously the technology in the past was not as effective as the industrialized genocide that the Nazis used, but the amount of murder as a percentage of the population was often very high—even sometimes absolute. There are even references to this kind of thinking in the Bible, such as Joshua 10:40:

> So Joshua subdued the whole region, including the hill country, the Negev, the western foothills and the

mountain slopes, together with all their kings. He left
no survivors. He totally destroyed all who breathed,
just as the Lord, the God of Israel, had commanded.

It is only in the last century that civilized people have
come to a more or less universal consensus that wiping out
entire populations is not only unnecessary but is downright
horrific and indeed the lowest form of human action. If this
change of thinking was the responsibility, even in part, of the
Jewish people, that might be the greatest endorsement of Jewish
action in world history. I can think of no greater moral accom-
plishment than persuading the world that mass murder is an
abomination.

"I don't want this to be a violent conflict," Cantwell insists.
"When people refuse to talk, that is what happens. If you and I
have a conflict and we can't have a discussion about it, violence
is going to ensue."

"You get attacked all the time, far more than me. But for me
to get attacked, sometimes in the basest terms, I have to say—
it's disturbing."

"I can see why it would be. But I can understand why people
are like, 'Get away from the movement. Get away because I don't
want to find out when the treason comes.' I genuinely think you
and [moderate libertarian comedian] Dave Smith are good
people. I grew up in Long Island; it's not like I could avoid Jews
if I tried."

"I'm from the Soviet Union. We have a paranoia built into
our bloodstream. We don't trust anyone. But to me there's a difference between skepticism and seeking me out and being like,
'You're a covert neocon.'"

"It happens. I have better things to do and maybe they don't.
I've never been one to deny anybody the joy of trolling."

"If the big fear is that there is a secret Jewish cabal controlling the government," I said, "how can someone be pro-Trump when two of his children married a Jew? He *is* the Jewish cabal!"

"If Adolf Hitler had been in the primary, I would have voted for him. (I'm 90 percent kidding about that)," Cantwell quickly points out. "I went into that primary thinking I'm just a too-cool-for-school ancap who isn't going to participate. Then I thought Rand Paul, but then he started with the whole 'the drug war is racist!' crap. Then I was sort of pulling for Ted Cruz before I got convinced that Trump was sincere. I was never under the impression that Donald Trump would solve the Jewish problem. I just didn't want to suffer through a Hillary Clinton presidency."

"But it seems like some people on the Alt-Right mirror leftist arguments and say Trump is a Nazi. But he's a really bad Nazi when literally every one of his kids is marrying a Jew."

"I imagine that Trump is more informed about anti-Semitism than he lets on. And I imagine that he isn't 100 percent happy about the Jewish influence in his own family, quite frankly. I can't say that with any certainty. But look, anti-Semitism is *not* 'there's no such thing as a good Jew.' It's not 'we have to exterminate them down to the last drop.' It's skepticism, and I encourage skepticism and I think it's healthy. To the extent it turns into other things, it's unfortunate, but the problem is since it's such a taboo to discuss, it's almost impossible for anyone to have an intelligent opinion about the subject. People who research this stuff end up in the darkest corners of the internet, so what they end up with is 9/11 truther stuff and it becomes paranoid, incomplete, and sometimes outright false. That is what happens when you drive a school of thought underground."

"So how would you describe yourself? You're obviously not in the Klan, and you're not a white supremacist. Would you describe yourself as a Nazi or neo-Nazi?"

"No. 'White nationalist' is the most appropriate term. It would not be entirely inaccurate to say I'm a Nazi sympathizer at this point. I'm still foundationally a free-markets guy. I'll convert to Islam before I call myself a socialist, and not because I'm anxious to pray five times a day."

15

★

THE ROAD AHEAD

> Every normal man must be tempted, at times, to spit
> on his hands, hoist the black flag, and begin slitting
> throats.
>
> —H. L. MENCKEN

So what does this all mean? Are these people a threat, a boon? Both? Neither? Let me first address this from the personal, anarchist perspective. When people ask what the law would look like if it were private, the answer I give is, "What would fashion look like if the fashion industry weren't run by the government?" Of course the fashion industry isn't run by the government. The point is that if it *had* been, it would be impossible to imagine what the free alternative would look like. We see this in sci-fi, where every alien population of snails has architecture based on shells, while the lizard people have scales everywhere—as if humans would make buildings that looked like hands and feet. The common law—government at its basest and least objectionable—is akin in this sense to architecture and fashion. It is the sum total of literally millions of attorneys, clients, lawyers, judges, and politicians making marginal changes over decades.

No one mind can deduce it in its totality and simultaneously contain all the infinite threads woven throughout.

In this sense, any political prediction I might make is almost surely doomed to failure. In the age of Trump, virtually no one possesses any certainty about where we're going as a country in the future or even what's happening at the moment. There are, however, some broad long-term trends that can be projected with some degree of certainty, due to basic asymmetries.

The first is the erosion of trust in the Cathedral and its respective elements. The days of America huddled around the radio and listening to FDR's fireside chats with nigh-universal consensus are very much a thing of the past. In part this is a function of the velocity of information and the fatigue that quickly sets in regarding most politicians. In the last thirty years, there have been only two presidents who achieved broad national agreement: the first president Bush regarding the Gulf War, and George W. Bush after 9/11. The first was defeated for reelection; the second dropped to the lowest approval rating ever recorded by Gallup since Truman, even below Nixon's during the Watergate scandal.

Similarly, we will no longer ever have an America that sits down together to watch one of the three network anchors. For leftists, invoking "Fox News" is enough to get them to dismiss something out of hand, as it is for right-wingers and CNN. Thanks to the emergence of social media, websites, newspapers, and all other aspects of the press are publicly held accountable by their respective ideological enemies in real time, twenty-four hours a day, seven days a week. Even if "corrections" levied at any one of these were *false*, the impression left over time would be that the source being critiqued is disreputable. After all, there's a constant stream of criticism directed toward them.

Trust once lost is very hard to regain. One lie isn't equivalent to one truth: a friend who says nineteen true things for every lie would be regarded as untrustworthy despite being honest 95 percent of the time. The claim that "we are more divided as a country than ever" is demented in light of things like the Civil War. But we aren't exactly united either—and the tools that do work to unite us are, for perhaps the first time, under conscious, intentional attack.

For an anarchist who believes in absolute decentralization, this is a wonderful development. For those who are opposed to this idea—i.e., the vast majority of Americans—it is something to worry about indeed. Both Republicans and Democrats seem to want each other to cease to exist, yet each is simultaneously reticent about letting the other leave. Until quite recently, the concept of secession was intertwined with slavery. While not gaining much traction, current secessionist movements in California, Texas, and Vermont have done much to destigmatize such thinking. This is the necessary prelude to actually letting two entirely different ideologies go their own way.

This is the broader point. The Trump phenomenon specifically has a different meaning. In my view, the salient thing about the Trump presidency is how he has mainstreamed several formerly marginalized strands of right-wing thought and behavior. Ronald Reagan was the first president to have previously been divorced; Trump has two ex-wives, with each marriage tarnished by scandal. It is frankly shocking to see how comfortable Trump has made religious people with his vulgar New York vernacular—down to the four-letter words that they themselves would never say.

Nixon grumbled in private that the press was the enemy, and he was mocked for literally decades for attacking them in his 1962 press conference. Now when Trump routinely describes the press as "the enemy of the American people," he has a great deal of support among the population and, as importantly, among some media types. Indeed, the self-righteous indignation at being attacked reads as blatantly absurd when spouted by journalists who seem to base their entire careers on attacking the president and his supporters in the most vicious terms imaginable.

The sins of individual journalists have done an enormous job of creating a large divide between the media and the masses. Minor misstatements of fact and exaggerating one's past accomplishments on a resume are things that most people can relate to and forgive. To claim that one's helicopter was forced down by a grenade, as Brian Williams did, is such an egregious lie that it is hard to empathize with on a simple level. The average person can't imagine a situation where they would make such a bold claim in private, let alone on national television. Matt Lauer's years of sexual abuse and assault are too salacious to get into here. But in his case and Williams's, a culture that would produce and sanction such behavior is quite simply an alien one to most Americans.

Similarly, there is a growing understanding that the university system of bygone days is not what it used to be. Far too often someone's child goes off to college as a bright-eyed innocent and returns literally unrecognizable from the person they were before. College is a time for transformation and discovering oneself, to be sure. But far too often this "self" that one discovers happens to be exactly identical in essence to every other member of the evangelical left. This guarantees that families will become strangers staring at each other at the holiday dinner table, quite literally unable to understand one another's point of view.

Social media has allowed parents to see for themselves what is going on at various campuses, as the increasingly shrill tone is proudly broadcast on the internet for all to see. One doesn't need to be educated to understand blatant displays of rage and hostility; even animals know what shouting and baring one's teeth mean. The left is unintentionally furthering this attack on the universities, with the frequent complaint about how expensive it is to get a higher education. The recognition that a college education is often a terrible investment will, in my view, likely become more and more common. In the past, pretty much the only "business" a young person could start was forming a band. Now, it is quite easy—and becoming easier every day—for any given young person to open their own online store or business. There is no shortage of websites offering encouragement, tutorials, and the tools to make this happen.

In the same way that media fragmentation is so irreversible that it is impossible to even conceive of it stopping, political fragmentation is already following suit. The previous decades saw Coke and Pepsi roll out new varieties. For comedians, this came to be a source of absurdist humor: "What's next? Caffeine-free Diet Cherry Coke Zero, am I right?" In their own vapid way, what such types were recognizing was the increased fine-tuning of products to individuals. Milk that was available as skim, 1 percent, 2 percent, or whole can now be bought lactose-free and/or organic at any supermarket, with unpasteurized raw milk available where permitted by law. Orange juice is sold with pulp, pulp-free, or with—as Tony Soprano famously preferred—"some" pulp.

Past events in Europe have in many ways presaged American political events. Brexit was a repudiation of the entire elite class in the UK and in Europe, and it was followed a few months later by the Trump election. Margaret Thatcher's elevation to the prime ministership in 1979 was a foreshadowing of Ronald Reagan's conservative victory the following year. Now, nation after nation in Europe is finding it impossible to form consensus on virtually anything.

In late 2017 Angela Merkel led her Christian Democrats to victory in the German elections. For the first time ever there were six parties represented in the Bundestag. Both Merkel's party and the rival Social Democrats had their lowest share of the popular vote since the 1940s, if not earlier. The two largest parties only managed to poll 53 percent of the vote *combined*.

It took the Dutch a record 208 days to agree to a coalition after their March 2017 elections. Even so, the resulting four-party deal still only had a one-seat majority. These are four parties who quite obviously represent different interests and points of view. A situation in which any one member of parliament has the power to take down the government—whether via defection, death, or resignation—is not a governing consensus.

The Czech elections in December 2017 saw similarly unprecedented outcomes. The formerly first-place Social Democrats slipped to sixth, while the Pirates took third place despite never having been in parliament before. In 2002, four political parties were represented in the Czech Chamber of Deputies. When the new members took their seats there were nine, which has also never happened before.

We have started seeing these trends seep into American politics. The two political parties are effectively each composed of various blocs that change allegiance over time: conservative Southern Democrats became Republicans; northeastern liberal "Rockefeller Republicans" turned Democrat. The Senate filibuster, the need to find sixty votes before certain motions proceed, has been chipped away by leadership from both parties. Obamacare was eventually passed through reconciliation to bypass the filibuster, and Supreme Court nominations can no longer be held captive by the minority party.

Increasingly, there is a grudging admission that New Right ideas have validity. Leftists complain that these long-dormant strains of thought are being legitimized, but there is little they can do about it without control of the means of information. Right-wing pundits like Kurt Schlichter and sites like the Daily

Caller frequently use New Right ideas, jokes, and even slang. Unlike on the newsstand, there is infinite space for various publications to put their ideas forward. This fabled competition in the marketplace of ideas can only help the New Right, whose starting position was close to zero vis-à-vis popular discourse even five years ago.

What has completely passed without comment is that under President Trump, it is still the judicial branch of government that is by far the most radical. The growing trend among right-wing jurists for strict constructionism means looking at the Constitution directly and putting decades of decisions secondary to that. The greatest example of this was the Citizens United decision, which overturned decades' worth of law—even issues that the plaintiff wasn't asking for. The Obamacare decision was one vote away from being struck down *in its entirety*. The last time the Supreme Court had the nerve to strike down a major government program was in 1935, when Charles Evans Hughes (Woodrow Wilson's opponent in the 1916 election) led the Court in finding the National Industrial Recovery Act to be unconstitutional. Since then the Court has overwhelmingly deferred to the legislative branch. Now, this is decreasingly the case and *consciously and intentionally so*.

In 2015 Apple announced that it would create such tight security on its forthcoming iPhones that the government and even Apple itself would be unable to access the phone's data without the owner's permission. "No back door is a must," insisted Apple CEO Tim Cook. Though cloaked in buzzwords about privacy and security, this was a sea change in the relationship between corporations and the state. Though Cook is no anarchist, the Apple approach is exactly the techno-anarchist idea that the government is an engineering problem to be solved for. It was the market itself that persuaded Apple, not any debate or lengthy blog post—certainly not any election! Instead of the major corporate taboo of defying the edicts of law enforcement (aka "law imposement"), Apple has cleverly put itself in a position where it can't side with the law even if it wants to. Sorry, officer!

In the same way that technology implemented the promises of the First Amendment, Defense Distributed is coming pretty close to doing the same for the Second Amendment. The organization created and distributed instructions for creating a gun in one's home using a 3D printer. Being made of binding material instead of metal, the so-called Liberator will hardly be replacing the Colt in the next couple of years. But in principle, with some improvements (and the technology is improving far faster than governments can react), it will render gun bans moot.

The files were copied and spread throughout the internet, hosted across the world. Short of shutting the internet down, there is no way for the government to destroy these files. In addition, short of banning 3D printers—something that no one considers plausible—there is no mechanism by which to make such guns unproducible. There was no discussion, no debate, no attempt to persuade anyone of anything. There was information and technology—and there are many upset people who have been rendered completely powerless and downright baffled. Moms can demand action all the way. They'd be just as successful demanding all these young adult men clean their rooms.

Rather than being guised in the corporate veneer of law-abiding civility, the project's creator Cody Wilson is more explicit about his views and freely refers to his opponents as "the enemy." "You can adjust your politics to this reality," he told one journalist. "You will not ask me to adjust mine." For most people the idea that a law can be illegal is incomprehensible, like saying water can be dry. Yet there exists the constitutional guarantee that "the right of the people to keep and bear Arms, shall not be infringed." From this, any individual can choose to view gun control "laws" as having no legal basis. Yes, they might be enforced quite harshly in practice, but in a *moral* sense one can view it as if these actions don't exist as laws and are in fact *antithetical* to the "actual" law.

As for the right wing of politics, the New Right seems to be in full control at the moment. Neoconservative Mona Charen had to be escorted out by security after denouncing the right for endorsing an alleged pedophile, Roy Moore, for the Alabama senate. Ohio governor John Kasich—long a stalwart Republican—openly mused about a third party. They—and those who think like them—are being attacked and driven away from the Republican Party in the most personal terms. President Trump's approval rating among Republicans was over 80 percent in 2018; the "Never Trump" team are a statistical irrelevancy. At the same time, American politics has a way of reverting to the mean. George H. W. Bush didn't out-Reagan Reagan. Nor did Ford out-Nixon Nixon. It's hard to imagine any Republican president— heck, any human— being more Trumpian than Trump.

Since the New Right is reactive in its strategy, with its players disposable, it is impossible to predict where, say, Mencius Moldbug will be three years from now. But leftist attempts to dismiss the entire movement as a bunch of Nazis are doomed to failure, if only because the actual Nazis of today aren't the Nazis of the 1930s and 1940s. The subculture is by its nature a response to progressivism and the Cathedral. Though the mainstream has the numbers, historically speaking a self-aware tightly organized minority tends to prevail over a loose unthinking population. We've seen this everywhere from Lenin seizing control in Russia to the Constitutional Convention itself.

On the other hand, as any movement grows, infighting becomes inevitable and schisms necessarily happen. When the right wing in America consisted of small numbers of conservatives and libertarians, a natural alliance occurred. "I'm a libertarian conservative" or "a conservative libertarian" has given way to both ideologies having their own subculture, with subdivisions therein as well. Already there is tension between the broader New Right and the Alt-Right in terms of the veracity of claims, prioritization of issues, and strategy. And, of course, there is the issue of egos and backbiting.

Sincerely or not, the New Right holds out to young people the promise of being antiestablishment, edgy, and cool, things conservatism has historically had an issue with. Michael J. Fox's young Republican character from *Family Ties* was almost always clad in a suit. The increasing New Right focus on self-actualization will only further concretize the subculture's role in American society. Cleverly, there is a conscious and intentional attempt by its adherents to distance themselves from President Trump at various times. The New Right recognizes that the Cathedral played the long con, and they intend to respond in kind.

Ayn Rand's novel *Atlas Shrugged* featured the heroes sitting back and watching the American polity self-destruct before trying to fix it. At the end of the day I go back to the thoughts of Albert Camus and his philosophy of the absurd. In *The Myth of Sisyphus*, he describes the character forced to push a rock up a hill for eternity—only to have it fall away at the last possible second. For Camus, once Sisyphus accepts the absurdity of his condition, "[t]here is no fate that cannot be surmounted by scorn." To realize that we live in an absurd culture where we are taught absurd things by absurd people and threatened with absurd consequences for defying all of it is to achieve a level of contentment. As Camus concludes, "The struggle itself toward the heights is enough to fill a man's heart. One must imagine Sisyphus happy."

ACKNOWLEDGMENTS

You need a mess of help to stand alone.

There were several people instrumental in getting this book from concept to reality. I am blessed to have Joe Veltre as my agent, who is the rare person who goes above and beyond for all his clients regardless of their importance. My editor Adam Bellow had the idea to change the premise from third-person to first-, and he alongside Kevin Reilly helped shape the manuscript. Ryan Masteller's superb copyediting was the most precise and yet unpedantic I've yet experienced in the publishing world. Charles Ruten was instrumental in researching two key points. Natasha Simons literally held my hand that one day I needed it, and is very bad at obscuring her big heart and terrible political takes.

The following people were also instrumental in helping me fulfill this project, at the very least via emotional support. My acknowledging them should neither be taken as approving of the contents of the book nor as explicit endorsement of genocide: Ed Berlen, Marshall Boprey, Kris Borer, Frederick Bouchardy, Mark Bower, Topher Burns, Don Caldwell, Mike Cernovich, everyone at Compound Media, Jackie Danicki, Josh Davis, Pax Dickinson, Eric Dixon, Paul Ducko, John Durant, Bob Ewing, Jesse Forgione, Perry Metzger, Simoon Franek, Michael Fazio, Pat Flynn, Kmele Foster, Marcy Gallegos, the GaS Digital crew, John Girgus, Jim Goad, Michael Goldstein, Chuck and Amanda Grimmett, Andrew Heaton, Ryan and Samantha Holiday,

Charles Hope, the Hughes family and the Chileses, Jay Irwin, Harjit Jaiswal, Andrea Jamison, Kennedy, Annette Knezevic, Darrin Knode, Ali Lerman, Olivia Lilly, Maddox, Julie McGuire, Anders Mikkelsen, Weston Minami, Mencius Moldbug, Anna Nash, Charlie Nash, Carl Oberg, Camille Paglia, Andrea Pisani, Mott Pretchard, Patrick Reasonover, Stephie Russell, Tushar Saxena, Phil Saxton, Summer Saxton, Kurt Schlichter, Tom Shillue, Justin Stoddard, Cole and Amber Stryker and l'il Ayn, Dick Talens, Peter Vaihansky, Matt Welch, Chelsea Whittemore, Michael Wolf, Michael Woods, and last and certainly least Tom Woods.

NOTES

Chapter 1: This Is Your Welcome

1 Quoted in Amalgamated Clothing Workers of America, Documentary History of the Amalgamated Clothing Workers of America, 1916–1918: Proceedings of the Third Biennial Convention of the Amalgamated Clothing Workers of America, pg. 53, https://books.google.com/books?id=QrcpAAAAYAAJ&pg=PA53&dq=%22First+they+ignore+you%22#v=onepage&q=%22First%20they%20ignore%20you%22&f=false.

Chapter 2: The Lurker at the Threshold

1 Ayn Rand, Letters of Ayn Rand (New York: Dutton, 1995), p. 326.
2 Lysander Spooner, The Lysander Spooner Reader (San Francisco, CA: Fox & Wilkes, 1992), p. 77.
3 Spooner, The Lysander Spooner Reader, p. 121.

Chapter 3: The Strike

1 Pat Buchanan, "Yes, Mario, There is a Cultural War" Chicago Tribune, September 14, 1992.
2 Brian Doherty, "Best of Both Worlds: An Interview with Milton Friedman" Reason, June 1995.
3 Sam Tanenhaus, Whittaker Chambers: A Biography (New York: Random House, 1997), p. 500.
4 https://mises.org/library/toward-reconstruction-utility-and-welfare-economics-1/html/c/55.
5 https://mises.org/profile/murray-n-rothbard.
6 https://mises.org/library/egalitarianism-and-elites.
7 https://www.lewrockwell.com/1970/01/murray-n-rothbard/life-in-the-old-right/.
8 William F. Buckley, "Ayn Rand, R.I.P." National Review, April 2, 1982.
9 Justin Raimondo, Reclaiming the American Right (Wilmington, DE: ISI Books, 2008), p. 221.
10 R. L. Dabney, "Women's Rights Women" The Southern Magazine, Vol. VIII, January to June 1871, https://babel.hathitrust.org/cgi/pt?id=coo.31924065565693;view=1up;seq=335.
11 http://voxday.blogspot.com/2017/06/soiled-soiled-i-say.html.
12 Quoted in Jeffrey Hart, The Making of the American Conservative Mind

(Wilmington, DE: ISI Books, 2005), p. 104, https://www.nationalreview.com/2013/08/marching-time-editors/.

13 Digby Anderson, "Dead Issues" *National Review*, January 29, 1996.

14 Serhii Plokhy, *The Last Empire* (New York: Basic Books, 2014), e-book, chap. 10.

15 https://www.nationalreview.com/corner/working-class-whites-have-moral-responsibilities-defense-kevin-williamson/.

16 Patrick J. Buchanan, *The Greatest Comeback* (New York: Crown Forum, 2014), e-book, chap. 8.

17 Quoted in Murray Rothbard, *The Irrepressible Rothbard* (Brulingame, CA: Center for Libertarian Studies, 2000), p. 37.

18 Hans-Herman Hoppe, *Democracy—The God That Failed* (New Brunswick, NJ: Transaction Publishers, 2001), p. 193.

19 Private conversation.

Chapter 4: Meme Magic Is Real

1 http://takimag.com/article/why_i_publish_this_magazine.

2 http://takimag.com/article/the_talk_nonblack_version_john_derbyshire.

3 https://www.nationalreview.com/corner/parting-ways-rich-lowry/.

4 https://www.breitbart.com/big-hollywood/2011/08/22/politics-really-is-downstream-from-culture/.

5 https://twitter.com/astroehlein/status/818449125503094785.

6 https://www.politico.com/blogs/onmedia/0811/Right_calls_foul_on_Schultzs_Perry_remark.html.

7 Dorothy Herrmann, *With Malice Toward All* (New York: G. P. Putnam's Sons, 1982), p. 85.

Chapter 5: Airtight

1 https://www.socialmatter.net/2014/10/08/practical-workshop-groups-deal-females-beta-males/.

2 https://voxday.blogspot.com/2016/08/ben-shapiro-is-glad-you-hate-him.html.

3 https://voxday.blogspot.com/2016/08/the-littlest-chickenhawk-clucks.html.

4 Vox Day, *SJWs Always Lie* (Kouvola, Finland: Castalia House, 2015), p. 66.

5 Day, *SJWs Always Lie*, p. 182.

Chapter 6: The Case Against Democracy

1 Greg Lukianoff and Jonathan Haidt, *The Coddling of the American Mind* (New York: Penguin Press, 2018), chap. 11.

2 https://www.scottaaronson.com/blog/?p=3167#comment-1732159.

3 https://www.scottaaronson.com/blog/?p=3167#comment-1732088.

4 James Burnham, *The Machiavellians* (Washington, D.C.: Regnery, 1987), p. 131.

5 https://www.cato-unbound.org/2009/04/13/peter-thiel/education-libertarian.

Chapter 7: Penthouse Legend

1 Jim Goad, *Shit Magnet* (Los Angeles: Feral House, 2002), p. 10.

2 Goad, *Shit Magnet*, p. 17.

3   Jim Goad, *The Redneck Manifesto* (New York: Simon & Schuster, 1997), p. 55.

4   Goad, *The Redneck Manifesto*, p. 71.

5   Goad, *The Redneck Manifesto*, p. 71.

6   https://www.commentarymagazine.com/culture-civilization/the-actual
-pauline-kael-quote%e2%80%94not-as-bad-and-worse/.

7   Goad, *The Redneck Manifesto*, p. 16.

8   Goad, *The Redneck Manifesto*, p. 89.

9   Goad, *The Redneck Manifesto*, p. 236.

10   Goad, *The Redneck Manifesto*, p. 23.

11   Shannon Sullivan, *Good White People* (Albany: State University of New York
Press, 2017), pp. 6, 30.

12   Sullivan, *Good White People*, p. 58.

13   Sullivan, *Good White People*, pp. 129, 154.

14   https://thoughtcatalog.com/jim-goad/2014/06/hating-the-haters-in-the
-name-of-love/.

Chapter 8: The Vices of Gavin McInnes

1   https://www.nytimes.com/2003/09/28/style/the-edge-of-hip-vice-the-brand
.html.

2   https://thoughtcatalog.com/gavin-mcinnes/2014/08/transphobia-is-perfectly
-natural/.

3   https://ew.com/article/2002/07/11/candice-bergen-says-dan-quayle-was
-right/.

4   https://www.washingtonpost.com/opinions/20-years-later-it-turns-out-dan
-quayle-was-right-about-murphy-brown-and-unmarried-moms/2012/05/25
/gJQAsNCJqU_story.html?utm_term=.970daffad88f.

5   http://paulgraham.com/say.html.

6   http://www.rooshv.com/lindy-west-disease.

Chapter 9: Get in the Chopper

1   Patrick J. Buchanan, *The Death of the West* (New York: Thomas Dunne Books,
2001), p. 9.

2   Buchanan, *The Death of the West*, p. 10.

3   Buchanan, *The Death of the West*, p. 23.

4   Buchanan, *The Death of the West*, p. 17.

5   Buchanan, *The Death of the West*, p. 22.

6   Buchanan, *The Death of the West*, p. 34.

7   Buchanan, *The Death of the West*, p. 101.

8   https://metro.co.uk/2018/02/02/sexual-assault-survivor-created anti rape
-shorts-7281220/.

9   Buchanan, *The Death of the West*, p. 265.

10   Buchanan, *The Death of the West*, p. 243.

11   Buchanan, *The Death of the West*, p. 3.

12   Buchanan, *The Death of the West*, p. 13.

13   Buchanan, *The Death of the West*, p. 60.

14   Buchanan, *The Death of the West*, p. 22.

15   Buchanan, *The Death of the West*, p. 125.

16   Buchanan, *The Death of the West*, p. 232.
17   Buchanan, *The Death of the West*, p. 19.
18   Buchanan, *The Death of the West*, p. 37.
19   Buchanan, *The Death of the West*, p. 37.
20   Buchanan, *The Death of the West*, p. 199.
21   Buchanan, *The Death of the West*, p. 37.

Chapter 10: Second-Hand Lives

1   https://twitter.com/andrewbreitbart/status/33636278100561920?lang=en.

Chapter 11: Ego

1   https://www.huffingtonpost.com/ryan-holiday/dear-dad-please-dont-vote_b
_10990432.html.

2   https://observer.com/2017/02/i-helped-create-the-milo-trolling-playbook
-you-should-stop-playing-right-into-it/.

3   A similar case can be seen with Cody Wilson. In late 2018 Wilson was arrested for "sexual assault of a minor." The term, though legally accurate,
sounds as if he forced himself onto a child as opposed to what actually happened, namely paying a girl for sex and not knowing that she was sixteen years
old.

4   http://www.latimes.com/local/lanow/la-me-ln-berkeley-security-20170916
-story.html.

5   https://www.buzzfeednews.com/article/josephbernstein/heres-how-breitbart
-and-milo-smuggled-white-nationalism.

6   https://www.businessinsider.com/robert-mercer-letter-milo-yiannopoulos
-steve-bannon-2017-11.

7   Andrew Breitbart, *Righteous Indignation* (New York: Grand Central Publishing, 2011), e-book, chap. 1.

8   Thomas C. Leonard, *Illiberal Reformers* (Princeton, NJ: Princeton University
Press, 2016), p. ix.

9   Leonard, *Illiberal Reformers*, p. 10.
10   Leonard, *Illiberal Reformers*, p. 15.
11   Leonard, *Illiberal Reformers*, p. 17.
12   Leonard, *Illiberal Reformers*, p. 20.

Chapter 12: The Divine Miss C

1   Ann Coulter, *¡ADIOS, AMERICA!* (Washington, DC: Regnery, 2015), e-book,
chap. 15.

2   Coulter, *¡ADIOS, AMERICA!*, chap. 1.
3   Coulter, *¡ADIOS, AMERICA!*, chap. 4.

4   E. Digby Baltzell, *The Protestant Establishment* (New York: Random House,
1964), p. xi.

5   Coulter, *¡ADIOS, AMERICA!*, chap. 4.
6   Coulter, *¡ADIOS, AMERICA!*, chap. 10.
7   Coulter, *¡ADIOS, AMERICA!*, chap. 11.
8   Coulter, *¡ADIOS, AMERICA!*, chap. 9.
9   Coulter, *¡ADIOS, AMERICA!*, chap. 17.

10   Coulter, *¡ADIOS, AMERICA!*, chap. 16.
11   Breitbart, *Righteous Indignation*, chap. 9.
12   Coulter, *¡ADIOS, AMERICA!*, chap. 2.
13   Coulter, *¡ADIOS, AMERICA!*, chap. 16.

Chapter 13: The New Hwite

1   https://www.reuters.com/article/idUS74746206720140627.
2   https://www.newstatesman.com/2014/01/1914-to-2014.

Chapter 14: Charlottesville or Bust

1   https://www.huffingtonpost.com/entry/daily-stormer-nazi-style-guide_us_5a2ece19e4b0ce3b344492f2.
2   Quoted in *Anarchy!* (Washington, D.C.: Counterpoint, 2001), p. 76.

INDEX